Raising Hell

Raising Hell

STRAIGHT TALK WITH
INVESTIGATIVE JOURNALISTS

*Ron Chepesiuk,
Haney Howell
and Edward Lee,*
INTERVIEWERS

McFarland & Company, Inc., Publishers
Jefferson, North Carolina, and London

British Library Cataloguing-in-Publication data are available

Library of Congress Cataloguing-in-Publication Data

Raising hell : straight talk with investigative journalists /
   Ron Chepesiuk, Haney Howell and Edward Lee, interviewers.
      p.   cm.
   Includes bibliographical references and index.
   ISBN 0-7864-0356-X (softcover : 50# alkaline paper) ∞
   1. Investigative reporting.   2. Reporters and reporting.   3. Journalists —
United States — Interviews.   I. Chepesiuk, Ronald.   II. Howell, Haney.
III. Lee, Edward.
PN4781.R35   1997
070.4'3 — dc21   97-18934
                                                                                                                                CIP

©1997 Ron Chepesiuk, Haney Howell and Edward Lee. All rights reserved

No part of this book, specifically including the table of contents and index, may be reproduced or transmitted in any form or by any means, electronic or mechanical, including photocopying or recording, or by any information storage and retrieval system, without permission in writing from the publisher.

Manufactured in the United States of America

McFarland & Company, Inc., Publishers
  Box 611, Jefferson, North Carolina 28640

For Ann, Elizabeth and Ola Lee

For Magdalena and Anne Chepesiuk

For Carol Howell and all colleagues who put up with
absences both physical and mental during this project.

With a remembrance of thanks to Put Sophan,
CBS soundman and expediter in Cambodia,
who eventually lost his life because of his work and dedication.

Acknowledgments

Many people helped to make this project possible. Dr. J. William Click, Marilyn Sarow, Robert Pyle, Dr. Larry Timbs, Stewart Haas, William Fisher, and Zeta Sistare, our colleagues in the Mass Communication Department at Winthrop University, put up with the massive printer runs and our odd schedules. From the Winthrop library, Ann Thomas helped with interlibrary loan, and Genie Poag checked bibliographic citations. Gina Price White, Winthrop Archives, and Dr. Michael Kennedy, History, provided strong support through all phases of the project. Dr. Anne Beard, Winthrop speech professor, gave invaluable advice in transcribing the audiotapes. Charlotte W. Tyson, the Winthrop History Department's administrative assistant, helped us meet our deadline commitment. And two graduate students, Michael T. Coventry of Georgetown University and Micheal J. Pereira of Winthrop, gave us a fresh assessment of our project. Alisha Cob, assistant in the Winthrop Archives, helped type the index and allowed us to meet our deadline.

During critical points in our research, many people across the country stepped forward to assist us: Bonita Hickman helped in Seattle, Carol Williams provided much needed transportation and encouragement during the San Francisco leg, Brad and Carol Conger put us up in New York, Leon and Barbara Howell made their Nags Head cottage available for the big writing crunch, and Charles H. Fant, press secretary to U.S. representative John M. Spratt, Jr., shared the wisdom he has gained from 13 years in the nation's capital.

The only authors whom I acknowledge as American are the journalists. They, indeed, are not great writers, but they speak the language of their countrymen, and make themselves heard by them.
—ALEXIS DE TOCQUEVILLE (1805–1859)

Contents

Acknowledgments	vii
Introduction	1

1. TIM WEINER
   Digging for Truth — 5

2. JOHN CAMP
   Following the Money — 19

3. MARJIE LUNDSTROM
   Exposing the Child Killers — 35

4. GERALD POSNER
   Against the Grain — 49

5. DOUGLAS FRANTZ
   Investigating Friends in High Places — 63

6. SYDNEY SCHANBERG
   Lessons from the Killing Field — 75

7. DAVID BURNHAM
   Investigating Bureaucracies — 91

8. BYRON ACOHIDO
   Covering the Company in a Company Town — 103

9. DAN MOLDEA
   Investigating Organized Crime — 117

10. EILEEN WELSOME
    Always Check the Footnotes — 133

11. DAVID BROCK
   Investigations from the Right   145

12. BRIAN ROSS
   Big Stories from Simple Pictures   157

Selected Bibliography   173

Index   177

Introduction

In 1977 the nation's press rummaged through T. Bertram "Bert" Lance's financial records like an eager shopper caresses merchandise at an early morning yard sale. The bright sunshine of media scrutiny revealed flaws in the Carter administration's director of the Office of Management and Budget, and Lance, despite President Jimmy Carter's "Bert, I'm proud of you" embrace, was forced to resign his OMB position. Lance's sin was that in post–Watergate Washington (a city labeled "ethics happy" by Senator John Glenn) the press — and the public — expected to be spared even the appearance of corruption as well as substantiated deeds of wrongdoing.[1]

The press had held up the Georgian for inspection and found him tainted by whiffs of financial corner-cutting such as a questionable $3.4 million sweetheart loan, a cozy relationship with the Teamsters Union, and unpenalized overdrafts for friends and relatives at the Calhoun National Bank which he controlled. And Carter's defense of his pal, "just a country banker," failed to save Lance's OMB career. Watergate and the trauma of Vietnam had so polluted the political atmosphere that Lance, never found guilty of any crime, could not pass the strict ethics test administered by the media. As Professor Suzanne Garmet has written, "In modern political scandals, the show is not considered over until the accused is carried bleeding from the stage."[2]

A year after his ouster, Lance had a chance to enter the lion's den to respond to his critics. He warned the American society of newspaper editors in an April 1978 speech that censorship could follow closely behind the efforts of overly zealous journalists:

> The press has always had its share of professional cynics, as quite properly it should. But that once healthy dash of cynicism appears to have become a pervasive and destructive cynicism, another sad legacy of Vietnam and Watergate.
>
> Along with this unhealthy climate of suspicion is a change in the standards governing publication of allegation, rumor and gossip, and an intense post-Watergate competition among investigative reporters. There are more muck*rakers* around these days than muck*makers*.[3]

Lance's political demise at the hands of vigilant investigative reporters documents a tradition which spans most of this century. "Muckrakers" trace their ancestry back to the era of Theodore Roosevelt. They personify the debate between advocates of First Amendment guarantees and the rights of the quarry — such as the embittered Bert Lance — cornered by the blinding lights of journalistic scrutiny. This debate, which focuses on the proper societal roles of the press, business community, government, and individual privacy, has been emotionally argued since 1906.

Upton Sinclair's goal of converting Americans to socialism failed, but his powerful indictment of the meat-packing industry, graphically depicted in his 1906 novel *The Jungle*, had a profound effect on our country. Disease, unsanitary practices, abuse of workers, and an absence of government regulation of the Chicago stockyards were exposed in Sinclair's book, in which he wrote:

> Let a man so much as scrape his finger pushing a truck in the pickle rooms, and he might have a sore that would put him out of the world; all the joints of his fingers might be eaten by the acid, one by one. Of the butchers and floorsmen, the beef boners and trimmers, and all those who used knives, you could scarcely find a person who had the use of his thumb; time and time again the base of it had been slashed, till it was a mere lump of flesh against which the man pressed the knife to hold it. The hands of these men would be criss-crossed with cuts, until you could no longer pretend to count them or to trace them.
>
> They would have no nails, — they had worn them off pulling hides; their knuckles were swollen so that their fingers spread out like a fan. There were men who worked in the cooking rooms, in the midst of steam and sickening odors, by artificial light; in these rooms the germs of tuberculosis might live for two years, but the supply was renewed every hour.[4]

The meat-packing industry, cozy with inspectors who ignored the conditions described so vividly in *The Jungle*, treated its workers like the slabs of beef that were hoisted on unclean hooks, dangling above cesspools of filth. And Upton Sinclair's book created a public outcry which climaxed with the establishment of the Food and Drug Administration and the march toward protection of laborers. Sinclair found much "muck to rake" because there had been, unfortunately, much "muck" made. Thus his vigilance brought about societal change and greater government regulation of business.

Sinclair was not alone in his journalistic crusade. As editor of *McClure's* and author of *The Shame of Our Cities*, Lincoln Steffens wrote eloquently about the corruption of America's municipalities, teeming with "new immigrants" who too often found themselves trapped in industries like those chronicled in *The Jungle*. Joining the muckrakers was Ida B. Tarbell, author of the series *History of Standard Oil Company*. She wrote about the pollution of the nation's political environment by the steady flow of campaign contributions from the "trusts," monopolies controlled by men with names like Rockefeller, which purchased politicians with the same eagerness that they bought railroads and oil leases.[5]

Stories of misconduct appeared in the pages of *McClure's*, *Collier's*, the *American Magazine*, and *Cosmopolitan*. These publications, easily affordable at 5¢ or 10¢ an issue, educated citizens about misconduct in the U.S. Senate and monopolistic tendencies at Standard Oil. As historian Mark Sullivan has observed, "All the writers of exposure accepted the epithet that was meant for some of them, and in the eyes of most of the public, 'muckraker' became a term of approval."[6]

Interestingly, President Theodore Roosevelt seems to have given these journalists their moniker. While laying the cornerstone for the new House of Representatives Office Building in April 1906, Roosevelt seemed to criticize the efforts of these early investigative reporters. He cited Bunyan's *Pilgrim's Progress*, in which a "Man with the muck-Rake" forfeited a "celestial crown" because he was concentrating on "the filth of the floor." The president urged that journalists look upward and temper their antibusiness efforts. Roosevelt, similarly to Bert Lance, raised the question of balance between "muckrakers" and "muckmakers." In his comments, Roosevelt clearly set forth the parameters for the investigative journalists of his era as they went about their tasks of exposing our country's impurities:

> The men with the muckrakers are often indispensable to the well being of society; but only if they know when to stop raking the muck, and to look upward to the celestial crown above them, to the crown of worthy endeavor. There are beautiful things above and round about them; and if they gradually grow to feel that the whole world is nothing but muck, their power of usefulness is gone.[7]

In researching our book *Raising Hell*, we have conducted interviews with investigative reporters from across America. They come from print and electronic media. Gender seems not to be a factor. On the following pages, you will read about journalists who have relished being "politically incorrect" (as in the case of David Brock's thoroughly researched *The Real Anita Hill*), have methodically shattered cultural icons (David Frantz's exposé of Washington insider Clark Clifford in *Friends in High Places*), and have revealed startling cold war experimentation on unsuspecting citizens (Eileen Welsome's Pulitzer Prize–winning stories). Some of these reporters are pursuing quite obvious — and narrow — political agendas. Bert Lance, and perhaps Clark Clifford and Anita Hill, would point out this heavy-handed abuse of the First Amendment. Other interviewees maintain their sense of Rooseveltian balance and seem inoculated against cynicism. They cite as their mentors a diverse group such as H. L. Mencken, acerbic writer for the *American Mercury* in the 1920s; Seymour Hersch, who broke the story of the 1968 My Lai massacre; Bob Woodward, who with his partner Carl Bernstein doggedly uncovered the Watergate scandal; and William Safire, former speechwriter for Richard Nixon and currently a *New York Times* columnist.

All of our subjects profess their allegiance to Justice Louis D. Brandeis' dictum "Sunlight is the best disinfectant"; they just wish to control the direction and intensity of the rays. They raise the curtain on a variety of ills and hope the glare of sunlight may heal the ailments. On the threshold of the twenty-first century, the "new muckrakers" employ computer technology and old-fashioned rolodexes bulging with sources. They are the professional descendants of Lincoln Steffens and Ida Tarbell and they, like their ancestors, are shaping the craft of journalism for all Americans.[8]

Notes

1. The charges against Lance surfaced at his confirmation hearings and culminated with his September 1977 resignation. President Carter later wrote, "I can see now that this situation — someone accused of wrongdoing who was high in government and an intimate friend of the President — was an investigative reporter's dream" (Jimmy Carter, *Keeping Faith* [New York: Bantam Books, 1982], 132).

2. Carter, *Keeping Faith*, 129–30; Suzanne Garmet, *Scandal: The Culture of Mistrust in American Politics* (New York: Times Books, 1991), 44; *Washington Post*, August 18, 1977.

3. *Washington Post*, April 19, 1978; in his memoirs, Carter alleges that the *Washington Post* had a vendetta against Lance (*Keeping Faith*, 131); ironically, Clark Clifford, who later was pilloried by investigative reporters, tried to salvage Lance's Washington career (*Keeping Faith*, 132).

4. Upton Sinclair, *The Jungle* (1906; reprint, New York: New American Library, 1960), 100.

5. In addition to *The Jungle*, see Lincoln Steffens' *Autobiography* (New York: Chautauqua Press, 1931), Louis Filler's *Crusaders for American Liberalism* (New York: Harcourt, Brace, 1939), and Harold S. Wilson's *McClure's Magazine and the Muckrakers* (Princeton: Princeton University Press, 1970).

6. William Safire, *Safire's Political Dictionary* (New York: Random House, 1978), 435.

7. Theodore Roosevelt, *Presidential Addresses and State Papers* (New York: The Review of Reviews Co., 1910), v, 712.

8. Arthur M. Schlesinger, Jr., ed., *The Almanac of American History* (New York: G. P. Putnam's Sons, 1983), 477.

1

Tim Weiner
Digging for Truth

> Journalism is a lot like making a bouillon cube out of an ox. You boil it down and boil it down. You want it to taste good, and you want it to taste like beef.

Investigative journalist Tim Weiner is not one to seek the headlines, but in his low key way he typifies the trail blazed by investigative journalists like Bob Woodward and Jack Anderson.[1] A 1978 graduate of Columbia University's journalism school, Weiner worked for the *Kansas City Times* before joining the staff of the *Philadelphia Inquirer* in 1983. Today Weiner reports for the *New York Times*, concentrating on coverage of the Pentagon and the Central Intelligence Agency.

Although barely 40 years old, Wiener has already won two prestigious Pulitzer Prizes for his investigative reporting. He garnered the first one as part of a team effort at the *Kansas City Times*; the other was an individual award for his three-part *Inquirer* series that investigated the Pentagon's so-called "black budget." The black budget, Weiner's investigation revealed, is a secret stash kept by the Pentagon that costs the American taxpayer $100 million a day. The Pentagon keeps it hidden by maintaining two sets of books: one for itself and other for the eyes of the American public.

Weiner's investigation was not without controversy, however. The publication *National Journal* claimed Weiner's winning series of articles were derived from a piece the magazine had published in 1986. The Pulitzer committee rejected the *National Journal*'s claim of "recycled journalism," however, and unanimously upheld its award of the 1988 Pulitzer Prize for national reporting to Weiner.

After the *Inquirer* published Weiner's articles, the reporter continued his investigation and published a book, *Blank Check: The Pentagon's Secret Budget*, which appeared in 1990.[2]

During our two-hour interview, Tim Weiner, articulate and deliberate in his thinking, spoke candidly about the controversy surrounding his Pulitzer, as well as the nuts and bolts of the craft and the issues affecting investigative journalists and the journalism profession.

* * *

How did you get interested in the journalism profession?

First of all, I wouldn't call journalism a profession. I consider journalism more a trade than profession. It's not like being a surgeon or a lawyer. There is no specialized language or methodology. If you can write a simple declarative sentence and are able to do detective work, you can be a newspaper reporter. It's a job where you are paid to get an education.

Both my parents are college professors, so learning is very important to me. I saw journalism as a way to get paid and still continue my education and learn about how the world works. I also wanted to use journalism as a craft to point out the wrongs of society and to educate people about the world. I also thought journalism would be the way to see the world. I've been lucky; I have seen a lot. I also love to write. It's incredible to earn a living and still be able to write.

So would you advise a young person who wanted to be a journalist to go to journalism school?

I would definitely advise them to take any undergraduate classes in journalism. I would advise them to study history because one has to have a background or a framework to be a journalist. Learning about history is the best foundation for a journalism career. Also, it's important to write as much as possible. Learning to be a journalist is much like learning to play an instrument. You have to practice every day to get good at it.

Do you consider yourself lucky? A lot of journalists are laboring at jobs in small towns, wishing they could be working as an investigative journalist for a newspaper like the New York Times *and see the world as you have.*

I think that's true. There are a lot of talented journalists, who, for one reason or another, haven't been as lucky as I have. They are laboring in obscurity for bad wages. But presumably they are people who love what they are doing or they wouldn't be doing it.

Do you call yourself an investigative journalist?

That's really a redundancy. What any journalist does is investigative. A journalist who doesn't do that is nothing more than a stenographer. An investigative journalist is no different than a scientist, historian, a cop, or anybody else who is trying to dig beneath the surface of things.

So I guess you're saying that curiosity and persistence are two of the qualities a good journalist should have, whether he's characterized as an investigative journalist or any other type of journalist?

Let me tell you a story. The first long, long investigative work I did for the *Philadelphia Inquirer* took six months to report, and it had to do with what turned out to be an elaborate and far-reaching conspiracy in Camden, New Jersey.

I knew I was on to something so big and complicated that no one had figured out yet. But I didn't know what it was.

I went to see this guy in the Camden county government. I knew he was honest. I told him what I was investigating. He leaned back in is chair, took his cigar out his mouth and said: "Listen, sweetheart. You are opening up a real Pandora's box." But I did open it up and that was the beginning of what eventually led to my exposing the Pentagon's black budget. That is what a good journalist has got to do. He has got to have a burning curiosity and persistence to pry the lid off things and look inside.

So if a journalist has an insatiable curiosity and is willing to work hard, can that compensate for writing skills?

Yes, although it's difficult to report a complicated story if you write with your elbows.

You said earlier that you became a journalist because you wanted to find out the social ills of society. Does a journalist have a moral responsibility to find out the truth?

The U.S. Constitution protects the country's press. We [journalists] have a constitutional privilege in that the government can make no laws restricting our work. With that privilege comes a responsibility to find the truth and speak truth to power. It is a sad fact of modern life that governments lie, that politicians lie, that corporations lie, and that sometimes, unfortunately, the police lie. Each does that to protect the power it enjoys. But journalists armed with the sword and shield of the Constitution can pierce the veil of those lies. That's the moral responsibility of the journalist. I think we are obligated, as someone once said (I forget whom), to "comfort the afflicted and afflict the comfortable."

Does the press do a good job of it?

It does a very good job. There are a lot of pressures on the press to be "official"—to report the official version of things, to be a stenographer. I think the mark of a good reporter is how successfully he resists those pressures.

But how do you explain that according to opinion polls, the public has a low opinion of journalists?

First of all, I think the "media" is what people hate. I think "the media" is a loathsome term that lumps together newspapers, television, advertising, movies, and public relations, all of which are very different forms of the "media." I think television journalism is unintelligible and often difficult to distinguish from entertainment. Sometimes I don't know how the public tells the difference between the local news show and a true crime "docudrama." That has nothing to do with journalism and everything to do with entertainment. People should have a low opinion of that.

Well, what about print journalism? It is often unintelligible, too.

I've never really had any pressure to make my stories dumber, slicker, or juicier than the fact warranted. I've certainly been told to make my stories shorter [laughs]. I might be lucky. I haven't been affected.

On the subject of shorter articles: the public's attention span seems to be getting shorter and shorter. Because of the influence of television, we are thinking more in terms of sound bites, so newspaper articles are getting shorter. Given this trend, how were you able to spend so much time and do such a good job with a complicated subject like the Pentagon's black budget?

No way could I have explained that story in eight hundred words. It was enormously complicated. It detailed issues of secrecy, war, technology, the Constitution, and proper balance between military power and civilian leadership. But a lot of stories can be told in eight hundred words. The Gettysburg Address is eight hundred words. The first chapter of Genesis is probably shorter than eight hundred words. So I'm not arguing against short, terse, rat-a-tat writing. But some stories require extremely lengthy telling.

Your book Blank Check *was based on a three-part series of about ten thousand words that appeared originally in the* Philadelphia Inquirer. *How could you do justice to the topic in ten thousand words?*

I think I barely scratched the surface. That's why I keep writing about it today. But not, of course, to the exclusion of everything else.

One of the big points you make in the introduction to your book Black Budget *is that the best way to find out what the government is doing is to show how the money it handles flows. Could you elaborate?*

If you want to know how a system works, you follow the money trail. It's an old trick, a basic rule of investigative journalism. It's what Deep Throat told Bob Woodward. If you want to understand the weather, you look at the way air currents flow. If you want to understand a system of government or a business, you watch the money flowing. From there you can understand the architecture of power.

A lot of young aspiring journalists might think that investigative journalism is romantic, but you make it sound like there is a lot of drudgery involved.

Yes, sure. There is a lot of work that is the equivalent of going to the library and reading every book on a subject. Sometimes you have to go to a county courthouse and read every land record for a city project or go down to the Pentagon and read every budget book, briefing book, and explication of spending made in a three hundred billion dollar budget.

It takes time. It takes months. But you learn how the world works, and with any luck you explain it in a coherent way to people who don't have the time and energy to do the work on their own. You explain to the people some of the unseen facts shaping their lives.

So, in investigative journalism is there a lot more digging than writing?

I would say a basic rule is that you need an inch-thick pile of documentation for every inch of writing. You need to know ten times, a hundred times more than what you end up writing. When a geologist tries to understand what happened ten million years ago, what does he do? Take a sample of a mountain. From that sample he gets to understand the mountain. What I'm saying is that if you really do your homework, you get to understand the whole mountain.

In reading your book, The Black Budget, *I was impressed by your knowledge of the workings of the Pentagon and weapons systems. How did you get so knowledgeable?*

You read, read, read. Then you talk to people knowledgeable about the subject to understand what you are going to write about. I didn't know anything about the Renaissance when I was in high school and about ready to go to college. But eight years later, I knew a lot about Renaissance painters, musicians, architecture, and so forth. Journalists can get scared off from digging into this stuff because it looks impenetrable. But it's a lot like learning a foreign language or law or medicine. You learn the lingo and talk to the people who are knowledgeable on the subject.

What was the most difficult part of your investigation of the Pentagon's black budget?

Making sure every fact was supported by evidence and then choosing the best way to present the story. It took a lot of time.

Do you follow any procedures to make sure that what you write is accurate? For example, if you quote somebody, do you interview another person to make sure that what the source said was accurate?

I try to interview three people on any given point. It's even better if those three people hate each other, so you are not going to end up talking to one school or faction. If three people who hate each other say something is true, then it probably is.

What happens if two sources agree on a point and one disagrees?

It depends, but I would also quote the source who disagrees. If two people told me that the sun would most likely rise in the east tomorrow, I would probably go with it. If fifteen sources said the U.S. government has a secret plan to put political dissenters in concentration camps, I don't think I would go with it, unless there was documentation or there were plans on paper to do it.

Do you ever get it wrong?

Yeah, sure. The last serious mistake I made was in a story I wrote for the *Kansas City Times* in nineteen eighty-two. Two cops from out of state told me that some criminals, whom I had been following for some time, had been indicted for murder. I reported that. Actually, the indictment had been sealed but not handed down. I was about seventy-two hours ahead of the actual fact. The next day, of course, my newspaper had to print a retraction. I had two people indicted who hadn't been formally indicted. That's pretty awful. Fortunately, I don't get it wrong on a regular basis.

Today American society is very litigious, meaning people seem to be always suing the press. Do you have lawyers who look over what you write before it is printed?
   It depends, but I've never been sued. I guess I'm lucky. I know of colleagues who have spent years fighting off totally baseless libel suits. Of course, what you print has to be true. If you can't prove it, you shouldn't print it. When I write stories that I worry might defame people, I want our lawyers to look at them to make sure I haven't done anything wrong. I try to be careful, so I haven't had to correct an error in some time.

Do you have to go to your newspaper lawyers often?
   You sure have to go to the lawyer more often than you did ten or fifteen years ago.

I'm sure you acquire a lot of material in the course of an investigation. How do you organize it?
   It's important to spend some time organizing before you write. If you don't have organized files, you better have a good memory, and if you don't have a good memory, you better have organized files. It's very important in my case because I'm a pack rat and keep everything because you never know if you are going to have to use that one piece of paper.

Do you have researchers who help you?
   No, I don't. I would love to, though, but most reporters don't have them. Only very few do.

Do you use computer records in researching a story?
   Most of the material I'm after is not in a computer data base I have access to.

But computers have been impacting on investigative journalism more and more, correct?
   To a certain extent. Public records are becoming more and more computerized and reporters are having to use computers to unlock them. I seriously doubt that I will use computer data more in the future. The material that I'm after is generally not in the public record, and I have to get the cooperation of people inside the system. I need a lot of human resources, so I need to talk to a lot of people.

Let's talk more about your investigation of the Pentagon's black budget. How much time did you spend on the investigation?

About six months, from the time I conceived the idea for the project to its completion. There were a couple of interruptions. I took another year to do the book. During that period I uncovered a lot more material. It was my first book. Writing a book is very different from newspaper journalism. I didn't know how to write a book when I started out. I learned by trial and error.

Given the complexities of some investigations, time and money must be considerations in a newspaper decision whether to pursue a project. Did you have to spend a lot of time convincing your boss that the Pentagon might have a black budget and it was a topic worth investigating?

No, they thought it was worth investigating. I have been lucky to work for newspapers that have been generous with both time and money.

Have any of your investigations put you in danger?

I've been involved in some projects that had risks. I have gone into war zones and have been in some pretty uncontrolled situations. For example, I was in the Philippines during the fall of the Marcos regime in nineteen eighty-six and that was dangerous.[3] One story that I wrote about recently involved alleged misconduct of a U.S. Army officer working on a secret program. It led to a break-in at my house; some files were taken. Fortunately, the story had already come out. The individual or individuals who broke in were trying to find out my sources. Unfortunately, I think they got them.

Did all of your investigating and reporting on the Pentagon's black budget make a difference?

There have been some changes, but they haven't been revolutionary. I can't tell if those changes were the result of the system collapsing of its own weight or because my book had something to do with them. For me to claim credit for any changes would be like a rooster claiming the sun is rising because it is crowing. I think, on the whole, my investigating of the Pentagon's black budget has made little difference.

I'm concerned, though, about the impact of the black budget on our system of government. The Constitution of this country calls for a public budget. As a part of the constitutional setup of our country, the government, in exchange for funding, must give a full accounting of how it spends money. That information gives power to the people. The black budget, which is a creature of cold war secrecy and fears, violates the covenant that is our Constitution. Now that the cold war is over, I think we should turn to the basic principle of full, fair, and accurate accounting of the public treasury. I believe the day is past when we should spend billions of dollars for harebrained schemes to fight nuclear wars, to spy on anything that moves in the world, and to create new and better ways to blow the world into smithereens. I tried to say this in my investigation of the black budget, and I've been trying to say it ever since.

In investigating government all the time, isn't there a possibility of becoming cynical about our system of government?

One person's cynicism is another person's reality. I think it's true that governments will lie to preserve their power. That's true of all governments. I don't think that's cynicism. That's reality. Now if I tell you our government lies all the time, that would be cynical. The seeds of the fact that recent U.S. governments will lie are found in the cold war. President Eisenhower lied about the U-2 affair.[4] President Kennedy lied about the Bay of Pigs.[5] President Johnson lied about Vietnam. President Nixon lied half the time about everything, both in domestic and foreign policy. It got to the point where President Carter came into office promising he would never lie to the American people. He did a pretty good job at it, but did a rotten job on other matters and was thrown out of office. I think President Reagan lied about Iran-Contra and the secret funding of Central America. He lied to the American people a lot. Whether he knew it is another question. I think George Bush lied when he said he would never raise taxes. It's the journalist's job to tell the people the government is lying when it lies and to figure out what the truth is. The danger, of course, is that eventually the people will think everything is a lie. To go that way lies disaster for our system of government.

You are forty years old and already have won two Pulitzers. That's quite an achievement. What impact has winning a Pulitzer had on your career?

Winning the Pulitzer made me very happy and proud. I got lots of letters from people I haven't heard from in years. It's the best part of it. All the rest is crap. I certainly realize — and anybody who stops to think about it realizes — that winning a prize doesn't make your work any better or make the winner any smarter. And it certainly hasn't made my reporting any easier.

Is winning a Pulitzer Prize the top award you can get in the journalism profession?

The top award is the freedom to report on what I choose, to think, to travel, and to report on the things that fascinate me. The best award is knowing that good work gets you that freedom.

Did it sting when the controversy surrounding your second Pulitzer erupted?

It was terrible and very painful. It was nasty and a false accusation. It was a fuzzy charge. I wasn't accused of plagiarism, nor was I accused of ripping off someone else's work. I was accused of writing about a subject that had already been written about, which is a pretty weaselly-like charge when you think of it. The Pulitzer Committee threw out the charge in three days. They threw it out almost immediately. But it happens every year. It happened with Pat Sline, the *Newsday* reporter, who was falsely accused of ripping off the *Army Times*. When it happened to me, there were a lot of nasty things printed. It was interesting to be on the other end of the microscope. I think it has made me a more sympathetic and careful writer. Instead of just slamming someone in print, I now realize

I have to be fair and balanced. But I wouldn't recommend what I went through to another journalist [laughs].

Yes, when the public thinks of the prototype investigative journalist, it probably thinks of the team of Woodward and Bernstein of Watergate fame. Have they had any impact on your career?

No. What Woodward and Bernstein did twenty years ago was to show that a lucky obscure reporter, if he dug hard enough and deep enough and works his tail off, can have an impact on our system of government. He can even bring a government down. Watergate has become a myth. There will never be another Nixon, and there will never be another set of circumstances quite like Watergate. The fact is most public officials do not behave like Nixon did in Watergate. The myth about journalism is that we are all good guys and they are all bad guys, and we are the scourge of the venal and corrupt and mendacious. Journalism is not that simple.

Woodward has been criticized for the way he uses sources in his book. In reading Veil *one has to trust Woodward when he says that he had access to [CIA director] William Casey even though Casey's wife said Woodward didn't.[6] Many people doubted that Woodward really talked to Casey.*

It's clear who the major source in Woodward's book *Veil* is. It's William Casey. Bob Woodward has too much credibility. He's a boy scout. He's not going to lie about something like that. Why did Casey talk to Woodward? Woodward thinks it's because Casey wanted his spin or version put in the book he knew Woodward was writing. He wanted to make *Veil* as much a reflection of his worldview as possible.

So do you have any role models?

H. A. Liebling, a writer no one reads anymore, has been a big role model for me. Liebling was ferocious in describing the absurdities and stupidities of the press. In his columns, he pricked every pompous balloon of the self-satisfied and complacent press. He also wrote passionately about what he liked: food, street life, and heroic behavior. He is a great writer and journalist — a wonderful, wonderful role model, both in terms of moral principle and just plain good writing. He is funny as hell, too. The fact no one reads him anymore is a tragedy.

There is also a book that remains an inspiration for me. It's written by Thomas Powers, an excellent journalist who is now retired from the daily life of a journalist. The book is titled *The Man Who Kept the Secrets* and it's a biography of Richard Helms, who was director of the CIA for a number of years and was brought down by the Watergate scandal.[7] The book is a model of fairness and dogged reporting, probing interviewing and great writing about a serious subject: the abuse of power in an intelligence agency. I go back to that book time and time again.

Over the years investigative journalist Seymour Hersh has been an inspiration.[8] Hersh works both inside and outside mainstream journalism and that is enviable. Hersh once defined objectivity as practiced by most newspapers as going out to find a lie to balance the truth. An example of what Hersh is talking about is Reagan's statement, which he said over and over again: "We didn't swap weapons for hostages in the Iran Contra affair." As a journalist you have to respect that statement because the president said it, even though you know it's a lie. You can't say it's a lie because you can't say the president is lying.

Why do sources talk?

To this day I don't really know why people talk. Sometimes people talk because they want their version of reality to be reflected in a story. Sometimes they talk because they want the "truth" exposed. Sometimes people talk because they want to make a point or right a wrong. But I've never understood how I can call a perfect stranger on the phone and ask a pointed question and he responds candidly. I confess it's a mystery of human nature that baffles me.

Do you try to get your sources to say things on the record?

Yes, it's crucial to get people on the record. Why should a reporter trust an anonymous source, someone hiding behind a screen. Too many journalists, particularly in Washington, rely too much on anonymous sources. It's a disease and occupational hazard. I'm loath to use anonymous sources.

Do you have any tips on how to be a better interviewer?

I learned a lot about interviewing before I even became a reporter. I used to hitchhike a lot when I was in college. I would be put out in the middle of the country and people stopped to pick me up. Basically, they were bored and wanted somebody to talk to about the most interesting subject in the world — themselves. They were inarticulate, and you had to draw them out by asking questions and more questions.

People do want to talk. They want to talk about their lives, and they want to make them understandable to you. But you have to draw them out. That's the way it is with interviewing sources for a story. You get people to talk by being empathetic and really letting them run the interview and say what's on their minds. You establish empathy by learning to take good notes without looking at your notebook. You want to establish some human contact.

Do you read a lot?

I read all the time and everything I can get my hands on. My greatest fear is that I will die before I read everything [laughs].

[Laughs.] So it's very important for an aspiring journalist to read?

Reading is the most crucial thing there is. You have to read everything you can get your hands on. That includes good fiction. You can learn a lot about the craft of nonfiction writing by reading Melville, Flaubert, Mark Twain, Dotoyevsky, or Dashiell Hammett. All of them can sum up a life experience or a time or a place in a handful of well-chosen words.

How do you find time to read?

I make time to read. When I wake up, I read three newspapers. I read on the subway. I read at lunch. I take a book to bed. I read all the time. And I don't watch fucking television. Television will be the death of journalists because an entire generation has grown up watching television and not reading. Watching television is a passive existence. You sit there, and the images are beamed at you. Reading is an active existence because your mind is penetrating the word on the page and imagining the world that word creates.

Let's talk about the technique of reporting. Do you use a tape recorder when you interview people?

I generally don't because it makes people uptight. If I need to use one, I will never use it during the first interview. I make sure the interviewee understands I'm using the recorder for clarity. Sometimes I will read a source's words back to them when I'm drafting my article, not to get their approval but to make sure I've quoted them accurately.

Suppose a source wants to see what you've written before it goes to press. What do you do?

It depends. If the topic is controversial, I always make an effort to quote a source accurately, so I might read his quotes back to him, again not for approval but to make sure the quotes are accurate.

Do you have a network of sources?

Yes, I do. It takes trust to build one. You start off with complete strangers. They make a leap of faith and decide to trust you. You report what they said accurately. Over time, they come to trust you. Over time, you will be able to call them out of the blue, and with the reasonable expectation you will be told the truth.

How do you find sources?

It takes time to build up a network of sources. For the past couple of years, I've been trying to write about the Central Intelligence Agency, which is pretty much a closed society. There are many people who used to work for the CIA and are now retired. You call them up and try to convince them to talk to you. You write the story and quote them accurately, and the next time they will be more willing to talk to you. Then ask them if there are any other colleagues, present or former CIA personnel, who would be good to talk to. Hopefully, they say: "Why don't you talk to Don or to Joe? Here are their numbers." Pretty soon two sources become four and four become eight and you have a good, reliable rolodex of sources, who are a part of the collective mind of the CIA.

What about ethical considerations? Some journalists have used duplicity to get a story. Does the end justify the means?

No, never. You can't lie. You can't call someone up and say you are from the police or the morgue. If you do, you are worse than the people you write about. This whole business is based on trust. The first time you lie, you destroy it. You risk destroying your credibility.

Is there a lot of frustration in being an investigative journalist? A lot of your ideas don't lead to stories, do they?

Yes, there is a lot of frustration. But if one idea doesn't work, you move on to something else. You save the research materials you've gathered and maybe something will happen one day that will push the story along. I have one story I've been trying to get for three years. Maybe I will, maybe I won't.

Describe the process by which an idea becomes the story that makes its way into a newspaper.

I try to put some meat on the idea before I present it to the editor. I'll often spend some time chasing a hunch. I'll chase first and discuss later. Every story involves a different pattern of facts. That makes reality rich and complex. There are stories everywhere. Often it's just a matter of luck and having the time and energy to pursue it.

I'll give you an example. I got a call back in January [1992] from a very respected government official who told me: "You got to look into the story the Puerto Rican senate is investigating about the alleged government death squads that were set up in the 1980s. Several people who supported Puerto Rican independence have been targeted." I said, "What!" You can imagine things like that happening in Guatemala or El Salvador but not necessarily where the U.S. flag is flying because Puerto Rico is a commonwealth under the U.S. hegemony. A week later and a quick trip to Puerto Rico and I had an extraordinary set of documents detailing the investigation and on-the-road interviews from members of the Puerto Rican senate, investigators. They were an amazing set of documents. No one had heard of such a story. But it was there waiting to be reported. The *Philadelphia Inquirer* published it last January [1992]. There are stories like that everywhere.

Is having a healthy dose of skepticism a prerequisite for being a good investigative journalist?

I get calls all the time from people who've seen flying saucers and believe the government is covering it up. Or believe that the government of Vietnam is still holding thousands of Americans and that the United States government is covering the story up. Or believe the government is covering up the story behind the assassination of J.F.K. The tragedy of the U.S. government using the shield of secrecy to hide behind its actions is that no one believes anything the government says anymore. Everybody believes Oliver Stone's ridiculous revisionist history — that a cabal led by Lyndon Johnson and the Joint Chiefs of Staff assassinated John F. Kennedy.[9]

There is a big difference between realism and cynicism. The realism is that, yes, governments lie. The cynicism, which affects most people these days, tries to tell you that everything the government says and does is a lie and everything is shielded by falsity and illusion. It's just not so.

Among journalists, is there a lot of competition for stories in Washington?
There's not enough.

There are more stories than journalists pursuing them?
There are so many more stories, but too many journalists here are into what the president had for lunch. Too many are hooked on the visible and ordinary mechanics of an enormous bureaucracy. Not enough journalists have the freedom to dig below the surface.

Is Washington an exciting place to work?
It's different from a real city. It's a small city. A great deal of the city is obsessed with the comings and goings of the vast bureaucracy here. But this is where the money is and a great deal of the power. This is the place where the most interesting organs of government are based — the CIA, the Pentagon, the intelligence branches. It's where the documents are. It's where the hidden architecture of power and policy lie buried.

What about your future? What are your career goals?
I would like to see more of the world. I would like to continue to have the freedom to write about what I want to write about — about the subjects that fascinate me. I would like to write a really good book. I have a topic, but I don't want to jinx it by talking about it.

Do you see yourself being an investigative journalist for the rest of your life?
Yes, there is no way you can beat this job. I have a great deal of freedom to investigate. I'm still learning a lot about the subject that fascinates me: the secret workings of government. Every day I learn more about the world. I have the greatest job in the world.

Notes

1. Bob Woodward and Carl Bernstein were the investigative journalists who broke the Watergate story, which involved the break-in at the Democratic National Headquarters in Washington, D.C., and other illegal activities to help President Richard Nixon win reelection in 1972. Jack Anderson is the dean of investigative journalists. From his base in Washington, D.C., he has covered the national scene since 1947.

2. Tim Weiner, *Blank Check: The Pentagon's Black Budget* (New York: Warner Books, 1990).

3. Ferdinand Marcos served as president of the Philippines from 1965 to 1986. In 1986 he was forced to leave his country after protests broke out against him.

4. The U-2 affair, an incident that occurred in 1960 during the presidency of Dwight D. Eisenhower (1952–1960), involved the Soviet Union shooting down an American U-2 spy plane over the Soviet Union.

5. On April 19, 1961, the Bay of Pigs on the south coast of Cuba was the scene of an invasion by 1,300 Cuban refugees trained in Central America under the CIA's direction.

6. Bob Woodward, *Veil: The Secret Wars of the CIA* (New York: Simon and Schuster, 1987).

7. See Thomas Powers, *The Man Who Kept the Secrets: Richard Helms and the CIA* (New York: Knopf, 1979).

8. Seymour Hersh is the famous American investigative journalist who first rose to prominence with his investigation of the My Lai massacre during the Vietnam War.

9. Hollywood director Oliver Stone made a movie, *JFK*, about the Kennedy assassination.

2

John Camp
Following the Money

> Swaggart addressed me directly in his confession on the Sunday morning after he was caught. He said, "John, I love you, and despite our differences I think you are one of the finest investigative reporters in the world. I really mean that."

John Camp hit the national spotlight as the man who laid the groundwork for the downfall of evangelist Jimmy Swaggart.[1] Few other investigative reporters can claim that their subject cited them by name during a tearful farewell. Yet John Camp still sees the good in Jimmy Swaggart and understands the televangelist's pull on the faithful.

While Camp enjoys retelling the events leading up to Swaggart's fall, he is quick to point out that this was not his first story that brought about major change. His first major story on a Louisiana bank landed several people in prison and garnered him a Radio Television News Directors Association International Award.[2] It was the start of a most impressive investigative career for a man who almost left it all in the bottom of a bottle.

John Camp was born in Nashville, Tennessee, and attended the University of Alabama for a short time before joining the U.S. Air Force in 1953. After his discharge in California, Camp decided to give radio a try. He knew he had the voice. He also attended Columbia College in Los Angeles.

We caught up with Camp at the CNN Broadcast Center in Atlanta.[3] In a way that seems symbolic of the maverick network, the building combines a state-of-the-art television facility with a lobby and visitors' area that ranks as one of the top tourist attractions in the city. From short-order food in the lobby to a discreet Italian restaurant catering to the taste of CNN chief Ted Turner, the CNN Center seems to have it all.[4]

Our interview was interspersed with phone calls about stories and time-outs for breaking stories on the CNN monitor in his fifth floor office. One wall is covered with major awards and a magazine cover which featured Camp. The office looks out over the open interior, and a steady stream of visitors rode the escalators as tour groups passed through the building. In many ways, Camp seems to reflect the attitude and culture of CNN. He's a self-made man and

John Camp. Photo by Haney Howell.

investigative reporter, and his presence will fill a room. At the same time, he is very up-front about his struggles and his gratitude. We decided to start at the beginning of his broadcast career.

* * *

How did you get into investigative reporting?
I started as a full-time investigative reporter in Baton Rouge in nineteen hundred seventy-two. I had been in the business for almost ten years. I started in nineteen hundred sixty-two at a little 250-watt station in Sanora, California. I had no plans of getting into news. My ambitions were to do play-by-play, be a disc jockey. None of this stuff involved any element of becoming a news reporter.

Two weeks after I was hired, the news director at the station quit. There were only three of us there: the news director, the station owner, and me. We had two sponsored newscasts, and the owner asked me if I was interested in doing a newscast. I told him no. He said, "Good, we'll let you do it." We had to do it because the sponsored newscasts were revenue producers.

We had no wire machine; it had been repossessed. I looked at previous newscasts, and I went around with the boss for two days to the sheriff's department, the police department, the highway patrol, and did the normal small, local news market gathering of those things. We called the local funeral homes and found out who had died. We had no morning daily newspaper. There was a little afternoon tabloid, so you had to depend on your own devices to gather the news. I spent three and a half years in that little market.

I wondered how people gathered the news for the newspapers. I bet they go to these meetings and do things. I learned how to cover council meetings, board of supervisor meetings, the courts. I went to the county courthouse and discovered how you run title searches and check out lawsuits and learned about the criminal docket. Little did I know that from Tuolumne County, California, to Manhattan, these didn't change. In some fashion, Tuolumne County was more advanced in its reporting than Manhattan. That got me interested in reporting.

After a one-year stop in a larger market, I was hired as a real news director for a news department in Chico, California. I really began to enjoy news. In nineteen hundred sixty-seven an old friend of mine had moved to Lake Charles, Louisiana, and he was the manager of a station. He ran into the manager of a station in Baton Rouge, who asked if he knew any news people to hire. I was that person. I was brought back to anchor a statewide newscast and run a small news department. That statewide newscast essentially focused on the legislature and capitol news. That was my first exposure to a capitol or state house.

Was that the start of your investigative career?

No. I began to develop a little bit of a reputation in Baton Rouge. I had a talk show that ran in the afternoons, kinda news oriented ... we had a guest each day. It focused on a lot of public affairs and political issues. Along about that time, John Barleycorn started catching up with me.

I was drinking pretty heavily, showing up drunk on the air. I went into DTs. In nineteen hundred seventy-one, I called up the station manager at four A.M. and told him what he could do with the radio station. I left, and when I got back, there was no job. The only job I could get, because my reputation preceded me, was with a black-programmed radio station. I set up a news department. I worked there a year, got involved in AA, and was doing very well at staying sober. The word got back to my old radio station, and they hired me back.

They didn't know what the hell to do with me because they had another news director. I became director of special projects. That was in nineteen hundred seventy-two. I produced a couple of radio documentaries and stumbled across a nice little news story, which ended up getting a state official fired because of the backstabbing he was doing to his boss. I got quite a bit of publicity around Baton Rouge, so I scratched out "director of special projects" and wrote in "investigative reporter."

What was your first, true investigative story?

At that radio station, I began doing the most classic investigative story I've ever done. It had all of the elements of someone calling me, meeting me outside of this place, "I'll be wearing a white carnation" type of deal. I meet the guy, and he hands me a tattered newspaper clipping. He says find out what's behind this, and you'll have the biggest story in Louisiana.

The clip only said that the Louisiana state auditor had issued a report criticizing a bank for failing to deposit money in interest-bearing accounts and criticized a state official for putting money in this bank and not in interest-bearing accounts. I began looking into that. The upshot was that the bank was a depository for his campaign funds. I would later discover that they got a disproportionate number of SBA loans for customers, and more importantly, they paid more than one hundred twenty-five thousand dollars in bribes to a state official in order to have two and a half million dollars left in non–interest bearing accounts.

The story ended up with a half-dozen indictments. The attorney general calls a news conference, credits me with breaking the story, and I end up the much-acclaimed investigative reporter. That year I won the RTNDA International Award. Remember, this was still radio. That is what got me to Miami.

How did you win your first Peabody Award?[5]

The first Peabody was on an investigation of the Miami state attorney's office. We did undercover filming of him meeting with gamblers. That led to the establishment of a statewide grand jury, and there were a lot of ramifications from this. The gamblers would meet with the state attorney, or district attorney for Dade County, then meet with Myer Lansky and others the following week.[6] There were direct links between Lansky and other gamblers and the ones who were meeting with the city attorney and a judge. I put that together in a fifteen-minute show and that was the Peabody Award Winner in nineteen hundred seventy-four.

In nineteen hundred seventy-five, I did a companion piece, which was an exposé on the FBI chief of the Miami office and his association with organized crime figures. Then in nineteen hundred seventy-five, the award was for a kinda "Know Your Neighbor" Mafia series. I went around doing undercover video of various Mafia figures.

The Jimmy Swaggart story brought you national fame. How did you get onto it?

The Swaggart story was really the key story. I consider it to be a major, well-done effort. That documentary was a high point, I think, in my career. It lifted me up from everyday investigative reporting both in style and substance.

When I returned to Baton Rouge from Boston, they said we've got this guy Swaggart out here. This guy is really weird. He has millions and millions of dollars coming in. He's one of these guys who can turn on the tears just in an instant. Channel two (WBRZ) had provided a studio for his first programs, and he was just legendary.

I would be sitting there, when he would suddenly turn on the tears. It was like a faucet. He could cry for money and do all of these things, everything. He was a talented musician. I didn't know much about Swaggart. I'd heard his name. I'd read that he was the cousin of Jerry Lee Lewis, so I had that much knowledge of him.[7]

What made you start looking into the Swaggart ministry?

I began to think about doing something, and just about that time, somebody walks in. He's a truck driver out at Swaggart's, and he's talking about how un-Christian he was treated by the Swaggarts. That in and of itself was not much of anything. His wife had complained about being sexually harassed, that she was fired and so was he.

I thought it was pretty outrageous, but that kinda reflects an attitude. That raised my threshold of interest a little bit more. Two weeks later somebody came in who became one of my key sources. He was able to bring with him document upon document showing this pattern of abuse of employees, of exploitation, of how they run their operation. That's when I began to take a major interest.

I began looking around basically from source to source. If you've got a name or two who you know will talk, then it mushrooms. You call up and you see if the person is willing to talk, and then after they give you information, the last question is, "Is there anyone else you know that would be willing to talk with me, and who do you think I should talk with?"

I had two sources. Then two made four, four made eight, eight made sixteen. Some of them called Swaggart and said we have this reporter asking questions about the operation.

Then somebody told me about a lawsuit that had been filed and a countersuit that I had just overlooked. It was basic. When you go through indexes of lawsuits, you just may glance at the initial page of the pleading rather than go through them. In this particular case, the lawsuit wasn't even titled properly.

It was filed by the Swaggarts, the Swaggart Ministry, against a musician named Duane Johnson. And Duane Johnson had countered. The elements of the lawsuit were that Duane Johnson was the lead musician of Jimmy Swaggart's band, and Duane was one of the people who'd brought this Nashville sound, particularly the guitar sound, into the Jimmy Swaggart music.

He had an agreement with Swaggart that the ministry would finance a home he bought in Baton Rouge, and he could hold that home in perpetuity and pay for it so long as he was an employee, up until he left of his own volition.

In this case, what had occurred was that he was fired, and they were trying to evict him from the home, and he had countersued. He said this was not of his own volition, that he had to leave because they kicked him out of the house. And the question came, why did they kick him out of the house? He got caught in bed with Jimmy Swaggart's son Donnie's wife, and in the pleading they talked about how Jimmy had come and threatened to break his legs, to hire somebody to do this. It was the typical nasty bullshit.

This became a really strong piece of leverage for me. When I first called Swaggart to tell him, he comes on the phone, typical Jimmy Swaggart. I've been waiting for your call, John, I know you've been asking around. You want to find out about us, and I just want to tell you that we are just as open out here as we can be and we want you to come in and ask any questions you want, we want you to see this ministry and on and on and on. He said that the best way for me to learn is to travel on a crusade. Then you'll be able to see it for yourself what we do and how we're doing this. I said, fine. It was to be in Hampton, Virginia.

I began talking to other people within the ministry, and it became known that I knew about the Duane Johnson lawsuit. I always assured them that I was not using that, that it wasn't any of my business, and so on. But it became something that they feared greatly. As a consequence, if I ran into any roadblocks, I would say, look, guys, we're being fair with you. I'm not using the Duane Johnson lawsuit. There would be an immediate acquiescence to any request I made. It was probably a sophisticated form of extortion of information, but I bided by my word.

Was that where you got all that fabulous video? The money counting?

It was unbelievable. It was on that trip. We just went along. For instance, getting in the money baskets, where they were all singing and dropping the money. Donnie Swaggart didn't want us in there. It was again, Donnie, your dad said we could have everything, we have an agreement, I'm trying to be fair with you people, and now you're trying ... He'd say, OK, go in, but he didn't like it.

The only time I really ran into a roadblock was after we got back. I wanted to shoot some B-roll before I do my confrontation.[8] We do the ministry, we do the interiors, shooting and so forth. We get into what is really, what was the big vault of the place, where they were running the money into the machines.

We were shooting in there, and we shot for about ten or fifteen minutes, and his top guy comes in and says, "I've got to ask you to leave. They don't want you to shoot here, we have security problems." I assured him that we are going to show nothing as to what the security devices are. They threw us out, but we'd gotten the video by this time. I argued with him long enough to get the video, and he's still very unhappy about it.

How did you structure the interview with Jimmy Swaggart?

Every time I lecture to a journalism class, I say the same thing. You structure your interview by knowing the answers to the questions you are going to ask. You build that around how you are going to get answers to questions you don't know the answers to.

With Swaggart, I had plotted it out before we went in. I had a young black photographer who field produced this thing, Sailor Jackson. I told Sailor, I want to burn off twenty minutes throwing softball questions and you shoot some B-roll. I'll give him the softball questions, but be set to do a close-up, to zoom in, to do all the things you need to do when we start on the second tape.

We had planned this, and when we moved over to tape two, I began asking harder and harder questions. There's a sequence of questions that were kinda devastating to him, building that sequence of money they received.

I said, "Jimmy, the first thing people want to know about ministries, televangelism, is, what's your salary?"

He said, "I'm not quite sure, John, I think I make about thirty thousand dollars a year."

I said, "I understand you get a check each month for sixty-eight hundred dollars."

He kinda backs off and says, "You're right, John, every month I get a check for sixty-eight hundred dollars, but I turn right around and I write a check back to the ministry for thirty-five hundred dollars."

And I said, "That's to pay off a loan, isn't it?"

"That's right," he said. "My son and I, we borrowed some money to build a house at such and such a place, I don't know what the interest rate is."

I said, "Fourteen percent." And he kinda does his third thing. From there, it was like taking candy from a baby. Every question I asked, he figured I knew the answer anyway, so why lie. I asked him about the jewelry that was being sent to the ministry. I knew a little bit about that because one of my sources handled all of the insurance for the ministry and had told me about how much jewelry they had.

And he said, "People give us gifts." He says, "This suit I have on, it was given to me, and these shoes were given to me, and this watch," and he pulls off his Rolex, gold Rolex, and he says: "This watch, it was given to me by a jeweler in California. They say it's worth five or ten thousand dollars. He got it wholesale, and I don't think it's worth that much." Then he puts the watch back on.

I ask him about the salaries, and then I asked him about Frances.[9] He says, "Frances has been given some things; she was given a coat the other day, a mink coat, I think."

He answered all of the questions that you'd ever dream of. This guy, you know, is pathological. He's like a kid. And the pathology is, if you catch him like he was caught in New Orleans and elsewhere, it's, "I, ah, ah, I did it, I'm sorry, and you're right."

There are people who would say you were responsible for bringing Jimmy Swaggart down. Do you feel any responsibility for that at all?

Nah. You know, the funny thing about it is that I feel sorry for Jimmy. I liked him personally. There was something about him contrary to the cynic's characterization that he was out ripping off people. I think Jimmy had a true calling. He turned down opportunities to go with Jerry Lee Lewis and Sun Records and become a rock and roll star. I think he was misguided in many of his attitudes, but more importantly, there was an underlying pathology.

One of the things that hasn't been reported is that Swaggart's adventures down into the red light district were not at nighttime. He wasn't operating under the cover of darkness. This was during the middle of the day, going for nooners. A rational person, whose picture is on the cover of *Time* and *U.S. News and World Report*, which was the case at that time, and with other spreads inside magazines with full-page pictures; who's appearing as a commentator on religious affairs in nightly network news programs, wouldn't do that.

I was really surprised. Everybody with sources intimately involved in that ministry, within his inner circle, never once raised the issue of sexual misconduct. They always felt that he would never do that.

But I'd always felt that the issue here was beyond sexual misconduct, and his little sexual peccadilloes, that it went to the issue of accountability. You had a guy taking in one hundred sixty million each year, manipulating rich widows and others, and no one to come in to say, "Jimmy, you can't do this, this is wrong."

If you have a sense of gratitude for things that have happened in your life, you don't want to go off on the deep end of challenging somebody else who is offering some kind of spiritual sustenance to large numbers of peoples. I had some real reservations about where I was going with this story.

Did something change your mind?

Yes. One of my sources told me a story about two sisters who were contributors to the ministry. He had received their letter, and the substance of the letter was that for years they had contributed to the ministry, that they were real concerned about feeding the children in these third world countries. They said we know that it is more important than our own welfare, and inflation has taken its toll on our social security checks. Our question is: Would it be a sin if we committed suicide and left our insurance to the Swaggart ministry to feed these children?

After receiving the letter, he took it in to Jimmy and said this is really urgent, you need to talk to these people, this is an emergency situation. He said it was not that Jimmy refused to do it, it was the cavalier fashion in which he looked at it. He said that was the end of their relationship. Jimmy said, "Oh, yeah, I'll try to give them a call in the next day or so." That was a fallback when I sit there and ask, "Should I be doing this story?"

I said, hey, these people are sending their money to Jimmy Swaggart, thinking they are feeding starving children in third world countries, when only one cent or two cents on the dollar is getting to them. They think all of these missions he shows are part of the Jimmy Swaggart outreach effort, when in fact he was contributing a million or so in nineteen hundred eighty-three of his seventy-five million dollar income, to the Assemblies of God missions, and they were putting it into their one hundred sixty-three million dollar outreach program. I think these people had the right to know. Then they can make their choices.

Swaggart addressed me directly in his confession on the Sunday morning after he was caught. He said, "John, I love you, and despite our differences I think you are one of the finest investigative reporters in the world. I really mean that."

All those things combined gives the impression that I broke the sex story, but "Nightline" actually broke it.

Do you believe in "following the money?"

I think the most astonishing "follow the money" story that I did was on that fourth Peabody, "The Best Insurance Commissioner Money Can Buy." It ran in December of nineteen hundred eighty-eight. This was one of those stories that I almost shrugged away. I had done an exposé on the longtime insurance commissioner in Louisiana by the name of Sherman Benard. How he qualified for this position I have absolutely no idea, but he served sixteen years, and everybody wanted to get rid of him. With his name beginning alphabetically with a B, in this obscure position, people just voted for him.

It got so outrageous that in nineteen hundred eighty-seven, a candidate named Doug Green ran for insurance commissioner. Green was supposed to be the clean-cut guy who was going to come in and get the department in shape. I got a little suspicious when private detectives working for an insurance company supporting Green came to me for a copy of that documentary. I provided them a script as a courtesy, as we generally did anybody.

As the campaign progressed, I began getting calls not from Green's people, but Benard's people, saying, "You should take a look at this Green. He's got one insurance company paying for everything. They're doing his printing, they've hired the payroll, they're doing it all. The company is called the Champion Insurance Company."

I thought it was election rhetoric. They were desperate and in the final weeks of the campaign. I wasn't going to jump into a campaign in the final days with some sort of story, even if it were true, unless it was really egregious, as it turned out to be.

Green is elected, beats Benard, takes office, and two or three of these people still call me. They'd say, "You'd better look at that campaign, look at where all that money came from. That guy spent $2.3 million, the most money ever spent in a campaign for insurance commissioner in the country."

A couple or three weeks after he takes office, I get a call from a detective who says you might want to check the sheriff's department. The chief examiner of the Insurance Department has just been arrested, charged with theft. I told the desk, since it's a daily story, and I don't pay too much attention to the story until I hear it that night.

He's charged with petty theft. Petty theft is a citizen's warrant for some minor little charge. He'd written a letter to Champion Insurance Company on a departmental letterhead two years before, asking them to take a look at the delay in settling the claim of his son. It was poor judgment to begin with, but Jesus, is this all these detectives could find after looking at this guy for all this time?

I started asking questions. I learned that two-point-one million of the two-point-three million used for his campaign came from this same insurance company. They were laundering these loans through other people and then putting the money in there. I wondered, why would one company spend two-point-one million to get an insurance commissioner elected?

I began calling people, and they tell me, why don't you talk to the former claims manager? I call, and he asks to come in and talk, but he must bring somebody with him because he didn't want to talk to me alone. After the chitchat, I asked him why they would spend two-point-one million to support this campaign. He says that's because they're running behind in the payment of their claims at the rate of forty-three thousand dollars a day. That translates into whatever the figure is for the year.

I asked, "How are they staying open?" He told me that it's a one hundred fifty million dollar a year insurance company and that you can hold it afloat. He told about all of the devices they used to beef up their reserve to stay afloat and get a clean bill of health from the insurance commissioner.

I said, "Jesus Christ, can you prove it?"

He opens his briefcase. He flaps out ninety days worth of tapes showing how they paid their claims, every one of them, shows the amount of approved claims, where a person goes out and has his car checked, and they say this approved for payment and they send it in. It's the company's obligation within a period of time to pay that. He showed me ninety days of those claims.

Every day the claims ranged between fifty thousand and eighty thousand dollars. Yet on only one day in ninety days did they ever pay more than twenty thousand dollars in their claims. My source said he almost got fired on that day for exceeding what was the arbitrary limit of twenty thousand dollars. He was told, instructed, that the daily payout was to be nineteen thousand eight hundred dollars, nineteen thousand seven hundred fifty dollars, nineteen thousand nine hundred fifty dollars. They were falling behind forty thousand dollars, then another forty thousand dollars.

I began looking at their assets. I discovered they had floated a law through the legislature that essentially allowed them to issue their own paper to show as their assets of the company. They were flowing the money through a Grand Cayman bank account. You always call in favors at the right time. I had a bank president who owed me a favor, and I asked him to just check the accounts and see where the deposits were going. He called me back and said, "They've got a bank in the Grand Cayman Islands."

It ended up with all of the people getting indicted. The father and the son and two daughters and the wife in the insurance company, plus a couple of other people. The insurance commissioner, the deputy insurance commissioner, and somebody else all going to prison for a lengthy period of time.

It shows the toughness of WBRZ. We opened with just me on camera, black background, dramatic lighting. My lead line into that story was, "In nineteen hundred eighty-seven, a wealthy Baton Rouge businessman bought the office of insurance commissioner for a close friend. In this report we will tell you why."

We laid the thing out. A consultant once told me that on these complicated stories, if you really want to help yourself, about every ten minutes stop and review what you've told them so far. In that particular piece, since it was so complicated, I just did it straightforward. Let's talk about what we've reported now and what it means. We'd give a review of each one and move on to the next phase. That's another of the Peabodys that I'm really proud of. I'm told that that piece is used at meetings of First Amendment lawyers, who gasp when they hear the lead line to that story, and see the commissioner's face coming through a hundred-dollar bill.

You've been criticized over your relationship with the late Barry Seal, the reputed drug smuggler.[10] *What's your position?*

Barry, you know, has become something of an icon in recent years. If you don't believe in the resurrection, look at Barry Seal. They dig him up every two or three years.

Seal came to me after that one CIA operation he was involved in. I read these stories and I have to laugh, because number one, I'm the only person who really ever traveled with Barry Seal. I'm the only reporter who had any close insight as to what he was doing. I mean, I flew in the C-123 that was later shot down in Nicaragua. I have video of Barry and me in the plane. I was consultant on the movie that was made on HBO. I got a lot of criticism for that story.

It happens if you take up the banner of a guy who's supposed to be the most notorious drug smuggler in the United States. And I said I wasn't taking up his banner. I said that this story was not about Barry Seal, it's about the U.S. government, and what steps the U.S. government would take to basically convict somebody whom they deem a crook.

As I understand the justice system, the crooks are suppose to violate the law, and the cops are suppose to enforce it. We had a flip-flop here. We had Barry Seal out working as an informant, seeking to enforce the law, and we had the cops in Baton Rouge violating the law trying to get him.

There was a lot of controversy about my involvement in the story. As I clearly pointed out, it wasn't about Seal's guilt or innocence. It was about the treatment, and about the methods and techniques of law enforcement people. People don't seem to understand that.

Do journalists have a responsibility to be moral? Is it fair to bend the rules a bit to get the story?

It's a hard question because you hate to refer to situational ethics. I have found myself doing things in the past that I wouldn't do today. Because I made the decision instantly based on a piece of ... hell, to be honest about it, based on my own desire to get the friggin' story. If after I do a story, I feel guilty about the way I handled the story, I reassess how I did the story.

I think in Swaggart, I stayed away from making any judgments on Swaggart and his followers from an elitist view of fundamentalist religion. After all, we're protected by the same amendment to the U.S. Constitution, so I wasn't going to go questioning the theological basis for Swaggart's ministry. I dealt with the accountability, and in a more globalized fashion, that none of these television evangelists were held accountable.

Have you changed your view on the importance of visuals in television reporting?

When I went to Boston, WCVB, I was responsible for setting up what was one of the first, if not the first, multimember investigative unit. I went there in October of nineteen seventy-six, and I really fucked up that deal because I was beginning to believe that I was a real journalist rather than a television reporter. We set our unit up in October of nineteen seventy-six, and the following spring Westinghouse created their "I Teams"—bigger and better. Everybody was hiring folks that were supposed to be hard-hitting journalists but, when our reports would hit the air, people would say, "Jesus, this stuff puts us to sleep, this stuff is horrible."

I would argue with producers, "It's five minutes. Sure it doesn't move, but damnit, it's real news and we have to tell the story, we can't compromise." It was a lot of my own hardheadedness, and my inability to recognize that your story is not worth a damn if people don't watch it.

How do you justify using TV as your medium?

Television used properly can be the most effective medium there is for investigative reporting. In a newspaper article you can't capture the little nuances when someone who is lying to you is explaining the unexplainable. You can't show with the dramatic impact, the kinds of graphics in which you pull out those important numbers, that are needed to explain the story.

You've been known for your tough interview style. Have you changed your methods?

I've been disappointed in "gotcha" journalism. I was one of the originators of lurking behind bushes with hidden cameras, sneaking them into restaurants. Back in nineteen seventy-five, there was a story I was doing involving an official at a golf course, handling book making. Since it was a municipal golf course, we just walked straight down the hall with cameras. The guy was sitting in his office, working at his desk. We walk in, the lights go on, and with this booming voice, I say, "We would like to ask you about your book-making operation."

The guy is scared out of his wits. He jumps back, holds his hands out, and says, "I don't know what you're talking about." He's totally caught off guard and looks as guilty as hell. Presumably he was, but that's not the point.

When I got back and put it up—this was in film days—when we racked it on the projector and looked at it, we were all orgasmic because it was a classic "gotcha" situation. After I used that, I thought, how would I react if somebody walked into my office, a light flashed on, and they began asking me some questions? Is that fair journalism?

I start looking at this gotcha mentality, of tracking people down, and the one thing I am absolutely sure of is that a private citizen has no requirement to speak to the media. They can tell you to fuck off.

I'm ambivalent about public officials because I think they have an obligation to be responsive. But I think first you have to make a good-faith effort to talk with these people before you hit them with a question. When I ambush somebody, my question is always, Mr. Smith, you are whoever you are, you are an elected official, I think you have an obligation to answer this, why won't you answer this question?

It's still a little bit of a cheap shot, but by the same token an evasive public official is violating his public trust, so there is a degree of justification there.

Do you feel pressure from the TV tabloid magazines?
I don't watch it, number one. It's only by accident that I watch "Inside Edition" or "A Current Affair" or any of the tabloids. So I don't consciously see them. On the other side of the ledger, I know some of the people who work for tabloids and they are good reporters, do some pretty decent stuff. When you have stories where the priorities are being "viewer friendly," I think that it creates problems. This is not only for the tabloids. Viewer-friendly stories — I don't know where in hell that phrase came from, but I've heard it so many times. Not all stories are viewer friendly. There are stories that need to be told. It goes back to this old argument, do we tell people what they need to know or what they want to know? And how do you strike that balance?

Has all this made you cynical? All of this digging?
When I talk to journalism classes, I tell people that what's wrong with journalism today is there are too many cynics out there. Skepticism is what makes a good investigative reporter. Cynicism is what makes a bad investigative reporter — when you go in believing that they're all crooks. The most important thing that probably influenced me, or one of the most important things in investigative reporting, was when we scratched off the "director of special projects" in nineteen hundred seventy-two and put on "investigative reporter."

I then took off pursuing some think-tank kind of boondoggle deal, and I was just convinced that I was going to find all sorts of corruption, corrupt relationships with the state of Louisiana at a research institute. I looked at it for five weeks, and I gathered documents and I brought in things, and I finally set them all down and I said, what's the news peg on this thing? and I couldn't find it. What I had found was a bunch of chickenshit little things that involved somebody overspending his lunch budget by five bucks. I'd wasted six weeks, and I'm looking at this thing and they're expecting me to do big things here. This is one of my first investigative efforts.

I walked in to my news director, who was more my colleague, and I said: "Phil, I hate to say this, but I wasted six weeks. There's no fucking story." He told me to make the call. And I said, no story.

It's the most important thing that ever happened to me. Now when I go out, I'm not fearful of saying it's not there. Too many reporters are going out with a cynicism that says not only that "I've got to come up with a story," but the belief that when they're talking to a public official, and the public official has Jesus standing on his right shoulder and the Angel Gabriel standing on his left shoulder and is talking about what he did and how he did it and the investigative reporter is saying, "Hah! You lying son-of-a-bitch." When you have that kind of cynicism, it causes you to lose sight. Enter the story with a presumption of something there, but with a belief that there may be extenuating circumstances or there may be explanations for all that you see. I've taken their suggestions and taken a look at the other side and have seen that it's one hundred eighty degrees from what I'd expected.

How important is writing in what you do?

I used to think that writing the story was writing. You don't write television. You basically describe television. That is one of the hardest lessons I had to learn. The word images occasionally help, but pictures really tell the stories. That's why with today's high level of technology in graphics, you can tell stories relatively easy. You've got to remember that you don't have to talk about the green grass. Everyone has a color television set today. They can see the green grass.

Any heroes? Any role models?

Oddly enough, my hero, my role model — and this would surprise him — was Doug Manship.[11] Back in nineteen hundred seventy-three, seventy-two, whatever, when I got hired after getting sober, I went out and I gathered information, a pretty decent story, on a right-wing, nutty congressman from Baton Rouge. In the course of gathering the information, it was during a campaign, I found an organization called the Supreme Court Amendment League, which was dedicated to the proposition of impeaching Abe Fortus, who was a Supreme Court justice. The congressman had taken advantage of his position as a conservative congressman to borrow large sums of money from this group and not pay it back.

I was given information, interestingly enough not by his political opponents, but by some people in D.C. who were unhappy about this thing. I put together this story about two weeks before the election in which he was a surefire winner. We run it past the lawyers, and then Doug gets called in, as was the case in all of our potential litigious stories. He reads the story and says, "Good story, John." There was only one thing that I was going to suggest. I knew this particular story was not going to have one bit of impact on the election. I told him that all we're going to get is a bunch of denials and allegations of trying to influence the election, and it's just going to be the same old rhetoric. I suggested that rather than go with the story in the hopper, that I know we have exclusively, let's wait until after the election.

Doug said no. He said our job is not to maximize the impact of the story, that our job is to tell the public what they need to know in a timely fashion. He says this guy is going to stand for reelection in two weeks, and both of us know it won't mean a thing in the election, but our obligation as journalists is at least to give that information to the public, and let them make their own judgment. That was probably the biggest influencing factor in my going back to WBRZ. Because I always remembered that.

The first major story I did went all the way on the libel case. We won, but it cost him a ton of money to try the case. I've been fortunate in that I've never had a story rejected because of the litigious nature. I've been sued a dozen times for libel and had three cases go all the way, and two or three others go the advanced stages of discovery. Just incredibly costly and time consuming. Yet Doug Manship stood by me through it all.

If a young person asked you about being an investigative reporter, what would you tell them?

I'm a bad person to answer that question because I'm so undereducated. I barely got out of Tuscaloosa High School. People say, "What makes you a good investigative reporter?" I can say, first, selling Bibles in back roads of Alabama and holding open the big picture of Jesus in front of potential customers and saying, "Ma'am, are you telling me you can't afford the price of a pack of cigarettes each day for this beautiful Bible?"

Then I improved that by selling the Great Books of the Western World. I've always said that if you can convince a plumber he needs to read Aristotle to operate his plunger better, you can sure as hell talk somebody into giving you some documents.

There are two things. Number one, investigative reporting requires you to—I don't like to say this, I don't like using technical terms—it requires you to be a bullshit artist. It's essential that you can talk with people, that you can carry on conversations that lead them to believe that you know what you're talking about.

The second is knowledge of what you are talking about. You need something more than a *Reader's Digest* knowledge of the subject you're looking at. My disappointment with young journalism students is that they don't read. My first question when anybody comes in to talk about an internship is how many papers do you read each day and how many news magazines do you read each week? It just shocks me the people who gain their information from either their local newspaper, from *People Magazine* or from *USA Today*.

How many do you read?

My commitment each day is to read the *Atlanta Constitution, USA Today*, which I just criticized, the *New York Times*, the *Washington Post*, and the *Wall Street Journal*. At home I take *Time, Newsweek*, I get *U.S. News and World Report* here, I take *Vanity Fair*, which is good for in-depth profiles, and I take *New Yorker* magazine because that's a sophisticated magazine and I'm supposed to be sophisticated instead of living in a trailer [laughs]. If they only knew.

Another asset. I really didn't know I had until I had used it and had become somewhat successful. When I first entered radio, I had no interest in journalism at all, but I had a tremendous amount of knowledge that I'd gained over the years from a lot of reading and that offset my educational shortcomings. The one thing that I had that I didn't realize I had was an almost photographic memory for facts, figures, names. I mean, I can go back and quote you names of people and events. I discovered this is something of a gift, to be able to just pluck out of the sky and visualize everybody who was sitting at a table at a meal I had twenty five-years ago and what was said and why it was said. That's been a real asset.

Notes

1. Rev. Jimmy Swaggart led the Swaggart Ministries from its base in a local church in Baton Rouge, Louisiana, to a nationwide television giant.
2. The Radio Television News Directors Association is a major national organization which represents news managers. The RTNDA Award is highly sought by local stations because it represents the views of their peers.
3. John Camp joined the Cable News Network (CNN) as a senior correspondent for the Special Assignment Unit. It focuses on special projects, including investigative reports.
4. When Ted Turner founded CNN in 1975, many observers doubted the market for an all-news network, especially on cable. It has now grown to become a major force in worldwide news gathering. At the time of the interview, Turner Broadcasting and Time-Warner were working out the details of a possible merger. Turner also controls CNN Headline News, TNT, WTBS and other cable properties.
5. The Peabody Award is given annually in a number of categories, including investigative reporting. It is one of the most coveted awards in broadcast journalism.
6. Myer Lansky was one of the top Mafia figures operating in Miami in the early 1970s.
7. Jerry Lee Lewis was one of the top Southern rock musicians during the 1960s. Both Swaggart and Lewis learned to play piano from the same blues musician, and their driving bass styles show their common background.
8. The "B-roll" contains pictures showing the setting for a story. They would include the wide shots and other necessary pictures that make up a visual story.
9. Frances Swaggart is Jimmy Swaggart's wife.
10. Barry Seal was a pilot and drug smuggler who later became a government informer. He eventually died under mysterious circumstance. John Camp was an adviser for a movie based on Seal's career.
11. The Manship family owns WBRZ television, along with other media properties. The Baton Rouge market is well known for quality television and tough reporting, mainly because of the support of the Manship family. The communication school at Louisiana State University is named for the family.

3

Marjie Lundstrom
Exposing the Child Killers

> I am very demanding, a real perfectionist. I also know that I was harder on myself than anyone could ever be on me. I remember that with the reporters. When they screw up on something, I don't really need to come down too hard because they'll do most of the heavy lifting for me. It's true. Especially with the good ones.

Marjie Lundstrom's years as a street and feature reporter laid the groundwork for the story that led to a Pulitzer Prize for national reporting.[1] She'd seen child abuse and its results on many levels, and a different look at an old topic led to the award.

On the surface, Lundstrom's career reads like a storybook. Born and raised in Nebraska, she attended the University of Nebraska where she majored in journalism and was selected for Phi Beta Kappa.

Lundstrom's climb up the journalistic ladder started in Fort Collins, Colorado. It then led to Denver, Sacramento, Washington, D.C., and back to Sacramento. She has extensive experience in most areas of print journalism, working as a reporter, editor and publisher finally moving into management. She covered stories that ranged from the Super Bowl to the execution of Ted Bundy, gun violence, and to attacks on Israel during the 1991 Gulf War. These reports led to numerous local and regional awards in Colorado and California.

Yet the path wasn't smooth. More than once Lundstrom turned down the money and glamour of television to remain in print. She fought other people's visions of who she should be and what role she should play, at a cost.

The same determination and clear vision led Lundstrom to where she is now. As an assistant managing editor at the *Sacramento Bee*, Lundstrom works with young reporters and is still concerned with the basics of writing and editing. She has led sessions at the Poynter Institute and is active in numerous professional groups.[2]

Our lunchtime interview on the Sacramento River was a reunion of old friends. I was then in television and was one of those who tried to get her to change media. We discussed the new phases of her life: her marriage to

Sacramento Bee political reporter Sam Stanton and the joys of raising their son Nicholas.

* * *

How did you get interested in writing? In journalism?

I ran out of majors in college. My mother was a frustrated writer. I grew up with *Writer's Digest* around the house, and in the background I heard my mother say that she always wanted to write. She was a math and physics professor, which is the antithesis of being a writer, but there was that creative side to her.

By college, I was going along one of those tracks, following in my mother and father's footsteps, thinking I wanted to be a teacher, heading toward math. I got into dance and art and things like that and realized that the creative juices were much more satisfied through those sorts of endeavors. By my junior year, I didn't have a major, and if I was going to graduate on time, I'd better pick one.

I told a college counselor I was a generalist. I like everything, and I'm pretty good at everything, which was a bad spot to be in — to be pretty good at everything and not particularly exceptional at anything. I wasn't good enough to make a career out of dance by a long stretch. I certainly wasn't good enough in theater.

Then they shipped me right over to the journalism school. Someone said, if you're a generalist, this is where you should be. I landed in the office of an adviser named Jose Weber, who I think was the first minority hire at the University of Nebraska. Tremendous. She got me started, and I knew after my first class that this was absolutely where I belonged.

My second mentor in college was Jim Patton.[3] Between the two of them, they were so nurturing. I hope that's still happening in journalism schools now, where they take a real interest in students beyond the papers you turn in. That they really help shape you as a responsible journalist with values. I know that's what Jim and Jose did for me. I got a really stringent journalism education, and it was always a shoe that fit. I think that because my mother was a frustrated writer, once I landed there, both of my parents were encouraging, too.

Where did you start in newspapers?

At the *Fort Collins Coloradan*. Gannett sent a recruiter around to college campuses to pluck off people they felt showed promise.[4] Again, I think my mentors were very laudatory of me and really promoted me to Gannett. I wanted to be in Colorado more than anything. When you grow up in Nebraska, Denver's the Emerald City, by God. Gannett had one newspaper in Colorado, in Fort Collins, and when they recruited me I told them they had to get me into the *Fort Collins Coloradan*. It was a small daily.

What did you learn there?

I'm a perfectionist, but I really learned the importance of accuracy. One of the first stories I did at the paper was on how Fort Collins was changing zip codes in the city. We ran a little graphic which showed what the new zip codes were going to be, and I got one wrong. The editor called me into his office and ripped me a new asshole. He was jumping up and down, screaming, ranting, and raving. I don't think anyone in my entire life had yelled at me like that. I was stunned. It was like out of the movies, the wrath of the old city editor.

He asked me, "What is the most important story for everybody in Fort Collins today? What is the story that everyone will clip and save, that will have impact on their lives?" I remember thinking, this is only a zip code story. I should be off doing big and important things, not this zip code story. He was right. It was the single most important story in Fort Collins that day, and I blew it.

I also learned that I was not a beat reporter. I don't have the attention span or interest to do beats. I'm very much a generalist, in the true sense. I get bored. When I come in, I want to do a variety of things. I don't want to keep going back to the same people at the same place. Now as an editor, when I hire, one of the key questions I ask a reporter candidate is, do see yourself as a beat reporter or a general assignment reporter? They have two separate mentalities, both very valued by newspapers and both very important, but two totally different kinds of people.

The beat reporters want to have ownership, to have a small piece of the turf that's theirs. They want to fiercely protect it. They want to mine it, they want to develop it. They don't want to stray far outside of it. Whereas generalists will get pissed off if we ask them to follow their own story. They're already bored with it. That's the other thing I got out of that, a better understanding as to how I function in the business.

It helped you focus on who you wanted to be?

Yes. Nowadays, young people who come to my door, and they're no different than I was, want to be at a large newspaper when they graduate. They want to land on a metro. I keep telling them that there is not only no shame in going to a small daily, they might be better off. You get better clips, you get better exposure, better stories, and you don't get sent to the local festival like you do at a big metro.

After Fort Collins, what did you do?

I chucked it all. I chucked newspapers at that point because there was an opening at the *Denver Monthly* magazine. You know, that whole segment of publishing has gone away, our city magazines. The ones that have survived are by and large advertising tools. They're slick; they don't do a lot of hard news. This magazine was started by some renegade editors and writers from the *Kansas City Star*. It was oriented toward real hard news and investigative, tough stories. So that really appealed to me.

What did you learn at the Denver Monthly*?*

Oh, God. I think that was the best job I ever had. It was just a ball. The magazine was a weird collection of eccentrics, and we worked in a Victorian mansion in a seedy part of Denver. It was supposed to be a haunted mansion. It was just the absolute freedom to go pluck off stories that we wanted to do. And we really shook them. We really shook things up back there. Of course, that may be the way I choose to see it, and if I were sitting at one of the dailies, I would have thought the work we were doing over there was a little silly.

Any stories stand out?

Clayton College, the orphanage. Absolutely. That was an incredible story that I just tripped across.[5] I was going to do a short item in the magazine, and someone suggested a sort of "here and now, whatever happened to ..." There was that huge, sprawling campus out near the airport, with all these old, ornate incredible buildings. And everybody said, what is that? It was called Clayton College for Boys. I was just going to do a short item for the magazine on what it was, but when I started digging into it, I found much more.

There was a campus left in trust to the city when the benefactor died eight years earlier, and the city had just pilfered it. It became the city's own private little account, and they had let the school go to hell. It was great. I remember the "aged orphans," all these people in their fifties and sixties, who got all behind it.

It brought about a lot of change. I think that was my first taste, not of the power you have, but the ability you have, to not even right wrongs, but to just expose and allow others to right those wrongs. And that did happen. I don't know what has happened since, but these orphan boys who had left the school fifty years earlier had a renewed purpose in life and banded together and fought. It was exciting to see that happen.

How did you research this story?

There were boxes and boxes and boxes of records filed in the county building. We just plowed through it one document at a time. We had to go through bank records. I was in way over my head. John Hoffman, the publisher, helped me with it, and I suspect we made mistakes along the way. That was the kind of document work that at the tender age of twenty-two, I certainly was not skilled in. But we pieced it together, and it was substantially correct.

I remember a story during that period on the street life in Denver.

That was a story on escort services, which now when I think back, that is the kind of story a twenty-two-year-old would find interesting.[6] "Oh, wow! There's prostitution out there!" Can you believe that! I kind of cringe now, but at the time it was quite an adventure. Yes, the cops talked me into that. I wanted to talk to a john, or a pimp. I wanted to talk to one of the two of them, and the cops said, "Well, you'll find one if you'll stroll down this section of Colfax [a Denver street], and within three minutes ... " I bet the vice cop a steak dinner. Sure enough, it didn't take three minutes. I owed him a steak dinner. That was typical twenty-two, twenty-three-year-old stuff, but it was important.

Most of us have to learn that by doing.

I suspect I thought that was pretty neat back then, but that was a lot of voyeurism and a lot of growing up in the business. I certainly wouldn't do that story now, and I sure wouldn't assign it. I sure wouldn't let a reporter dress up like a hooker and walk down the street to see how long it would take to find a john, or a pimp, or whatever the case was at the time.

Then you went to the Denver Post. *What did you do there?*

You would ask that. Let's see if we can get through this quickly. They hired me as a feature writer. I wanted to go to news, but they hired me as a feature writer, which was OK because I could write for the Sunday magazine. They had two at the time.

Six weeks after I got there, *Times-Mirror* had just bought the paper, and they wanted to start this three dot column, "About Town." They had a vision that Denver could have a column like the *Dallas Times-Herald*. Well, Dallas is a different kind of city, with so-called celebrities and movers and shakers, and that's what they wanted. I was absolutely miserable. Basically, it was, "You take this job or you will not have one." Well, I managed to wiggle in there and say, "If I don't like it in six weeks, can I get out of it?" They gave me a half-hearted "Yeah, yeah," assuming I would like it and that it would grow on me.

I just marked off the weeks on my calendar, I couldn't wait to be done. It was the absolute pits of my career. I hated it, I hated it.

What did you learn about yourself as a journalist?

Well, I learned I was not capable of — this sounds really arrogant, and I don't mean it to — but frivolous news. I like features, everybody likes to do soft stories, but frivolous news didn't appeal to me as a steady diet. I couldn't handle that.

I learned I was a more serious person, and I was more serious about my craft, and I was certainly more serious about issues than who was wearing what at the Carousel Ball. I couldn't deal with it. People fantasize about being a columnist with their picture in the paper. My picture was in the paper — the column was entitled "Marjie" — and it was not an ego booster. It really tore up my self-esteem, and it took me a couple of years to build back confidence because just that six-week stint had taken a toll.

Then it helped you define your career. It showed you what you didn't want.

Yeah, that's true. But I tell you, it was such a painful time because I was really at risk of losing my job for refusing or coming close to refusing to do it. I think I also learned about the power of management and the power that they can have over you. I remember toward the end I was willing to be unemployed. I just couldn't continue. It was really an awful, awful time. I know that sounds whiny now, but it was just a bad match for me. I knew that the person suited for that job was somebody who couldn't take things too seriously, and I just did not want to be thought of that way.

What did you do at the Post *after that?*

I was there for seven more years. It was an unpleasant departure from the column, and for the next year or two, it was tough to work there. I'd let them down from their point of view. They'd wanted the column to succeed, and I had not made it succeed, and I stayed in features. Then I got a transfer to the city desk, metro, where I wanted to be, and I started at the bottom of the heap down there because they were very dubious of me. At that time, shortly after I got transferred, a new editor came in, and he wiped the slate clean. They banished me to Douglas County, which is the farthest-flung suburb, where nothing ever happens, right? The message I got was, "prove yourself."

The editor was willing to give me a shot, and coincidentally, there was a big "mom and pop" murder. Not long after I got to Douglas County, an eighteen-year-old was accused of executing his parents on a lonely country road. I just dug my teeth into that story, I just shook it, and got out of Douglas County as a result. I just did good work, I kept my head down and laid low, and I dug myself out of the hole.

I worked my way up in Denver doing general assignments. I was competing with older and more accomplished reporters for the good national stories, and I would peel off a couple from time to time. But one by one, those guys, and they were all guys, started to leave the paper and I worked my way up in the pecking order and became national correspondent. That was my job, and I traveled all over the country. Then Singleton bought the paper.[7] At that point they said there probably isn't going to be a lot of money for a national correspondent, so that's when I went to the desk. The last year in Denver, I was an assistant city editor working with the general assignment reporters. The *Post* had another management upheaval, and I was tired of dealing with new bosses every two months or three months or two weeks. That's when I went to Sacramento.

Why did you go back to reporting?

I'd been an editor for a year, and I realized that I wasn't ready for it. I had not done all I wanted to do in reporting. When Gregory Faure hired me in Sacramento, he asked me, "Do you want to be an editor or a reporter? We can accommodate you."[8] I said there was more that I wanted to do as a reporter, I'm not done yet. So I came back here as a reporter for a little over a year, then went to Gannett News Service in Washington.

That's where you won your Pulitzer Prize.[9] Wasn't it a team effort? How did the story come about?

I did it with Rochelle Sharpe. A terrific reporter and researcher. She's teeny, tiny. About four foot ten or four foot eleven, she's very tiny. They called us "Mutt and Jeff" because here I was lumbering down the hall with little Rochelle by my side. She's a product of Gannett. She's now at the *Wall Street Journal* as a result of the Pulitzer. She has always covered social issues, which in many ways is my bailiwick as well.

One of the Gannett editors came to us and said that she wanted us to do a national story on child abuse and she wanted us to win a Pulitzer. We groaned for a couple of reasons. First of all, being told to do a national story on child abuse is a little like being told, like I was told once in Denver, to go do a story on the suburbs. It's like, "Can you be a little more specific about what you want?" [Laughs].

That was the only assignment we had. Do a national story on child abuse. To her credit, she sensed that there was a lot to mine there, that reporters were staying away from traditional women's issues–type stories. I think there was a real strong feminist push in the story, for which I credit them.

If you think about child abuse, it has largely been treated by newspapers and broadcast as a local issue, for obvious reasons. Every single state social service system is different. There's the famous Bradley-McGee case in Florida where the stepfather used the kid as a toilet plunger, smashed his head open, and he died. It became a big story in Florida because they were able to track back through the system. This social worker did this, that social worker didn't do that, et cetera. Here you have real villains and real avenues for change when you expose a problem on the local level. You track back and figure out what went wrong.

When you're handed a mandate to do a national story on child abuse, what do you do that has meaning in Hawaii and New York and in Denver and Sacramento? That's what we were up against.

Rochelle was determined to do a database project. We had those two parameters — one from our bosses and one from Rochelle. Trying to marry these, I felt a little bit like Solomon.

We realized early on where we would cut the deck. When you're dealing with that much data, you have to take a slice. We decided on child abuse deaths, kids who died. There's a limited number of those, it's definable, and surely it's getable, we thought. How many people died of child-abuse related deaths in America last year? Then we'll define our population, and then we'll figure out what we are going to do, what the story will say once we get our deck cut.

Believe it or not, we thought we'd do a profile on each and every kid who died. We really thought that that would be interesting. You can imagine what our editor said. It was a ridiculous idea.

We thought we'd compare the sentences of those convicted of killing adults and children. It's long been thought that child killers get lighter sentences. We then spent about twenty thousand dollars on Nexus, and typed "child abuse" into the omnisearch of Nexus, which is every publication, and the thing printed out the entire night. When I came to work the next morning, we cut apart every single story and tried to look for patterns. It took us weeks to read every case of child abuse death and injury in the United States. Then we got the program, "Ask Sam," to input our sentencing data, and it quickly became apparent that it wasn't holding, that it just wasn't true.

We were desperate. People were making fun of us at work. Here was this motley couple, Mutt and Jeff, who couldn't pull the trigger. We were working for a wire service, after all, that's supposed to be filing four times a day. We had not written a story in three months because we were off on this goofy project that no one understood, and people resented it, and I don't blame them. What are Rochelle and Marjie doing today? It was awful.

I called a welfare investigator in San Francisco. I'd been in Sacramento, and I knew these people. I asked him, If you were assigned to do a national story on child abuse, what would you do? He said that he was troubled that in California, the difference between rural areas and San Francisco is cataclysmic in terms of how children's deaths are treated. You've got coroners up in the hills that are sticking babies into the ground without even bothering to find out why. They don't know enough to ask for an autopsy. They're bus drivers and bowling team members who are elected.

That tip was coupled with a curious phenomenon, which I think is absolutely essential to investigative reporting. It's not so much what people tell you at the time, it's what they don't tell you. What really had troubled Rochelle and me, when we were off on this weird patch, was when we'd ask, "Where are the stats?" We figured that it was a basic call, that you'd only have to call once. Nobody had it. Not only does nobody have it, we tried to call every single state, to get it on the state level, and the door was essentially slammed in our face. We were told that was confidential. We were horrified. Confidential to whom? The kid's dead. It's a child abuse death, the kid's dead. Who's being protected here?

The second thing was that all the so-called child abuse experts were really pissed off that we were focusing on fatalities. They, almost to a one, chastised us and scolded us for focusing on the extreme. "Just like journalists, you're just ghouls, you only pick the negative"—like there's a positive to child abuse. "It's too late to help those kids. Why focus on child abuse fatalities, it's too late for them, focus on the kids that can be saved. Look at neglect. That was the big theme we heard over and over. They were really angry that we were investing a lot of time and energy into investigating child abuse deaths because in their minds they had written those kids off. We were getting a steady diet of those two things.

We didn't know what we had until that third thing fell into place. The welfare investigator saying you ought to look at the quality of death investigation. We realized that if there were discrepancies between rural California and urban California, then they had to pepper the landscape. That became the thrust of the project. We did a database.

The way we got around confidentiality was that Rochelle found that in every single state, while they would not give us their data on infant mortality, they're required to give it to the Feds for mortality statistics. That tape was available. That was the death certificate tape, every death in the nation. You can imagine how big that tape was. We had to contract with Johns Hopkins to put it on a mainframe and cut the tape for children's deaths. The results were shocking, what was going on.

What did you find?

Wildly erratic patterns of death investigations by states and by counties. This was truly the ultimate Gannett project because they have papers all over. We could break it down by counties, so each individual paper could look and see what was going on in their county and surrounding counties. We could give story ideas to papers in states where they could pursue their own investigations.

Basically, it was very inconsistent death investigations, where essentially children are treated differently from adults. When a child dies, there is still a belief in our society that children belong to parents and that there are privacy issues there and we don't ask too many questions.

Even more disturbing were the number of SIDS.[10] By definition, SIDS cases must be autopsied. It's standard medical practice. You can't determine a SIDS death until you autopsy because an autopsy will show an absence of findings, and an absence of findings is a SIDS death. They were burying these kids, saying, "Oh, it's a SIDS death, it's unexplained, so it's a SIDS death." If they'd bothered to look, what might they have found? Suffocation, you name it.

That, of course, became very controversial, and it's understandable because SIDS parents twenty years ago were treated like suspected murderers. Their movement became very powerful, to educate people that sometimes children do die of unexplained causes, but I think their movement pushed things too far in the other direction, where people became so politically correct that they never did question the parents.

Christ, Mary Beth Tinning in New York killed, what, nine kids?[11] She hid out as a SIDS mom. They eventually caught her, but she killed them. I think it was a valuable work. And I think it was a real valuable work. It was truly the real investigative story in the sense we discussed before.

Impact. Do you think this story had any impact?

Basically, nobody in Gannett used it. Only a couple of papers ran it. It moved at Christmas. Here's one of my greatest stories, and it's why I didn't like working for wire services. You would hit the button on your stories, and they'd go off into space.

Impact. Yes and no. For a lot of reasons, our timing was bad. To move a four part series on child abuse deaths at Christmas was not the most fortuitous of timing. Beyond that, wire service work, for reasons I understand, for a lot of newspapers that is a large commitment of space, and they're probably not inclined to give it to the wire services. What they peel off the wire service is, frankly, what they consider filler, we give them something that they can't do themselves. Something this massive lands on their desk and they just don't know what to do with it.

The story did have impact in professional circles. Medical examiner circles, the American Academy of Pediatrics, the CDC. The CDC took our research, we gave it to them, and five years ago they were still working with it, manipulating it themselves.[12] Obviously, reforms have taken place as a result.

It was the one time as a reporter that I felt truly vindicated. We really do take a beating in our jobs, particularly if you're doing investigative. People tell you that you're only after the negative, you're such a ghoul, you're such an asshole. They get real personal, and they make you question sometimes what you are doing.

But what we learned from our project was that, by God, you've got to focus on fatalities because if a parent gets away with killing Joey, chances are that Joey's got siblings. Those kids are incredibly at risk. If you don't bother to find out why Joey died, then Susy or Mary are being left in the hands of killers. It's not too late.

You've obviously learned a great deal from working with statistics. Any other stories come to mind?

Investigative reporting is using your brain to spot things that you're in a position to see. I think the story that I am most proud of that I did is not the child abuse project, but a story I did when I first came to Sacramento. I was just stunned by the amount of gun violence in California. You can't fathom it until you live here. Gun violence just pervades our culture. I wanted to do a story on guns, but not a traditional story on guns.

The medical reporter linked me up with a real renegade researcher at U.C. Davis Medical Center who was studying guns as a public health issue. If you take gun violence, and do not look at it as a justice issue, it becomes a different issue. How many people were shot? How many people carry handguns? What's the arrest rate? What's the recidivism?

But if you take that issue and turn it a quarter turn, and you say I'm going to look at gun violence as a public health issue, then you have a whole new set of parameters. Compare it to malaria or another public health threat. Then you have different ways of measuring it. Look at its toll on hospitals, look at the cost of rehabilitation, look at the physical pain of the victim. You start quantifying that. I spent months on that series.

The investigative side was we called every single public hospital in California and arranged to have a specific day when they wrote down how many gunshot wounds came into the emergency room. We divided it up by staff and had people calling every public hospital in California. We could start to get a sense of the cost in just a single day in California.

Beyond that, I went down to Oakland and spent an overnight run with an ambulance driver who only did gunshot wounds, just racing around town. She called them "scoop and runs," because that's literally what they did. It would be in some of the toughest parts of town, and people would go down, and they would literally scoop them and run. That was incredibly revealing.

Investigative? Yeah. Because that story, to my knowledge, had not been yet told in the popular press at all. The press has always looked at guns as a criminal justice issue, and I think we as journalists can bring something to the equation where we say, "No, let's look at a problem in a different way." I think this can educate in unheard of ways.

Investigative reporters are often accused of being obsessed with minute detail. How do you respond to that?

It's funny because sometimes all the work that goes into getting that one statistic becomes just that in a story; just one statistic. Yet it can become that one statistic that removes the story from the anecdotal realm into the real, measurable and quantifiable. It has a lot more impact than if you just go out and talk piecemeal to patients, rehab centers, people shot in Oakland, et cetera. It's terribly important to quantify where possible.

We in the media are very guilty of this, and the public justifiably accuses us of this, I think. We don't give people context. Sometimes we'll isolate a problem and then go out and only gather information that supports that premise and problem and illuminates it. But we don't tell them where it sits in the larger picture. How big of a problem is it? That's where your numbers really do that.

That's a problem for many traditional, old-school investigative reporters. Too often, all they had were the paper and the numbers and the stats. They did not go out and get the human dimension. And where you can make those two fit together, you have powerful reporting.

How do you define investigative reporting?

I'm a little turned off now by the label. It still conjures up in people's minds bringing down an institution, exposing somebody, getting someone fired, doing a big paper trail. There was a time in our business, in newspapers in particular, where investigative teams were formed. They were stuffed off in the corner in their own offices. You wouldn't see them at the paper for a year or two, and they'd be collecting every piece of paper that was ever related to a transaction, whether or not important to the story.

I guess to me the term "investigative reporting" has a negative connotation because I think of those people basically as gumshoes, as frustrated private eyes, people who approach their jobs that way. Our job is to get information out. To write stories, not to not right stories.

For the past few years, you've been an editor. Do you miss reporting?

Yes, I miss feeling like I have something that is mine, something that I can pursue, sculpt, craft, shape, and take in a variety of directions and have it be yours. It's not the byline frenzy as much as the sense of pride of ownership. You get a lot of that in editing too. When you see other people succeed, grow and flourish, and not because you do anything, but because you ask the right questions and you get them to think about things in a different way. That's rewarding, but not in the same way.

Has your reporting background made you a better editor?

Sure. I hope as an editor, I never become "ivory-towerish," if there's such a word, become so detached, where I don't remember the insecurities, fears, self-doubts, and all those things that all reporters feel while working on a story. The worst thing an editor can do is go in and "bigfoot" (assign a senior reporter to the story) somebody. You need support. You don't need somebody bashing you. You need somebody to bounce ideas off of, to talk to, to listen to you.

There are a lot of editors, fortunately not where I work, who really believe that reporters are there to get away with what they can get away with. Bullshit. Every reporter wants to do a good job. In my mind, every reporter wants to do well. They want to tell the whole story, they want to tell it well, they want to write it well. Nobody's trying to do a bad job. We've all worked for editors who assumed the worst. Yeah, I think being an on-again, off-again reporter has made me a better editor.

I am very demanding, a real perfectionist. I also know that I was harder on myself than anyone could ever be on me. I remember that with the reporters. When they screw up on something, I don't really need to come down too hard because they'll do most of the heavy lifting for me. It's true. Especially with the good ones.

What has the Pulitzer Prize meant to you?

Not a lot professionally beyond some nice opportunities to attend and lead some seminars, which is great. It let me get out of reporting. Remember, I told you that when I first left editing and returned to reporting, it was because I had not done enough as a reporter. I wasn't finished. Now I feel that I could say, OK, you can move on to other things.

Why did you decide to go into print? You've had opportunities to do television. You've been very loyal to print. Why?

I think that I was astute enough, even in my immaturity and youth, to recognize that broadcast was too volatile for me as a person. You could lose your job because somebody didn't like the way you looked on a particular day. That as you aged as a woman, you were going to get screwed in the business. I think I really learned that early on, even though I did not articulate it, but I veered away from it. It made me feel too uncomfortable, too uncertain.

I also didn't like the idea of writing for pictures. To me, when you're writing a story, it should be based on facts. What's important about a story should not be dependent on whether an asshole cameraman that day got the pictures to accompany the story. I really couldn't see how you could sculpt a story around something as inconsequential as pictures.

I think I understand that business better now and have more respect for it. But it ran counter to what I prized and valued about writing, which was going out and gathering the essence of something and communicating that to readers.

Who were your mentors?

Jose Weber and Jim Patton on the college level. Gregory Faure, without a doubt. He is the consummate newsman, without the rumples! When you describe the old city editor, who's just pure journalism inside and out, who also has the tie that doesn't match, and mustard on the shirt and the cuffs stapled together… Greg's all those things without those things.

He is an impeccably dressed, elegant human being, while inside beats the heart of a pure newsman. He's elegant, classy and very tough. He treats his people incredibly well. I watch the things he does for the people at the paper, the really kind things. He treats people in the office as human beings. It's rare to find that. Bosses become detached and get into their own worlds, but he's always connected with people. He's an amazing person… the business will be much poorer when he retires.

Do you treat writers differently because of him?

He's made me appreciate that no individual is bigger than the institution. That no person's personal problems or mistakes are bigger than the paper. The paper is the paper. But that we as individual people are terribly important and valuable. I don't want to suggest that it's one "touchy, feely" session at the paper. He's tough!

Your advice to someone thinking about newspapers as a career. What would you tell them?

Don't shy away from the small markets. There's no crime in that, no shame in that, and it can be really good for your career. Go cut your teeth at a smaller newspaper where you do have tremendous responsibility. They will give you City Hall when you're twenty-one or twenty-two at a small daily, and you will learn quickly and a lot faster than at the *L.A. Times*, where you're being sent out to cover the county fair in the suburbs. So many people I see just aren't willing to do that.

We're had so many interns come through who don't want to learn. I don't know what some journalism schools do, but they're just not convinced that you have anything to teach them. Teaching, as you know, is a two-way street. I always feel that I learn something from the young people who come in. I learn something from them, but they've got to learn something from me. That good things happen when both people are open to that.

I don't think that's happening with a lot of young reporters. Either they're not willing to teach me anything or they're not willing to learn anything from me. You've got to be open in both directions. Beyond that, being in newspapers is going to be incredibly tough in the next twenty years, and none of us know in which direction newspapers will ultimately go. The newspaper industry is struggling with that now.

My advice to young journalists is that the only path to survival is ethical journalism. In ways big and small, our industry is creeping away from that. We are being influenced by the sleazy operators. Little things are starting to encroach, even at reputable newspapers like my own, because of mass media being so pervasive and competitive.

When you're working with writers, what do you emphasize? Do you make them go back and work on the writing?

I do both. I make them go back and work on both their writing and reporting. I get real frustrated with the skilled writers who write so beautifully that they can write around holes a truck could drive through. Some can do that. They can stitch it together almost seamlessly. That's what a good editor should be able to do; spot the holes in the beautiful writing. I make them do both.

I'm a big believer in coaching. I don't like to tell them what to do, to fix their stories. As Don Fry, formerly of the Poynter Institute, likes to say, ask them the right questions so they understand what needs to be fixed, or changed, or improved. That's how I like to work. I don't like adversarial relationships with my reporters and writers. I like it to be a partnership, and I think that's what I've developed. Some people I work with better than others, it's just natural.... you get along with some human beings better than others. That's been my philosophy.

Gregory and I started an ethics brownbag session at the paper. I prepared two questions on real-life things that have happened in our newsroom, and twenty to twenty-five people go across the street, away from the building, and spend two hours hashing it out, cussing and discussing, and they have just been really great. I think that's the great hope of our business, transplanting and spreading the values.

I think flexibility is ultimately the key to survival. Don't be as entrenched as perhaps I am, because I have ideas of what newspapers should be, and they may not be that in twenty years.... But I'll be close to retirement then... (laughs).

Notes

1. "Getting Away with Murder." Four part series, Gannett News Service, Broadsheet, 1990.
2. The Poynter Institute for Media Studies is located in St. Petersburg, Florida.
3. Jim Patton was Lundstrom's professor in journalism at the University of Nebraska.
4. The Gannett Corporation is one of the largest media companies in the United States. They own over one hundred newspapers nationwide.
5. "Clayton College," by Marjie Lundstrom. *Denver Monthly Magazine*, March, 1981.
6. "Diary of a Teen-aged Prostitute," by Marjie Lundstrom. *Denver Monthly Magazine*, November 1981.
7. The Singleton Group own a number of newspapers in the United States.
8. Gregory Faure is the Vice President of News for the McClachey Newspapers, owner of the *Sacramento Bee*.
9. The Pulitzer Prize is an annual award that is considered the top prize for print journalists. Lundstrom shared the award with Rochelle Sharpe.
10. SIDS. Sudden Infant Death Syndrome.
11. Mary Beth Tinning was accused of killing her children after a long series of mysterious deaths in her family. She was convicted of murder.
12. CDC. Centers for Disease Control. The CDC is located in Atlanta, Georgia and investigates unusual medical situations as well as diseases.

4

Gerald Posner

Against the Grain

> If you are going to be a real investigative journalist, you can't just do stories [that are] based on library research and are easy to do. You have to research stories that are going to take you into the field and involve some risk.

In 1993 Gerald Posner published a book that many praised and others vilified. When he went on tour to publicize the book, picketers paced outside his hotel, protesting the book's publication. He received harassing phone calls in the dead of night, and radio talk show hosts accused him of being a CIA agent.

The vitriolic reaction was to Posner's investigative book, *Case Closed: Lee Harvey Oswald and the Assassination of JFK*.[1] More than two thousand books had been published about the assassination of President Kennedy on November 22, 1963, and most of them had concluded there was a dark conspiracy and a coverup involving the FBI, the CIA, the Mafia, Cuban exiles and even the U.S. government, depending upon the thesis the writer was trying to prove.

Posner, however, went against the grain, concluding that the Warren Commission report had been flawed but right all along. Oswald, alone, committed the assassination.[2]

Case Closed, many reviewers concluded, was based on a thorough investigation and meticulous research. Posner took a brilliant look at the famous Zapruder film, which captured the shocking assassination, using computer enhancements to trace the trajectory backward from the bullet wounds.[3] He interviewed hundreds of witnesses and, like a biologist in a lab, incisively dissected each of the conspiracy theories. *Case Closed* was a best-seller and received critical acclaim. *U.S. News and World Report* made it the subject of a special double issue, and it was one of the three finalists for the Pulitzer Prize in history in 1994. Most importantly, on the thirtieth anniversary of President Kennedy's assassination, it sparked a much needed debate about the evidence and who was responsible.

Born on May 20, 1954, Gerald Posner, as a young boy growing up in San Francisco, never dreamed he would be an investigative writer. Law, not writing,

Gerald Posner. Photo by Ron Chepesiuk.

seemed the career path that would lead him to prominence. In 1975 he graduated summa cum laude from the University of California at Berkeley, and three years later, he graduated with honors from the Hastings Law School. Posner became one of the youngest attorneys ever hired by the well-known Wall Street firm of Cravath, Swain and Moore. There, he stumbled on to the fascinating case of the missing Nazi doctor, Joseph Mengele, the so-called Angel of Death, and his career path changed.[4]

Without any real writing experience, Posner managed to get a contract and spent five years researching what eventually became *Mengele: The Complete Story* (McGraw-Hill, 1986), the definitive biography of the infamous doctor. Posner followed up his initial success with an ambitious investigation of the multi billion dollar underworld empire of the Chinese Triads and the international heroin trade. *Warlords* was translated into half a dozen languages and optioned for a motion picture.[5]

Posner has also published *Hitler's Children: Sons and Daughters of Leaders of the Third Reich Talk About Their Fathers and Themselves*, a book involving interviews with a dozen adult children of Nazis.[6] The *Los Angeles Times* wrote that *Hitler's Children* was "a mesmerizing, blood-chilling book ... enough to make you weep."[7]

Our interview took place at Posner's modern and antique filled apartment in downtown Manhattan. It was mid-morning and Posner was nattily attired in blue tie and blazer. After pleasantries and coffee we moved from the living room to the dining table, where, once our interview began, it became obvious that Posner relished the opportunity to talk about his passion: investigative journalism.

* * *

When did you first get interested in writing?
   In 1981, through my legal work, when I had just started my private practice. I have a friend named Mark Berkowitz, who was representing the (U.S.) Justice Department, and he called me and said the department had been approached by a twin who had been subjected to the medical experiments of Joseph Mengele, the Nazi doctor. The twin wanted the U.S. government to bring a suit against Germany because the subjects of Mengele's experiments didn't get compensated for their injuries resulting from those experiments. My friend said the Justice Department didn't want to handle the case, but I might want to do it pro bono, since I was starting out and looking for work.
   I thought it was a great idea. I got hooked. I was always interested in World War II; in fact, I've had a fascination with it. So the case was a perfect match for me. I discovered there were about one hundred survivors of the estimated twenty-five hundred people Mengele had conducted experiments on. They didn't want a million bucks each. They just wanted the German government to pay their medical bills.

So what happened?
   I began to collect some good material on the case. I got the Red Cross file on Mengele by constantly harassing them in Geneva, Switzerland. When I went to Argentina to do research, I arrived within four to five weeks of Raul Alphonsin's takeover of the government.[8] There were rumors that the [Argentine] federal police had the Mengele file. The Argentine people knew about it, but no one had ever seen the file. Now this was nineteen hundred eighty-four, and I was just thirty years old. Only someone thirty years old can be so foolish and brazen as to go to the police and ask to see the file and then go wait in his hotel room.
   The police had rebuffed other researchers who had wanted to see the file, but Argentina was in the spasms of democracy, and so one night the police picked me up in a blue Falcon. I took a translator with me, and he was frightened out of his mind.
   They showed me the file. There was Mengele's application to enter the country, his marriage license, ten years of documentation. Six weeks later a British journalist tried to get into those files and couldn't. The police had got their act together again.

You were at the right place at the right time?
   The police were angry I got in. I wouldn't say the reason I got to see Mengele's file was because I was brilliant. It was just that the window of opportunity was there, and I jumped through it.

You exhibited some of the important qualities an investigative journalist must have — namely, determination and aggressiveness.
   I didn't feel scared, but the element of danger is exciting to me. I loved it

when I worked on the book about Chinese Triads. I would love to research a book on terrorism, about the Iranian financing of terror groups, and I would love to do a book on Scientology.[9]

Those types of investigations don't dissuade me. They almost attract me. I think a lot of journalists are turned off by a story because risk is involved. That element of risk, though, makes for a better story. We American journalists are actually lucky. In countries like Colombia, journalists have to give up their lives. I know because I'm a member of the Committee to Protect Journalists.[10] But we [American] journalists are basically protected.

If you are going to be a real investigative journalist, you can't just do stories based on library research that are easy to do. You have to research stories that are going to take you into the field and involve some risk.

Could you describe the qualities an investigative journalist needs if he is going to be successful in his craft?

More than anything else, stubbornness. You have to keep coming back if you don't get the answer you want, and you have to find the information other journalists can't find. You have to be innovative to come up with ways of getting information that other journalists haven't thought of before. You can't be intimidated, and you can't worry about being a pest or that somebody might not like you because you called them a dozen times. I would rather have a potential source say in the end, "I'm still not going to talk to him. He's a real pain" than "He didn't bother us again. He's a rather nice, considerate journalist."

Another thing — the problem with some investigative journalists is that they tend to go down the same path as journalists did before them. When I begin an investigation, I read all the books about it I can, and then I think about what has not been covered. Instead of just looking at the names of people who have been interviewed and interviewing them as well, I'm always looking for a different angle.

Also, you should never think of something as impossible to get. I've asked for information through FOIA [Freedom of Information Act] requests from the National Security Agency and the CIA.[11] Often it's very difficult to get that information, but you never know. Files from these agencies have to be declassified some time, and you may be the lucky one who gets access to them.

I wrote a letter to Jacqueline Kennedy asking for an interview for my book [*Case Closed*]. I wrote a wonderful letter, and I didn't even get a response. She didn't want to talk to me. All right, fair enough. But if I didn't try, I would always be wondering: could I have gotten that interview? My feeling is try for everything.

I get the feeling that to be successful as an investigative journalist, the intangible qualities of boldness and tenacity may be as important as writing skills, or they may, at least, be able to compensate for writing skills.

I used to be convinced that the research is the key. I don't care how wonderful a writer you are, if you don't come up with something, it's going to show. You will pad your book, if you don't have the goods.

But as I write more and more and see how my writing has changed over time, I'm now convinced that writing is equally as important. If the writing isn't good, you'll have a limited market. People in this country don't buy books in vast numbers to be educated. That's the problem with this country. So I'm now convinced that I have to take my information and put it in a format that is readable. If you don't have the research, you can't get to the second part, writing. But if you have the dynamic research and the writing is bad, you're going to limit your market.

Were you writing before you discovered the great story about Mengele?
No, I was just a lawyer, which should be a real disadvantage because legal writing is so awful.

[Laughs.] Yes, it's called "legalese."
[Laughs.] Yes, like a foreign language. So I essentially had to learn the English language. It's great how life takes such twists. I had never set out thinking, "I want to be a writer," but now I can't imagine doing anything else. I'm so on fire with what I do. Sometimes I get the feeling that someone is going to come down from up high, tap me on the shoulder, and say, "Time to get back to work."

So how did the Mengele case jump start your writing career?
Well, I was collecting all this wonderful information as the federal lawsuit was going on, and I thought maybe I could turn the case into a book. But I was naive and didn't know what publishing was about. I thought because I had such wonderful information there would be no problem getting a book published. I didn't realize how difficult it is to get a publisher and how tough it is to write.

I'll show you how naive I was at the time. Around the end of nineteen eighty-three or the beginning of eighty-four I went to a bookstore, located near the *New York Times* between Forty-Fourth Street and Forty-Fifth Street, and looked at a wall of nonfiction books, trying to decide which publisher was putting out serious historical works. I decided it was McGraw-Hill and wrote the publisher, saying I had all this information about Mengele.

I got a letter from the editorial assistant. At the time I thought it was a big deal, but now I realize she was handling the slush pile. She wrote me back, saying, "I find your idea interesting and I'm going to bring it to the attention of an editor." And she did. The editor arranged a meeting with me, and I convinced him that the fact of being a lawyer was a big plus. I verbally sold McGraw-Hill on the book. This was the end of nineteen eighty-three or the beginning of nineteen eighty-four.

The publisher told me to do a book proposal for the book idea. I did a twenty-page proposal. McGraw Hill said: "Okay, but you've never written before. We would like you to do the book with a writer. They suggested Robert Moskin, who wrote *Among Lions: The Battle for Jerusalem* and a number of other books.[12] We met, but he wasn't interested in the Mengele story because he didn't think it was that interesting. The publisher said, "Fine. You find somebody." I talked with John Ware, who had done a great documentary. He thought about it and said fine, but he hadn't done a book either.

McGraw-Hill offered us ten thousand dollars, but I had spent that much on my research already. They said that wasn't important to them. So I found a [literary] agent, Pam Bernstein of William Morrow, and when she got involved, McGraw-Hill went up to a forty-thousand dollar advance. I thought an agent was the best thing since sliced bread [laughs]. We signed a contract, and the publisher said, send me what you've written. I told the publisher I hadn't written anything. They said, "You're kidding" [laughs]. But the book turned out okay, and I was hooked.

You were thinking about a career change?
I told my law partner I was going to do another book proposal. Thus began my precarious existence. I got a forty-five thousand dollar advance for my second book on the Chinese Triads, but my research ate that all up.

You were taking a chance, or did you have another income?
No, I didn't have any family wealth.

We talked earlier about "legalese" writing. But isn't it an advantage for an investigative journalist to have legal background? A lawyer has a propensity for precision and rigorously follows through on investigations.
I agree with that. The best training I had inadvertently was my legal training at Cravath, the reason being my involvement with a case in which the government was going after IBM in an attempt to break it down as a monopoly. Cravath was on the defense's side, and I came on board in nineteen seventy-eight. The case had been pending since nineteen sixty-eight. It was the largest trial record in history. Still is, and I don't think it will ever be matched. Over a million pages of exhibits and material. My first year there, I had over three thousand six-hundred billable hours. We worked like dogs. But I learned that if I wanted to be on the fast track at that firm, I had to immerse myself in documents beyond belief. So after working on a massive project of that size, no writing project dissuades me because of its size.

My book on the Kennedy assassination, *Case Closed*, involved more than a million documents. I knew I could organize it. I think some investigative journalists are dissuaded from certain projects because of their massive size. They don't want to be buried in the paperwork.

Lot of journalists don't like to immerse themselves in court records because they seem kind of dry. But I guess that's not true in your case?
They are indispensable. They are gold mines. I much prefer projects that involve court records. I love to do research. It's the writing that's the real work. To sit across the table from a DEA agent who is working undercover or a

two-bit punk in the heroin trade is fascinating to me. It's great material, and I'm going to get paid to research it.

For you, what is the most difficult aspect of being an investigative journalist?
Getting people to open up for interviews on delicate subjects. Also, you often have to make judgment calls about where you are going to spend your research money. That's tough, too.

Could you give an example?
In researching the Kennedy book [*Case Closed*], I dealt with the KGB via fax, letters, and telephone calls. If I had had my druthers, I would have gone over to Russia, but I couldn't afford to put up money for airline tickets and hotel bills and then go over to Russia and not have the KGB talk to me. There are times I wait until five P.M. to make a call because the rates are low then [laughs].

You've talked about sitting across from some fascinating people. One of the most interesting things about investigative journalism is why sources talk. Why do they open up and say such incredible things?
It has to do with the interviewer and his level of skill. I've become a better interviewer as I've progressed in my career. When I listen to my early interviews from the Mengele book, I realize I talked too much and talked when I should have been listening to the interviewee. As I get better and better at interviewing, I hardly talk at all. We have a wonderful conversation, but the interviewee dominates it. After a while they forgot they are talking for a book.

Clearly, though, not every interview is going to be a home run. For every good interview you conduct, you may have five duds.

Does that ratio apply to the number of interviews you get compared to the number you don't?
Some investigative journalists are better at getting interviews than others. I never mislead an interviewee. I don't want the interviewee to say: "Posner misled me. He told me he was going to do a profile that was favorable and he ended up doing one that was terrible." Too many investigative journalists mislead their sources. The good ones don't. I'd rather have an interviewee say no than get an interview under false pretenses.

My calling card is my reputation. I love the fact that sources think I'm fair with them.

The credibility factor is important because an investigative journalist needs a network of sources, doesn't he?
Oh, yeah. If I burn a source and the word gets out, I cut off my lifeline. I once had an interview with a source who said some astonishing things and then ended up saying to me, "Of course, you can't use anything of what I just

said for publication." I tried to convince him to let me use the information, but he wouldn't let me. That's the nature of the business. You hone your sources, even if it means not getting the explosive story you want.

Do you tape record all your interviews?
Yes, everything. If someone doesn't want me to do it, I don't. But I do my best to convince an interviewee to let me tape him.

Does the situation where the interviewee doesn't want you to tape the interview happen often?
Actually, it seldom does. When a tape recorder goes on for the first time, an interviewee can feel a little uncomfortable, but he gets used to it. You put the tape recorder aside and try to make it as inconspicuous as possible. It's important, though, to tape record interviews for my protection and that of the interviewee. You have it on tape, if someone tries to say later that you misquoted him or you put something out of context.

Has that happened to you?
No, although some interviewees said bad things about me, especially after I published *Case Closed*.

How do you decide if an idea is worthy of becoming a book? For example, do you have a checklist against which you test the idea?
You just got to have faith in the project, once you have committed yourself to it. But as far as writing a best-seller, it's a guessing game. It's impossible to predict what will sell well. Anyone would be able to write a bestseller, if you could do that.

Let me add that once I'm committed to a book project, I view the researching of it as if I was a student who was going to school. I love school and the thought of being the eternal student. I view the editor as being my professor and I'm his student, who tells him he's interested in researching a subject. He tells me it's a good idea and gives me the go-ahead. I research the book for two years, come back, and write it up.

Actually being an investigative journalist is better than going to school because the publisher gives me some money [an advance] to research the book. I may get lucky, sell some books, and make some more money. What an ideal world. Someone actually pays me to learn about Chinese Triads or the Kennedy assassination.[13]

You won't undertake a project you are not enthusiastic about, even if a publisher gave you an advance of two hundred thousand dollars?
No. I'll give you an example. After I had finished the Mengele book, my agent asked me if I would be interested in writing a celebrity book. It would have paid me more money than I made from my first two books. I told my agent,

"No. It's not for me." If I was offered a five hundred thousand dollar advance to write a diet or a fitness book, I wouldn't do it. I hope to do this [investigative journalism] for another twenty or thirty years. I know some of my books will be hot and some will miss, but I've got to be interested in the subject matter to proceed.

Are you a fast researcher and writer?

It's easy to get a book in under deadline when you have two mortgages to pay as I do. I like deadlines, being under the gun. Researching the Kennedy book was great because I had a self-imposed deadline: the thirty-year anniversary of the Kennedy assassination was coming up. I knew that if I missed that deadline I would be cutting my throat. The last year on that book was madness, but it was worth it because I never missed the deadline. Now I'm contracted to write a book about the nineteen hundred ninety-six elections, and I've got to finish it in a year. That's fine with me.

Getting back to the subject of developing a network of sources, what's your opinion of the way Bob Woodward does investigative journalism?[14] You have to trust him on sources because they are nameless in his books. Is that good investigative journalism?

I think it's legitimate, but I don't do it myself. For the Kennedy book, I had two unnamed sources, and I was really reluctant to include them in the book. I don't like to use unnamed sources.

Naming sources should be the way to go. If I read the reference in a book or article, "a senior White House source said," I don't know if that's the third assistant to the press secretary or the press secretary himself who said that. But if you are Sy Hersh or Bob Woodward and you have built your network of sources over a period of time, many of them won't go on the record.[15]

For me, more important than the issue of unnamed sources is the question of how many sources does an investigative journalist have for a particular point. It's important to have two. I haven't talked to Woodward about it, but I understand that his standard was two when he was researching the Watergate book. Now he is often down to one source for a particular point. That's dangerous.

Is that his standard now because he's a celebrity and is lazy?

I don't know. Here is what I think Woodward would say — and, of course, I'm guessing — I'm good enough to know whether my sources are reliable or not.

But the point is, we still have to trust Woodward.

That's right. There are very few writers that have that kind of respect. Woodward is one of them. Sy Hersh, another. Who else? Maybe Frederick Danner, who wrote a book about the corruption in the recording industry.[16] I trust Danner when he uses unnamed sources because I know him. There are a lot of journalists, though, I wouldn't feel comfortable saying that about.

Have you had any role models?

Yes, Sy Hersh and Jim Phelan, who broke the Howard Hughes–Clifford Irving story.[17] He also broke the Jim Garrison story a long time ago.[18] He's an investigative journalist of the old school. He is now eighty-eight and lives in California.

Is it more difficult being a freelance investigative journalist than an investigative journalist working as a staff reporter for a newspaper or magazine?

Nothing beats freelancing, if you can pay the bills.

But you don't have the resources of a staff investigative journalist who is regularly working for a publication.

That's true, but in terms of personal life, freelancing is the way to go because your time is your own. Sure, it's an unstable life. You worry if someone is going to employ you.

Let's move to your big book, Case Closed. *Where did the idea for the book originate?*

Before I completed *Hitler's Children*, I proposed *Case Closed* as one of several book ideas to Random House. I knew it was good story because a lot of junk had been written about the Kennedy assassination.

Are you a Kennedy assassination buff?

Not really, although I've followed the controversy surrounding JFK's death. I had read about half a dozen books [about the assassination], and I knew they couldn't all be right. So I went to Bob Loomis [Posner's editor at Random House] and told him that as a lawyer, I thought it would be great to go through and examine all the evidence there was on the assassination. Then we could say I've written a book that you would have to read before reading any other book on the Kennedy assassination. Loomis said, "We don't know if there is a market for such a book." That was 1989. I did *Hitler's Children* instead.

Then I got the go-ahead on *Case Closed*. Random House told me to go out and find whatever I could find on the assassination. It would have been great if I could have proved there was a conspiracy. I would have become the next Woodward and Bernstein because I had cracked the most difficult case of our generation.

After I had sent the manuscript in to Random House, Loomis arranged an editorial meeting. He said to those present: "How many believe Oswald alone killed Kennedy?" Nobody raised their hand. Nobody.

Then he showed the new material I had uncovered, and they got enthusiastic, caught fire, and pushed the book. Harold Evans, the head of Random House, had been editor of the *London Times* for twenty-five years. In that position, he set up an "inside team," a special group of investigative reporters whom he sent off for months at a time to research stories. Evans wrote a letter to magazine editors saying, "I'm Harold Evans, a journalist by trade and the head of

Random House, and I believe the book [*Case Closed*] to be journalistically correct. I'm not just pushing it." It was very unusual for him to do that. No fact checking had been involved. He put his faith in me.

You say your investigation uncovered new research. What did you find that scores of other researchers missed?

First, I got information from the KGB, although they did not show me Oswald's entire file. To get me off their backs, they kept giving me tidbits. Secondly, I made an effort — as many journalists had done before me — to talk to Yuriy Nosenko, the KGB defector.[19] He spoke to me first and then spoke to the *Washington Post*. He didn't want to talk before because the KGB had a death warrant on his life and he was afraid. Now he was no longer afraid.

I talked with witnesses to whom other journalists had talked before and who had said the most sensational things. I interviewed witnesses who said, "I haven't talked to anyone in twenty years." Ruth Payne who lived with Marina [Oswald] hadn't talked with anyone in fifteen years because she told a story journalists didn't think was fascinating enough.[20]

Also, I got the Warren Commission testimony and found it had no index. Sylvia Meagher had done the only index in the early 1960s, but she also wrote a book in the early 1960s that said Oswald was innocent.[21] It had relied on the Warren Commission material, and I feared her belief in Oswald's innocence had affected the index's accuracy.

I did my own index for the first book of [the Warren Commission] testimony and then compared it to hers. There was a big difference. Regarding Oswald's tendency to violence, the first volume had no citation at all, but I found twenty references. I had to go through the entire Warren Commission's volumes — all twenty-six of them, a million plus words — and make a new index.

Combine Meagher's index and mine, and you have a complete index. No other writer had done what I had done. Writers had relied on Meagher's incomplete index and kept making the same errors.

Were you prepared for the condemnation that came down on you after Case Closed *was published? I read Harold Weisberg's book* [Case Open], *which accuses you of distorting.*[22]

And of being a liar, a scoundrel.

Yeah, everything an investigative journalist doesn't want to hear.

I didn't quote Harold in my book, although I did talk to him. I think he felt terribly betrayed when I came out with a book that said Oswald did it alone. That was heresy. I must add that I have nothing against him personally, even though I think *Case Open* is a travesty — just junk. I think he is very angry and bitter, and I think the conspiracy theorists are bitter and angry because my book did well. I would not have received any condemnation if my book had been ignored.

Did the angry reaction to your book reach the point where you had to worry about danger to your life?

It got hairy. We weren't prepared for the abuse, the foul language left on my answering machine, the picketers in Boston where I was doing a lecture. I did books on the heroin trade and Nazi war criminals and never had the trouble I had with this book. I was on a radio talk show and was asked if I worked for the CIA. But I never felt physically threatened, although Random House did receive a case of dead fish. I became the Salman Rushdie of the Kennedy assassination debate.[23] Get on the Internet today and see what things are said about me.

I learned something, though, that is very important to an investigative reporter. You are going to make enemies all the time if you do your job. I know people are out there who hate me. My next book will be judged by them, but I can't worry about it.

But the controversy did help you sell the book?

I don't think people buy books for controversy. I think they buy books they are interested in and the book reviewers say are good reads.

So is your book the final word on the Kennedy assassination? How confident are you that your conclusion — Oswald did it alone — will stand the test of time?

I'm one hundred percent convinced it will stand the test of time. There will always be questions, of course, and we will never have the answer to every single question. More records will come out and more histories will be written about the assassination, and how the Warren Commission screwed up, and how the FBI and CIA covered up. But I believe my book will stand the test of time.

After researching and writing several books, you must have some thoughts on the role of the investigative journalist in society.

It's interesting that, without having planned it, my work is getting closer to being current. I started off with World War II. Then I moved on to the heroin trade, and then the Kennedy assassination. Next I will do a book about the nineteen ninety-six elections.

When you delve into more current subjects, you feel your work has added importance because you are doing investigative work that hopefully will uncover stuff affecting current events. I believe the role of the investigative journalist is to clarify the record and keep it straight, although at times one finds that difficult to do.

Is the new technology going to be a boon to investigative journalism?

I'm crazy about computers. I'm on my fifth one and I subscribe to computer magazines. I use e-mail and download articles off Nexus and Lexus all the time. I'm a techno junkie, but I know I've wasted hours on the computer. A computer is just another tool. In the end, your research and writing is the key. Technology will not make one a better investigative journalist.

What are your professional goals?

Here is my dream scenario: I hope to live to be in my eighties and still be doing what I'm doing now. This is the business I want to retire from. My fear is that new young turks — new lions — will come into investigative journalism and replace me.

I want to do another twenty books. Not every one is going to be as good as the book before. Not every book will have a big story. Some books will fizzle; some will do better than others. I want to avoid the trap of thinking that my latest book has to be bigger than the last. You force yourself to look for a story that's not there. I will never expect that every one of my books be a home run.

Notes

1. Gerald Posner, *Case Closed: Lee Harvey Oswald and the Assassination of JFK* (New York: Random House, 1994).

2. The Warren Commission, headed by U.S. Supreme Court chief justice Earl Warren, investigated the Kennedy assassination. In 1964 the commission reported that Oswald had acted alone.

3. Abraham Zapruder shot his film of the Kennedy assassination while crouched on a low concrete abutment between the underpass and the book depository from where Oswald shot President Kennedy.

4. Josef Mengele (1911-1979), a German doctor, personally selected over four hundred thousand prisoners to die in gas chambers at Auschwitz, a Nazi concentration camp in World War II. After the war, Mengele escaped to South America.

5. Gerald Posner, *Warlords of Crime: Chinese Secret Societies — The New Mafia* (New York: McGraw-Hill, 1988).

6. Gerald Posner, *Hitler's Children: Sons and Daughters of Leaders of the Third Reich Talk About Their Fathers and Themselves* (New York: Random House, 1991).

7. *Los Angeles Times*, May 21, 1991.

8. Raul Alphonsin's government took office in December 1983.

9. Scientology is a religious movement begun in 1952 by L. Ron Hubbard. It teaches immortality and reincarnation and claims to have a successful psychotherapeutic method for freeing the individual from personal problems and speeding recovery from sickness, injury, and mental disorder.

10. This group monitors the worldwide treatment of journalists.

11. The Freedom of Information Act of 1974 allows investigative journalists and others to get access to public documents.

12. Robert Moskin, *Among Lions: The Battle for Jerusalem, June 5–7, 1967* (New York: Arbor House, 1882).

13. The Triads are criminal gangs that flourish in Chinese and Chinese-American societies.

14. Bob Woodward collaborated with Carl Bernstein on the Watergate investigation.

15. Seymour Hersh first made his name with the investigation of the My Lai massacre during the Vietnam War.

16. Frederic Dannen, *Hit Men: Power Brokers and Fast Money Inside the Music Business* (New York: Vintage Books, 1991).

17. Howard Hughes was a fabulously wealthy entrepreneur and an eccentric recluse. Clifford Irving wrote a book that fraudulently claimed he had interviewed Hughes for a book about his life. The book was published but subsequently discredited when the fraud was discovered.

18. Jim Garrison is the controversial New Orleans district attorney who tried to prove there was a conspiracy in the Kennedy assassination. He wrote a book about his investigation called *On the Trail of the Assassins*.

19. In *Case Closed*, Posner wrote, "In June 1962, a thirty-five-year-old KGB officer attached to the Soviet disarmament delegation in Geneva approached an American diplomat and offered to trade information for money. That request was the beginning of one of the most controversial episodes in CIA history, the case of Yuriy Nosenko, a key to unlocking important pieces of the Oswald puzzle."

20. Marina Oswald was the wife of Lee Harvey Oswald, and Ruth Payne was the Oswalds' friend.

21. Sylvia Meagher, *Accessories After the Fact: the Warren Commission, the Authorities, and the Report* (Indianapolis: Bobbs-Merrill, 1967).

22. Harold Weisberg, *Case Open: The Unanswered Questions* (New York: Carroll and Graf, 1994).

23. Ayatollah Ruhollah Khomeini sentenced Salman Rushdie to death for the publication of his *Satanic Verses*, which the Khomeini thought blasphemed the Islamic prophet Muhammed.

5

Douglas Frantz
Investigating Friends in High Places

You have to corroborate everything. I started out reporting at the *Chicago Tribune* and the city editor at the time, a man named Bernie Judge, had this great sign over his desk. It said, "If your mother says she loves you, check it out." It's the same thing with every source, even my most trusted sources, you've got to check it out; you've got to realize that everybody who comes to you with an idea, or a tip, or a suggestion has his own agenda.

Published just one year before his fall from grace in the Bank of Commerce and Credit International (BCCI) scandal, Clark Clifford's memoir, *Counsel to the President*, paints a vivid portrait of a man of nearly ninety years of age who, through hard work, became one of the Democratic Party's wise men, Lyndon Johnson's last secretary of defense, confidant to Presidents Truman, Kennedy, and Carter, and successful Washington attorney. Clifford writes glowingly of his childhood in Missouri, his education, and his half century of service to our country. He adds, "At the end of my exploring I have arrived, in a sense, where I started. I see a young man whose career and life would be transformed by events on faraway continents, yet who would never change certain values and attitudes he had first acquired in St. Louis just after the turn of the century."[1]

These "certain values" seem to have become deformed over the years. As Douglas Frantz and David McKean tell us in their book, *Friends in High Places*, Clifford routinely brushed up against the borders of impropriety. His relationship with Supreme Court justice William O. Douglas is a good example of how Clifford's ethical values became numbed. Clifford loaned money to Douglas and then solicited from him favors for clients, becoming one of the country's most adroit influence peddlers.

Ethics — or lack thereof — are of major concern to Frantz. In an earlier book entitled *Levine and Company*, he dissects the murky Wall Street world of insider trading. Patricia O'Toole of the *New York Times* book review department says that the book serves as "a lucid and compelling introduction to the arcane world of corporate finance. Bankers ignored warning signs and permitted Dennis Levine to grow wealthy by manipulating stock purchases."[2]

Douglas Frantz. Courtesy of Douglas Frantz.

As the following interview indicates, Douglas Frantz is a true believer in ethics, integrity, honor, and accountability in government and finance. Cynic is not in Frantz's vocabulary. As he said in an interview for *Contemporary Authors*, his sense of settling for nothing less than the highest standards was formed during the social upheavals and credibility gaps of the 1960s and early 1970s.[3] He is disturbed about shady financial arrangements, such as those made by Dennis Levine, and warns, "Wall Street is out of control." This zeal to sweep our system clean of corruption led Frantz to focus most recently on a cultural icon, Clark Clifford, who betrayed his St. Louis values, practiced law before sympathetic judges whom he had befriended, and consummated questionable deals with shady Middle Eastern businessmen. Clifford, adviser to presidents, personifies what many Americans consider to be wrong with our nation's capital, a casual disregard for ethics in the pursuit of power and influence.

*   *   *

I was so impressed with Friends in High Places. *What were some of your other books?*

The first book I wrote came out in the fall of eighty-seven. It was called *Levine and Company*. It was about Dennis Levine and Ivan Botsky and the insider trading scandal on Wall Street. Then my wife and I wrote a book a couple of years later about Japanese investment in the United States. Then I wrote a book about a skyscraper in San Francisco. Then I wrote a book about BCCI called *The Full Service Banks* with a guy named James Ring Adams, and then my wife and I wrote a book about teachers and education; then I had this Clifford book.[4]

Of course I would think of Clark Clifford as being a Washington icon. Did you have any qualms about digging into this and seeing what you could come up with?

No, I've never had any qualms about any story I've ever been assigned or with any book project I've ever done, especially with a book; that's a choice that you make. You go out and solicit a book contract, or some publisher comes to you with an idea. There you've got a lot of choice, and all the books I've done, I've done out of a real passion for the subject, and I certainly had developed a passion for Clifford and what he represents about Washington.

Exactly. And that's very clear as I read your book. There is a passion — that's why I was so impressed with it. Do you mind being called an investigative journalist? I know some folks don't like that label; do you mind that?

No. I don't mind it. I think I'm an investigative reporter. I sometimes recoil at the term *journalist* because it seems to be a little grand for what we do. I'd like to think of myself as a reporter; it has more working-class roots, more association with the downtrodden than *journalist*. *Journalist* sounds a little highfalutin to me. And I certainly don't mind the term *investigative reporter*; it's an honorable calling, an honorable craft.

Who would be your role models? Perhaps reporters from earlier times in our history?

Well, I think all investigative reporters owe a great debt to H. L. Mencken and his muckraking friends and to people like Upton Sinclair, you know the people who really opened America's eyes to what good reporters could accomplish. More recently, I'm a longtime admirer of Sy Hersh and some of the work he's done. Two other guys I like a lot are Don Barlette and Jim Steele at the *Philadelphia Inquirer*. I think that they, perhaps more than any other working investigative reporters in the country, have developed an ability to change complex material and make it readable and understandable for all of their readers. They wrote this series of what went wrong with America in the *Philadelphia Inquirer*, which generated thousands and thousands of letters, and they turned it into a best-selling book. And I think the beauty of that was they took these complex subjects, looking at the eighties really, a whole decade, and they boiled it down into terms that everyone could understand. That's always one of my goals in investigative reporting, to take something and come to understand it and understand it well enough that I can make sense out of it for my readers.

How do you go about selecting a topic?

Well, there are a couple of different ways, I guess. I think it's often what I'm interested in. When I see something slide off of the news and think there might be room for digging, I'll pursue it. Sometimes suggestions come from editors; I think that the best investigative ideas often come from beat reporters. One of the things I do here at the *New York Times* is work with beat reporters who come across subjects on their beat, maybe a story or a broader subject that needs more work, so we free them up and the two of us team up together and we take a little more time. We take an in-depth approach, and that's very satisfying for the beat reporter because it keeps them thinking that they can do a lot of things, that if they find the right subject they will have the freedom and resources to pursue it.

It also means that most of the investigative stories I've been working on at the *Times* lately have been off the news, and I think that gives them an automatic momentum and impetus and relevance. Sometimes I think investigative reporters can kind of get lost in the forest. You tend to spend a lot of time working on things that are not really relevant to your readers; that's why I like teaming up with beat reporters. I've done it on four or five stories in the last six months, and I think it has been real successful. I guess I like working off the news a lot. I think the best story I've done since I came to the *New York Times* was in the fall of nineteen hundred ninety-four.[5]

I did a story on USAir's safety record with another reporter here, Ralph Blumenthol, and that was an assignment to the assistant managing editors here. It was right after the Pittsburgh crash, which was in September of ninety-four, USAir's fifth major fatal crash in five years. They assigned us to take a look and see whether there was any nexus between their very poor safety record and their difficult financial troubles.

I've done a lot over the years in terms of financial investigative reporting; I guess it has been sort of a specialty of mine. So Ralph Blumenthol and I began looking at that and what we found was perhaps not necessarily a direct link between financial troubles and safety problems, but we sure found enough links that I think it made a hugely compelling story. That's a story that again came off of the news. It had therefore an immediacy and an impact that stories we suck out of our thumbs don't always have.

You know, Doug, Winthrop is near Charlotte. You probably know that, and there was a tragic crash there a few years ago. My wife is an intensive care nurse and so she was on duty when the crash came. Of course, there were questions raised about cutting corners. I was not aware of your work on that topic.

Pull it up on your Nexus and show it to your wife. I think it's a compelling story, and it made some points about that Charlotte crash that were later confirmed by the NTSB in its final report. I think serious questions about USAir arose, and that was one of those stories that is really the reason that I got into journalism and the reason I developed this investigative reporting specialty. That's because I think we're here truly to serve the public. I don't want to make that sound grandiose, but I came out of the sixties and seventies and I believe that journalists are advocates for people that don't have a voice. That story to me was satisfying because USAir, despite their "harrumphing" at some volume about it, through ads, did most of the things we suggested in there.

That story talked about refueling changes that the airline had made to turn planes around faster at the gate, which was directly related to finances, and we showed that those refueling changes had led to some near accidents. The lead of the story was a plane flying from Washington to Boston that ran out of gas and had to make an emergency landing at La Guardia in New York because in their rush they had forgotten to refuel down in Washington. Immediately after our story they changed, they went back to their old procedures, with some changes, and they hired a retired air force general to come in and do an overall safety evaluation of the airline.

They hired outside independent auditors to come in and go through their safety programming and so, despite their sort of kicking and screaming about it, they responded, and I think the result is a safer airline today. So that's really a very satisfying accomplishment.

Now, I remember a muckraking journal of about 1915 had on its masthead that it wanted to "afflict the comfortable and comfort the afflicted." I've always liked that phrase. Is that how you see it, is it afflicting the comfortable, as perhaps in the USAir folks and the Clark Cliffords of the world and the Robert Altmans, and to comfort the folks who don't have a voice?

Well, I think that's part of it, that's only part of what we do. The phrase that's always been sort of in my mind is Justice Brandeis' phrase — that the sunshine is the best disinfectant.

I like that.

And that's really the way I look at it. I'm not a disinfectant, but I like to open the doors and let the sunshine in. I like to let people have the facts and make up their own minds. I spent all of nineteen hundred ninety-two on stories about United States policy toward Iraq before the Gulf War, and that was the story that grew partly out of my experience in the Gulf War.

I was working for the *Los Angeles Times* then, and I was the *Times*' bureau chief in Bahrain, Saudi Arabia, and, you know, one of the realities that came home there was that a lot of the weaponry that was arrayed against the American troops, while it was never used effectively, was developed with Western technology. So I came home from that war with the strong belief that that was something that needed investigating.

It sort of simmered around in my mind for a while, and then I hooked up with a freelance investigative reporter named Murray Waas [the *L.A. Times* hired Murray on a contract basis], and we spent a year doing those stories. They became known as Iraqgate. It was an important look at American foreign policy; it was really an attempt, as I said, to open that up to sunshine and let people have the facts. We tried to avoid being too judgmental; that's a difficult task, especially when you write as we did about a hundred stories over a one-year period. You do develop pretty strong opinions about things, and it's hard work to keep them out of your story.

How did the Bush folks, just by the way, react to that?

Well, it was interesting. I think it's hard to estimate the impact of those stories; they ultimately became a campaign issue. Al Gore raised them during the campaign, and Ross Perot raised them, and it came up in one of the presidential debates. I think what the stories did was weaken President Bush's ability to roll out the flag and claim that the Gulf War was a great victory because I think that every time he tried to do that, or thought about doing that, he was going to have to face the chorus of people saying, "But wasn't Saddam built up with complicity, if not direct aid from the United States?" So I think it took that issue away.

Now, how did they react?

They didn't as strongly as one might have expected. I think that's because almost all of those stories were built on classified documents that we obtained from various sources within the government, and those classified documents were really from the Reagan administration and the Bush administration voicing this policy and executing this policy in their own words. So that becomes a very difficult kind of story to attack. They had no legitimate line of attack on our story, as far as I'm concerned. Subsequently, it's been interesting. They started what seems to me to be a disinformation campaign. In the last couple of years, since they are out of office, to try and create a revisionist attitude toward Iraqgate and say that the stories and their theories were all wrong. That's been promulgated by some former State Department officials and by some other journalists. Stuart Taylor in the *American Lawyer* wrote a piece about it a couple of years ago. That's been interesting. But those stories, as far as I'm concerned, were factually unassailable when we were writing them, and so I have a low tolerance for this revisionism now.

When did they come out?

Well, the first package of three came out in the middle of February nineteen ninety-two and after that they sort of came out all year long, all throughout nineteen ninety-two and into nineteen ninety-three in the *Los Angeles Times.*

Do you have a network of sources? Do you have a rolodex on which perhaps you keep names of folks?

Oh, sure. In fact, I have an old-fashioned rolodex. It's not on a computer because I don't want it in a computer. Yeah, I have a rolodex that sits right here on my desk, gets locked in my desk when I go home at night, and I have a duplicate at home that I fax the sheets.

There are people I rely on who are experts if I have a question about the sorts of subjects. There are people I can call and say, What have you heard, have you heard anything interesting? There are people I call to run stuff by, people whose judgment I trust. Yes, I think a rolodex and sources are the lifeblood of any investigative reporter. They are absolutely critical, although you can be a terrific reporter without sources; then it's a lot harder.

I would think. How do you verify what they tell you? Do you call others to make sure that you're getting the story without any kind of slant?

Absolutely. You have to be skeptical of your own sources. You have to be skeptical of your own judgment. You have to corroborate everything. I started out reporting at the *Chicago Tribune,* and the city editor at the time, a man named Bernie Judge, had this great sign over his desk. It said, "If your mother says she loves you, check it out." It's the same thing with every source, even my most trusted sources, you've got to check it out; you've got to realize that everybody that comes to you with an idea, or a tip, or a suggestion has their own agenda.

And you have to be as aware of their agenda as much as possible, but you also can't discount it simply because they have an agenda. You have to check it out.

I think a story where a source was most perhaps most troubling of all was a piece, the last story I did at the *L.A. Times*, which ran in late December of nineteen ninety-three, and I did it with Bill Rimple. It became quickly known as Troopergate.[6] We worked on that story about four months down in Arkansas, and it involved allegations made against President Clinton by four Arkansas state troopers regarding his sex life and more importantly to me regarding his offers to two of them of federal jobs if they derailed the investigation that Rimple and I were conducting down there. The initial source on that story, and this is well known, I'm not divulging anything, was an Arkansas lawyer named Cliff Jackson, who is an enemy of Bill Clinton. They were friends once upon a time, and they're no longer friends. Cliff Jackson had come to Bill Rimple with the original outline for this story, and here, you know, is someone out to get Bill Clinton in any way he can and you have to treat everything he says with special care.

But that special care should be applied to any source you're dealing with, and what you can't do is be blinded to what we ultimately decided was the truth of the information that he brought to us. He basically provided the introduction to these four state troopers who told very convincing stories. Two of them wound up going on the record in our story, and they signed sworn affidavits. We had hours and hours of taped conversations with them and with two others who were off the record, although one of them sort of in a backhanded way wound up going on the record after our story came out.

Cliff Jackson is an example of a very tainted source, but, nonetheless, an extremely valuable one. If you're a sophisticated, smart, and most importantly, fair reporter, you'll take that information and you'll know how to corroborate it. Now sometimes you can't corroborate information, sometimes stories just go away. I spent about two months just this fall with another reporter here at the *New York Times* working on a story. We got firsthand information from somebody with what would have been a blockbuster story, but after two months we just could not corroborate this person's tale. We had no way of proving conclusively through any other sources or any other way that they were telling the truth. So we had to walk away from that story. It was very frustrating.

Sometimes that's what you have to do, and I think the most important freedom an editor can give an investigative reporter is the freedom to fail. The freedom to take the big risks, and if you don't come up with a story, to walk away from it.

David Brock said the same thing. He thought the American Spectator *gave him that freedom to do his research, but if he ended up at a dead end, nobody could get mad at him about it, he could move on to another project. He made the point that two of the troopers didn't mind being taped at all. Is that what you found out?*

Yeah, absolutely. The *L.A. Times* was working on that story first, but Cliff Jackson was concerned about whether the *L.A. Times* would actually print that story, whether the mainstream press would print a story. So he went out and reached out to David Brock and brought him in as insurance, I think. Cliff was pretty honest about it; David Brock was there to make sure the *L.A. Times* did the right thing. In fact, it was probably a very smart move on Cliff's part because in the end the editor of the *L.A. Times*, Shelby Coffee, got cold feet over that story. He got real concerned about the impact of it. So he was very reluctant to publish. It took the *American Spectator* going first to get Shelby Coffee to find the backbone to actually put our story in the paper.

So you feel that sometimes the mainstream press has to be nudged by these publications?

Well, not very often. Mostly I think the nudge is from the tabloid press and the ideologues are nudges in the wrong direction. If you read our Troopergate story alongside David Brock's Troopergate story, I think you'll find that ours is much different in tone. Ours is much more factual. Ours is, I think, a completely apolitical story. I think that David Brock has a political ax to grind in every story he does. I spent all of nineteen ninety-two going after the Bush administration. I spent four months of nineteen ninety-three just as happily going after Bill Clinton, although somewhat queasily, over the sex aspects of it.

So you would think of yourself as being basically apolitical?

Absolutely.

Do you use a computer in your research?

I do, some. Obviously I type on a computer, but I do computer research. I use the Internet lately. I like getting access to Security and Exchange Commission documents and other sorts of documents like that. We used computers to analyze the safety records of USAir.

Very helpful, I'm sure for that.

Yes, I think computers are a useful tool. I think there's a danger in computers becoming a crutch because I think computers tend to generate dry stories and they have to be humanized. I think one of the big failings of investigative reporting is that too often we don't put a story in human terms, in terms that readers not only should read but want to read. Too often investigative reporters tend to be sanctimonious in the sense that we think that this is such important information that no matter how we put it into the newspaper, people are going to read it and if they don't read it, it's their fault.

Well, we don't have that luxury. In fact, the more important the information and the more complex the information, the more important it is for the reporter to describe that information in a fashion that is understandable and simple and compelling to the readers. I develop some kind of narrative for every major investigative story I do. I try to develop a way so that the readers can follow it and that the information can build on itself toward some conclusion. I think that's one of the things I've learned from writing books.

Do you conduct the research yourself or do you use researchers?

I do it all myself. I often team up with other reporters or with coauthors but those are partnerships. They are small partnerships. I've never done a book where I've hired a researcher. I've never worked an investigative story where we've used a researcher to go out and do any sort of substantive work. This is a high wire act in many ways, and you want to be sure that you've strung the wire yourself and that you have built the safety net yourself and that you've tested it.

It's tricky using researchers. There are perfectly wonderful writers who do that. I know my good friend, Jim Stewart, is just finishing his book about the Clinton White House and its relations with the press, and he's used researchers and he's using fact checkers also. That's a little different from newspaper reports, I suspect. I don't use them here. It makes me uncomfortable. I want to know where everything comes from.

Now what part of the process do you like the best?

Oh, I like the digging. I like a sense that you get a fact and it's a revelation. You get one more piece of information and suddenly the picture in the puzzle comes through. I liked when we were working on the Clifford book when one of Clifford's partners had mentioned to David and I, we had a day-long interview with him, and he was a partner of Clifford's for forty years, was there at the start of the firm. He mentioned to us all the work they'd done for Justice Douglas over the years.[7] And that was one of those things that clicked in my mind. Justice Douglas. I knew Clifford had cases before the Supreme Court. So then I went up to the Library of Congress and started looking through Justice Douglas' letters, and lo and behold, we find these thank you letters that he wrote to Clark Clifford, thanking him for his financial help and thanking him for other kinds of help. That was a real revelation.

I think that's what every investigative reporter lives for. After that comes what for me, and I guess most of us, is the harder part, and that's writing. It's hard work because you have to restrain yourself, I think. You want to make sure that you never overwrite. I think whether it's a book about Clark Clifford or an investigative story about a black church in Harlem that owns a building where eight people died in a shooting and a fire a couple of weeks ago, you have to underwrite that, you have to understate it. There's very little room in the kind of writing I do for flourishes. So that makes it a little harder.

I enjoy writing the books a lot more than I do the newspaper stories because even within those constraints a book can be a lot of fun to write because you get to tell a story, you get to throw in all the stuff and set all the scenes. I like the digging. I like when I come across some fact that's a revelation. I think that's really what I live for.

Have you ever been sued for libel or maybe been threatened by these folks who are so powerful like the Clark Clifford folks or Robert Altman, perhaps?

Well. Mr. Clifford has never threatened us since the book came out. He's really too much of a gentleman for that. Robert Altman, in the end, decided not to talk to us and that damaged his standing.

I was sued once in Los Angeles when I was working for the *Los Angeles Times* for invasion of privacy. It wasn't a libel suit, but it was an invasion of privacy lawsuit by a guy who, speaking of banks, had gone out and registered a number of brass plate banks, as they call them, down in the Caribbean islands. They are financial institutions that are merely phone booth or mail drop operations. They are sold to shady people who want financial front operations. I wrote a story about him, and he sued for invasion of privacy, but it was dismissed on summary judgment by the judge.

Good reporters get sued for libel; solid stories can draw libel suits. That's part of the job. What you need to do when you're writing an investigative story or any other kind of story is to make it as accurate and fair and truthful as possible so that when that lawsuit does come up you can defend it successfully, and your lawyers can defend it successfully.

The *New York Times* has wonderful lawyers, and the *Los Angeles Times* had very good lawyers, too, as does as the *Chicago Tribune*. I've been an investigative reporter at all three of those places, and I've been threatened a lot with libel suits. And here lawyers go over my stories very carefully before they run, and I find the lawyers here, every single one of them, to be helpful. It's not an adversarial relationship. They're not trying to stop stories. They're not trying to keep facts from getting in the papers. They're trying to find the best possible way to get those facts into the papers, and a smart sophisticated reporter will recognize that and work with them because we really do have a common goal.

What have you learned about the way our country's government functions? Are you cynical?

No. I'm not cynical about it. That's a good question, and I wouldn't pretend to know much more than the average person about the way our country's government works. There are the wide majority of public servants there to serve the public. They're honest, hard-working people and I think when investigative reporters come in and find a rotten apple in the barrel, that's just it. There's just one rotten apple, and the whole barrel is not tainted as long as you're able to get in there and get it out. And that's the function that we serve.

I really think that investigative reporters have an important role to play in keeping government responsive and responsible and making sure that good people in government are able to work in an atmosphere where they can do their jobs honestly and that those who are corrupt don't stay in government long, whether they're elected officials or hired civil servants. I don't want to sound grand or immodest at all. But as long as people believe that sunshine is the best disinfectant, then government is going to stay as clean as it can.

What advice would you give young students of journalism?
Any story you approach, whether it's a daily news story or a feature or even a longer project, you need to think investigatively. You need to be skeptical about the people you're talking to, you need to get behind the scenes and understand how something works before you write about it. You need to understand that there's going to be more than one side to most of these stories, and you need to have the time and freedom to go out and get as many answers as you can before you sit down and write. Now that's a luxury not all reporters have. I've worked on papers where reporters have to do four or five stories a day. But as long as you retain that healthy skepticism, I think you're not going to get suckered on a story. The second bit of advice I'd give is that you don't usually, unless you're extraordinary, come out of a university and get a job as an investigative reporter. It's something you have to work your way into. I think an investigative reporter needs to have terrific judgment, and judgment is developed only through practice and experience.

I have worked for nine years in journalism. I've been city editor of a newspaper before I started working as an investigative reporter.[8] I think that served me well. I hope that I'm still getting better every day as an investigative reporter, that I'm learning new techniques, most importantly, that I'm becoming fairer.

Notes

1. Clark Clifford, *Counsel to the President* (New York: Random House, 1991), ix; Central Intelligence Agency official Robert Gates referred to BCCI as the "Bank of Crooks and Criminals"; see Douglas Frantz and David McKean, *Friends in High Places: The Rise and Fall of Clark Clifford* (Boston: Little, Brown, 1995), 354. The bank allegedly used Clifford and law partner Robert Altman as front men for money laundering and other questionable activities by foreign investors; see James Ring Adams and Douglas Frantz, *A Full Service Bank* (New York: Pocket Books, 1992).

2. Book review, *New York Times*, October 25, 1987; see also Bernie Shellum's October 14, 1987, review in the *Detroit Free Press*.

3. *Contemporary Authors*, Susan Trotsky, ed. vol. 126. (Detroit, Mich.: Gale Research, 1989), 110–111.

4. James Ring Adams is currently an investigative journalist reporter for the *American Spectator*.

5. In July 1994, USAir Flight 1017 crashed in a blinding rainstorm during an approach to the Charlotte, N.C., International Airport; thirty-seven passengers lost their lives. This disaster was one of three which plagued the financially strapped airline during 1994 and raised questions about USAir's commitment to safety.

6. See the interview with David Brock concerning Clinton's use of troopers to arrange sexual liaisons with various women when he was governor of Arkansas.

7. William O. Douglas was appointed by President Franklin Roosevelt to the U.S. Supreme Court in 1939 and served until 1975.

8. See *Contemporary Authors* for Frantz's complete résumé, which includes service at the *Albuquerque Tribune*, *Los Angeles Times*, and *New York Times*.

6

Sydney Schanberg
Lessons from the Killing Field

> Part of investigative reporting is not just digging up information. It takes persistence and tenacity to get data, figures, facts that haven't been uncovered before. It also takes a certain willingness to be out there all alone, by yourself.

Nothing makes a good reporter more uncomfortable than to become part of the story. That's exactly what happened to Sydney Schanberg, whose coverage of the war in Cambodia and his search for his Cambodian colleague was chronicled in the movie *The Killing Fields*. In 1975, Schanberg's reporting on the fall of Phnom Penh and the start of an Asian holocaust gained him the coveted Pulitzer Prize for international reporting "at great risk." His book *The Death and Life of Dith Pran*[1] was a personal memoir which became the basis for the Academy Award–winning movie.

Schanberg's work in Cambodia covered only a small part of his quarter-century tenure with the *New York Times*, which was followed by a ten-year stint as a columnist and associate editor for *New York Newsday*. He made his mark as a reporter, editor, and columnist, a true lover of his medium. Along with the Pulitzer, Schanberg won two Overseas Press Club awards, two George Polk Memorial Awards, the "25-Year News Achievement Award" from the Society of Silurians, and the 1991 Alfred K. Lowenstein Award.

Schanberg was born in Clinton, Massachusetts, and graduated from Harvard in 1955 with a B.A. in government. Drafted into the army, he started his newspaper career in Germany as a writer for the 3d Armored Division newspaper. During this time, he met a number of major correspondents who came to Germany to cover the cold war. He jokes that he chose journalism over the prospect of slogging through the snow and mud of Germany as a foot soldier.

After discharge, Schanberg applied at three major newspapers but was only interviewed by the *New York Times*. His was a classic print journalism education: from copy boy to clerk to news assistant, with stints on the metropolitan, foreign, picture, and makeup desk. In 1960, he was promoted to reporter, covering general assignments in New York City. Then he moved to Albany, the state capital, for a five-year tour, the last two as bureau chief.

Schanberg's career as a foreign correspondent started in New Delhi, India, where he covered the 1971 war between India and Pakistan, which led to the formation of Bangladesh. He then moved to Singapore, his base for covering all of Southeast Asia, including Cambodia.

Schanberg continues his campaign to recognize the indigenous reporters, photographers, and expediters in foreign countries who make it possible for the foreign reporter to cover the story. Because of their associations with and loyalties to foreign reporters, many of the Cambodians who worked for the wire services, newspapers, and networks perished after the fall of Phnom Penh. Dith Pran was one of the few to survive.

Schanberg's apartment was a welcome refuge from the cold winds of the upper West Side of New York City. The decor reflects his ongoing love for things Asian, and the certificates of his achievements are subtly scattered along the walls. At the end of one hallway hangs the haunting movie poster for *The Killing Fields*, which led into our discussion about his identification with Cambodia.

* * *

What drew you to Cambodia?

I didn't know a lot about Vietnam, but when I went there, that war was much more clearly defined.[2] For the North, in any case, it was nationalistic and ideological, and they were committed. In Cambodia, I don't think there were six people who knew why that war was taking place, who had really had thought it through. Why are we having this war?

Everybody could look at Cambodia and see how this was a country that was small in population and small in power and had been drawn in. The Cambodians were essentially pawns. In the end, the Cambodian leadership, which was supported by the American government, were pawns. They'd enjoyed power, and in some instances money, and sometimes it was money made from corruption based on American aid, but they too were pawns. Because Cambodia was simply a device for carrying out an American policy, at that point primarily the Nixon-Kissinger policy, extricating us from the Vietnam War.[3]

The White House decided that the way to do it was to draw in the Cambodians. After the coup that removed Sihanouk, the incursion, what Nixon called the invasion on April thirtieth, nineteen hundred seventy, they had a new leadership in Cambodia which was pro–Western.[4] At least that was the tag that they got. I think they were more feckless than anything else. They were less interested in appeasing the North Vietnamese, which Sihanouk had done.

In any case, they came in and said we need help, and they took help from the United States. They began to follow American policy, which was to create a light infantry army that would distract the North Vietnamese from their combat in Vietnam. To the degree that you could distract two or three North

Vietnamese divisions, to that extent, you would reduce American casualties in Vietnam and make it more possible to bring home more men and decrease the size of the American force in Vietnam. They were really used to this effect. In that sense, the leadership were like mercenaries. Pay them to build this army, perform this task. There was no one who could tell them that we were in the process of nation-building or democracy-building; that was the frosting on the cake.

They were used. And I think that's what drew me in. I felt, here was a helpless people who had lived through colonial rule under the French for eighty-some odd years, then the monarchical rule of Sihanouk and his father before him. Essentially, they had been governed by an autocracy, people whom they were supposed to worship, and they were used. They were conditioned to bowing to the elite classes, and they were doing it again. This time, the Americans were part of the elite class. They were being used. They were being used, of course, on the other side by the Chinese and the Soviet Union, who were using the communist side as surrogates in the Vietnam War and the cold war.

They were pieces on a gameboard, and suddenly, as years passed, they were dying in large numbers, and the civilian population turned into a population of refugees. The food supply dwindled, and the people were getting the symptoms of malnutrition, and eventually, by late nineteen seventy-four and early nineteen seventy-five, they were dying of malnutrition. First it was infants and the elderly, the weakest in the population.

That's what really hooked me. These people were in no way in control of their own fate and in no way had the capacity or the power to say that we don't want this, we want to get off this carousel. I felt really badly for them, and I felt that it was a great power failure. But it certainly wasn't the first time in history that it happened, that a small country was used this way. There's no excuse for it.

Why this interest in a little-known, third-world country?

Why was I drawn to Cambodia and not some other story? Why do I think the third world more interesting than the first world? Because I believe that more people are capable of looking after themselves in the first world. There are more identifiable places to go to air a grievance, more chances to have justice done.

Also, in the third world, they haven't had their industrial revolution yet, or they're having it now. A great upheaval is taking place, and I think it's exciting to watch and be able to report on it. By reporting on it, perhaps we help people avoid some of the mistakes of our own industrial revolution, although I doubt very much that the abuses will be avoided.

How did you build sources in Cambodia? What process did you go through there?

I had a colleague, Dith Pran, who had been a tourist guide before the war. He started out first as my fixer and interpreter, and then he became fascinated by, and committed to, the journalism. It was he who first introduced me to people, usually at the midlevel in the military or government bureaucracy, who had something to tell.

You have to have the interviews from time to time, but I don't think you learn a great deal from the people at the top. They are not about to tell you their administration is leaking like a sieve. Or that they have two hundred thousand phantom soldiers in the army that are being paid, but that the money is really going to the generals, and things like that. You learn that usually from the middle up, from the bottom up. Pran was instrumental in that process of introducing me to people.

I believe in using every bit of information you have. I think that if somebody else writes a story, you can start with that information. Somebody else whom you trust comes back from the front and tells you something. Everyone of us did this. We just used all the scraps and decided what was creditable and what wasn't. We checked it out against embassy sources, not just American Embassy sources, but other embassies like the Japanese or the Australian Embassy, people who had good reporting facilities and military attachés who would go out. You would check all of these gathered scraps against other people, and in the end select the meaning of it from those parts that stood up under scrutiny.

News conferences in Cambodia were called to condemn what you had written. How did you handle that pressure? You had the top U.S. official in Cambodia saying you were lying through your teeth.

I had no pressure from New York, from my superiors. I listened to everything they said when they criticized, to make sure I hadn't gotten anything wrong. If there was an area where I hadn't been as precise as I should have been, if there was some missing thing, I could find a way to write that and also to indicate that the earlier report was distorted in that fashion. But I can't recall anything I wrote that didn't stand up.

I didn't mind them yelling. I just thought I'd gotten their attention. My sources weren't yelling at me. It was someone at the top. And sometimes it was someone at the top whom I liked, who was taking enormous heat from Washington. No, I wasn't bothered very much. I just felt that I was an outsider, that I was not part of the embassy. I had top people at the embassy say to me, "You should be helping us." I said: "That's not my job. My job is to find out what you're doing, and if what you're doing stands up and is a good thing, it will stand up just by my reporting. My job is not to help you. You have a whole staff here to help you. That's not my job."

This particular person, who was the acting ambassador, would use that phrase all the time — you're not being helpful. I never saw that as my job. My job wasn't to make his life a misery, but at the same time it wasn't to be helpful to him. My job was to pass on to the reader what I was learning, what I came to believe was truth based on my reporting, to bring that reader into the story. Certainly that reader was getting a very different picture out of Washington every day.

When Henry Kissinger and his water boys would testify before Congress, they'd say things like "There's no refugee problem here." They would say things like "We don't need more refugee aid because there's a very strong extended family system in Cambodia. When the refugees flee to the cities, particularly Phnom Penh, their families there, their relatives there, take them in." Not bothering to mention that the relative has a fixed rice ration and that now meant that if there were twenty people in this little apartment instead of six or eight, that's how the rice would be divided. People's diets were going down the tubes.

Why did they not mention that? Because they had a very limited aid budget, and they didn't want to divert three hundred or four hundred million, they didn't want to divert a hundred million to refugee relief.

In the first year of the war in Cambodia, there was no refugee aid, and there was one million dollars in the second. By the end, there was something between twenty-five and fifty million. It was too late, of course. People were dying of malnutrition and other diseases. So the American public was getting a very steady diet of how well everything was going, and they were being told that nobody was dying of malnutrition. Yet any reporter could go to the clinics and see infants dying in front of you.

I wasn't worried about the pressures from Washington. I was going to write my story and see if it stood up. The reader had to decide which one they were going to believe, and that's OK with me. I accept that challenge.

Your Cambodia coverage led to a Pulitzer Prize. You also had to leave Dith Pran behind. The prize must have been bittersweet.

That's true. First of all, the Pulitzer is one of those defining things. Go to your grave and someone writes, "Pulitzer-prize winning so-and-so died yesterday." It's a prize in our profession that carries a large cachet.

There are two things about it. One, when you've lived through all that [Cambodia], and you've seen this upheaval, which I hope I'll never see again, a whole country turned on its head, a city of two million plus people evacuated. It's biblical and it's awful. Many of them going off to their death, and many of them your good friends. You've lived through it all, and there is no good cheer about it.

You don't reject the prize. But your closest friend is not there, the man who saved your life so many times, who looked after you in his society where you were a stranger, because he was forced to go off with the others. Again, the thought of did we do enough to save him, could we have done more? Then the prize comes, and he's missing. It's not a time for great celebration. It's a time to remember the people who did so much for you, to make possible your work, who aren't with you. And I accepted that, even though it doesn't say so on the piece of paper, the sort of diploma that says you won it.

I accepted it on Dith Pran's and my behalf; it was shared equally. The *New York Times* used to run a full page of all of the award winners, with a bio and some comments underneath it. In that, I said it as well. I said it the night of that award. I also received another award — the Overseas Press Club Award — and I said the same thing all over again. We honor our own, but we don't honor the journalists that make our work possible. We could not function in those countries without people like Dith Pran.

I mentioned Put Sophan in a speech.[5] That was the subject of my speech. We were honoring the war dead, and the war dead in Cambodia. The journalistic war dead in Cambodia were only about twenty-some odd people. I say only because it was greater in other wars — it's not a long list. There are so many of the unnamed, and many now unknown to people, Cambodian journalists, that helped us. I mentioned Sophan because of how he missed the evacuation flight because he was trying to round up all of his wives. Lovely Sophan. How much of his film was on the six o'clock news with Walter Cronkite?

The reporters who came out on the convoy agreed to hold everything for a certain period of time. Didn't you write the bulk of the material cited in your Pulitzer in a couple of days?

It was even worse than that. We came out on the third of April, nineteen hundred seventy-five. There was a second convoy to come, and there were some journalists among them. We had agreed not to send anything and we had signed a solemn oath not to do this. I thought it was very important.

There were some problems with that because people started to file little bits and pieces. And Agency France Presse filed a piece. Then Monde did it. I did not. I refused. To my paper's credit, they tried to hold the embargo together. Everybody was getting antsy. I called Agency France Presse because the guys were in Bangkok, and I screamed at them. "Who are you?" they said. I told them we made this holy oath, and the whole point is, we're not going to endanger people's lives. Why are you doing this? When they come out, we'll all publish and print. Then Monde printed a story that their reporter had filed in advance. He didn't even know about it, and he sued them through his union. It was very messy.

The other convoy finally emerged on the seventh. I had sat down over those three days in between to try to organize myself, but I couldn't think and I could not function. Pran was missing. I really was a wreck. I did every piece of procrastination that I could think of. I read through my notebooks, I outlined my notes. In any case, my editors kept saying, "Send something." I was just blocked.

On the day of the convoy's emergence, I'd learned that morning they were out. By two o'clock, I had about a thousand words written and there was a lot to go. All I was doing was clearing my throat. I just started in panic to write. You know, when you're in panic. What did Samuel Johnson write? Nothing clears a man's mind so quickly as the imminence of his execution? Which explains all deadline writing around newspapers or anyplace else, for that matter.

I just began to write. Big gobs of copy. Fortunately, I had people running it down to the telex office. At about two o'clock in the morning, I still had a ways to go. At some point, my head hit the typewriter, I was so exhausted. I knew I had to keep myself awake, so I asked our stringer in Bangkok if he would go get me some caffeine pills like NoDōz. I knew we'd done that in college to stay awake. He came back and said he'd been to the druggist and that this was just as good. Wrapped up in some Chinese newspaper were these six to eight pills. I took two of them with some soda, and I began to wake up and began to write.

To make a long story short, I finished writing at seven o'clock, which was like seven o'clock the previous night in New York. The copy was all in, and they had been editing and breaking it into pieces, and I was filing some corrections and was exhausted but wide awake. Bouncing, as matter of fact. Turns out the pills were benzedrine, and it came to a point where the mind was so clear, so focused. I knew exactly which notebook had something in it and which page, and I'd turn to it and there was the quote. I was just typing a mile a minute.

There was about ten, twelve thousand words put out in that time, and then I couldn't go to sleep because I'd had these pills. I went off downtown to try and get my Thai visa fixed. There were all kinds of people at the visa office because people who came over with our convoy needed visas. One was the Bulgarian wife of a Cambodian engineer, and he hadn't stayed, so now she was with her daughter here with no place to stay. Everybody needed a little help. So I spent the whole morning at the visa office, and I don't know when I finally fell asleep.

It was part adrenaline, but I think those pills helped a little bit. I don't think I could have become unblocked if it wasn't for the panic and the ability to stay awake from those pills. I didn't want to write any of it. I think inside I felt I had no right to do these stories without Pran here, without Pran being present.

What impact did your Cambodian experience have on your life?

After I came out in nineteen seventy-five, and wrote the story of what had happened, I went to Los Angeles. I told the *Times* that I needed some time off because I was in what felt like a decompression chamber. I didn't want to talk to anybody. I went back to L.A. because my then wife's family lived out there, and she was in an apartment there. I stayed there for about eight or nine months.

I really dropped out. I couldn't do anything. I couldn't have conversations with perfectly nice people whom you would meet socially, talking about what people talk about — their mortgages, their children. There's nothing wrong with that, but it made no sense to me. I was really mourning, and I was in a depression.

Finally, the *Times*, to get me to come back to the world, offered me a job as the deputy city editor, and I came back. I was an editor for a few years, then I became city editor, and so forth.

The high point was when Pran escaped. I kept searching for him through letters, through relief agencies, through mercenary soldiers I had contact with, and there were a couple of sightings, which is kind of strange when you think of how difficult it is to find one person in a rural, third-world country. There were a couple of sightings. The second sighting was for real because he had a picture of Pran. He was an East German correspondent who was part of an Eastern European delegation the Vietnamese had brought in. He didn't know whom he was meeting. Pran ran up to him with this note for me. He [the correspondent] called me in New York from Paris where he was based. That was the most exciting moment — that Pran was alive. I think it was a blessing. Someone said to me that it was a gift.

Much of your success came from covering wars. What was it like?

We don't talk much about how we cover wars. Nowadays we see it on television, and it looks very swashbuckling and exciting. We don't usually talk about how exciting war is, and that's a big part of it, and it's why many of us go back and do it again, to cover another war. We don't want to talk about how we get a thrill out of it when you're in the middle of a battle, and the bullets and the shells are landing around you, and you're hunkered down. You're on the one hand scared, and on the other hand you're sure of your immortality because you haven't been killed before. When the battle is over, you come away feeling enormously excited about being alive because you've escaped all this. Your adrenaline is rushing very high. You see this in soldiers as well. It's not just with reporters. It's something we don't like to talk about because it makes it sound as though war is fun.

I don't know about fun, but a piece of it has a certain excitement. At the same time that it's exciting, it's horrendous. Someone's being blown apart while you are saved. And you live with that afterward. You know that it was an exciting time, and you also know that you bear inside of you the effect of witnessing someone else's death while you escaped. Partly that's survivor's guilt. The question of whether you did enough to save somebody else.

As a New York Times *columnist, you did a lot of stories on a highway called Westway, which would have had a major impact on New York City. How did you come to reach the position you did on that issue, and didn't it cost you your job?*

I think it was one of the factors, but only one. I had written a lot of columns on the real estate industry. It was a pretty bad time in New York, the early eighties. The homeless population was growing. Part of the reason, and only part, was that there was a push to energize real estate apartment development in New York. There were a lot of abandoned buildings. The city put into effect a law giving developers tax abatements to renovate buildings. A lot of the buildings were SRO housing — single room only housing. In them was everybody from retired school teachers to drug addicts. The neighborhoods saw only the unsavory side.

But there were fixed income people in there, and they were all thrown out by very unscrupulous landlords, taking advantage of these tax gifts. They did some pretty unscrupulous things, including violent things.

I'd become interested in the real estate industry because in New York City the real estate industry is the engine that makes the city run, even more than the financial industry. It always dictates to a large degree city policy on rents and on tax policy. There was a lot of overbuilding in that period, buildings that are now empty because of the glut of office space, not residential space.

Westway came along, and the waterfront was in a mess. Everyone from Pat Moynihan on down to the city fathers thought it was a great way to get federal money.[5] In other words, to build a highway on the cheap. The point was, do you need a six- or eight-lane highway, much of it underground, with amazing construction cost? Only a little piece of the waterfront would have been a park. All of it was going to be large apartment houses in which the developers were going to get tremendous breaks and tremendous location.

The money was huge. They'd already spent a couple of hundred million, and the price tag was, I believe, one-point-four billion dollars. I believe in creating jobs and public works projects, but this was not a giveaway to the construction workers, but a giveaway to the real estate industry, among others.

All the big real estate types were in on this, and the big engineering companies were making big, big money. The beneficiaries were not going to be average renters or co-op buyers. This was going to be luxury housing. There was no evidence this highway was needed on this lavish of a scale.

In the beginning, I didn't know all of this. I began to write about it because I was curious. It turns out that even Robert Moses was against this idea.[6] At the time it was about ten years old but only now got this federal financing. It did not make any sense. You're going to rip up a whole section of the city. The more I learned, the more I felt it was not good public policy, and I began writing about it and digging at it and seeing who was getting the money.

You can't make a federal court argument by saying this is going to benefit real estate developers. You have to show a fracture of federal law. Opponents held onto the conservation law about striped bass that were spawning underneath these rotting piers. Of course, that's not what it was all about. It wasn't about saving the striped bass, and I never even wrote it that way. They used the conservationist arguments in their court cases. What happened was, the other side, promoting this highway, would come in with fake information about this striped bass and lots of other things.

In a way, it was almost like "Watergate." I don't want to overuse or abuse the word *Watergate*, but in a sense it was the cover-up afterwards, more than the actual act, that got these people in trouble. They were finally exposed over time as people who were trying to get their snouts in the public trough. It wasn't going to be two billion, it wasn't going to be four billion. They finally admitted it was going to cost four billion. By the time they got through with delays, it was going to be twenty billion to build this three miles of highway, the most expensive highway in the goddamned world, ever. Twenty billion. That's what killed it finally. The role I played in this was simply to write about it. But there finally came a moment in Congress — maybe for the wrong reasons, to bash New York or something — it was killed.

I wouldn't want to take credit for bashing New York, and I wasn't doing that. But sometimes, some of the things you stand up and holler against do get killed, and one should be happy about that, I suppose. But sometimes it is for the wrong reasons. I don't think that Congress really cares that the developers are going to benefit.

It was a lonely process because the editorial page editors of the *New York Times*—I wrote on the opposite page—were gung ho for this. Every time I wrote a column, they would come up with a new editorial. It was funny in a way, but I felt there were just two competing voices and let's see who is right. All I'm doing is throwing some facts out there.

You know, part of investigative reporting is not just digging up information. It takes persistence and tenacity to get data, figures, facts that haven't been uncovered before. It also takes a certain willingness to be out there all alone, by yourself. Not just within your own newspaper, because that I was, but also because all of the major political figures in this state wanted that highway. They were always looking for a way to get federal funds because New York state is federally deprived. We pay more in taxes than we get back, so, any way they can get it seems OK. So, I can see that point of view. Yes, it's nice to get the money back, but not for a wasteful purpose. We didn't need this highway. I don't take it as any feather in my cap. I just see it as another thing that I had to see to the end.

Do you consider your work on Westway, in Cambodia, and elsewhere as investigative reporting?

Some of it was. The term *investigative reporter* gets overused because if a reporter is doing his or her job, he is carrying out some type of investigation, intellectual or otherwise. Some investigative skills are very complex, like document research, and these days many are using computers to do document research. Those are special skills.

But all of it really is a search to start off from scratch and to put together a picture—a piece here and a piece there—something like a mosaic, of what's really going on. You never get all of the pieces. The picture is never complete, and there comes a time when you know you're never going to get all of the pieces. You have to decide somewhere in your viscera when you're going to write.

What is it that you believe that your reporting, your research, your investigation, has told you? Who has done what to whom? Where does the preponderance of the evidence lie? I think at some point you unfreeze yourself, and you write as much as you know, while at the same time telling the reader what you don't know. It's very, very important to say that very high in whatever story you are writing; this is what I saw, or learned, or confirmed, and this is what could not be confirmed. It's not just a fire escape, a life preserver to get you off the hook. It again brings the reader in, and says he or she is not posturing, they're telling us what they don't know.

What attracted you to journalism? What are some of the things that we don't talk about as reporters?

We don't talk about how part of our fun is being high-grade gossips, knowing a lot about important people. Not necessarily using it, but being around important people. There's something exciting and also scary about that, too. It's very vicarious, in the sense that we feed off of them, but some of us mistakenly take our own importance from being around power. It's a mistake. You must really try to understand who you are and keep your distance. It's a running problem in journalism. Keeping your distance and not becoming too involved with the people that you cover. We don't talk much about that, and I think that is a mistake.

I think that when we don't explain the process, or that we don't explain that we're just human beings, there's nothing particularly special about us, that some of us, like in any profession, become special for being particularly tenacious or gifted, or just better than others at the trade.

How do you build and protect your sources?

Everyone builds sources differently. And I think you do it differently at different parts of your life. I know that when I was younger, and I had uncovered a story that no one else had because this or that source wanted to talk to me on the record, I just wrote that down and I wrote the story. Sometimes people become so outraged by what is happening, about some injustice, they say, I want this out, I want to tell you about this. Now I don't do that.

Now I tell them to go home and think about it. Do they want their name in this story? A lot of people, especially when you're talking to people without a lot of experience with the press, don't understand the possible result. When you're talking to the secretary of state, he's a big boy. He knows how to play the big game, and if he tells you something, you don't have to worry what is going to happen to his sensitive skin the next day. He knows what it's like when it appears in the press.

A lot of people don't have any idea what happens when their name, and their remarks with their name, go into the paper or go on the air. There's no way they can know it. They haven't done it before. But they're angry, and they want to get back at someone they feel who has done them an injustice. So they say, yeah, I want my name there. Now I say to them, think about it. Because you could wake up tomorrow morning, and while you'll have the satisfaction of having struck back at your tormentors, they'll still be around. Your job might become a holy hell, your family life could suffer, and you could become obsessed with this fight inside your career, your workplace. I've seen all this happen.

It's a process by which you do see what power you have and what havoc you can wreak, even unintentionally. You don't wish to do these things, but it happens. I don't think it makes you less energetic covering stories. I just think it makes you a little bit more careful about the individuals who are at the bottom of the food chain, who don't understand that the roof is going to fall in on them. And you protect them. Sure, it would be nice to have their name in the paper, but you don't need it. You can triangulate your information, you can get it confirmed some way else. You use your information while doing your best to protect your source.

Should the news media turn the spotlight on itself?

I think we are a very complex group of people. I don't think we're given to public introspection. For all of the confessional books that are written by reporters, I don't think we examine our profession very much. Very few papers have a serious beat committed to covering the press. Sometimes they have people covering the media, but more often than not, that's coverage of the economics of the media, how well they're doing and how well newspapers are doing vis à vis radio and television. These days it's about how large corporations are buying large media companies and running them like large business corporations. We don't often talk about the product or the process by which the product is arrived at. I think that is a big gap.

You're talking about more than accountability.

It's accountability because we have an enormous amount of power. In many ways the press sets whatever agenda there is in government. An independent candidate for the presidency can come down the road, and the press can decide whether that candidate is credible or not, and you may never hear his agenda. Especially on the local level, in the cities, the newspapers set the political agenda.

We have a lot of power, a lot of ability to hold an important institution's feet to the fire, and I think it would be very, very healthy if we had a discussion in our own pages on how we work and what it is we do. It would show us with clay feet, but the healthy side of that is that we would probably try to get a little more concrete in the feet.

Was writing your column a natural transition? What did you learn from this part of your career?

I really think what we do is a continuum, and not just in our work lives, but in our personal lives. We are at any given moment a sum of all of our parts. We are our childhood, we are drawn to certain pursuits.

I think reporters are often a certain breed of people. They share something in common. Not all reporters, but there are some common strains. They are outsiders, they are people who like to observe, who like to make sense out of the world. Maybe we are not doers in that sense. We're not the people who say we're are going to erect a building or go into government service and do "X" or whatever.

We're going to write about it. We are explorers in a way. But outsiders, I think that is an important ingredient. I think the best journalists are outsiders. That makes it lonely, and it also denies you certain things, certain friendships you can't have, because you can't do both. You can't cover a major public official and be his social friend at the same time. It's virtually impossible. I really think that what we do is a continuum.

I think we get into things not because reporting is some saintly profession, but because it is an avenue of protest along with teaching. It's a place where people can say, "Hey, wait a minute. Didn't you forget the history here?"

In a democracy, it's a place where people can holler when they are in pain. Not the reporters, but the people through their reporting. I think it all forms us. It's been a grand life. There's plenty of pain in it, but it's a grand life. When you think about it in many ways, it's a child's profession. I say this not to put us down, but it's full of adventure and curiosity and discovery and learning. It's like being paid to go on vacation, to go find out about something. Usually you pay to learn. You pay to go to school.

You've mentioned that several times: finishing what you start. Is this a problem in journalism?
I think that that's an important part of the craft. We are often correctly accused of skimming the surface of stories and then going on to the next story, and skimming that surface, then going on to the next disaster and doing the same thing, and never coming back to see what happened.

Take Vietnam. We had, over time, thousands of American journalists there in shifts. Yet when the war was over, when the soldiers were gone, our soldiers, we didn't have anybody there. Not that the Vietnamese were allowing reporters back in droves, but people weren't even trying to go back in there. The interest was gone. We should have found out how it came out. We should have been almost as interested in how it came out as we were in what was going on during the combat. And we weren't.

What that shows to me is that our national interest only existed because we sent soldiers there. There wasn't any national security interest. There wasn't any national interest of any kind in Vietnam that would warrant a war. It was backwards. We sent soldiers there, so we had a national interest. All backwards.

And we didn't care about them. That's not a sin when it's a distant society and we don't know about them. It's sad that we aren't one world. We are getting better at that, but we didn't care about the Vietnamese. We didn't care about the Cambodians. That's OK, as long as you don't pretend while you are there that you're making the world safe for democracy and that you're building democracy in Vietnam, which had no history with it. Democracy doesn't take root in a day.

That's part of the reporting process, pointing these things out and saying, "Whoa, what are we doing here?" Not just the day-to-day reporting, but what are we doing here? That doesn't happen the first day you land. You're there a year or two, and you began to say, why? I think that's when reporting takes on its public service cloak, when you began to say, why? It takes a while because you don't know enough in the beginning.

What do you think of television?
I think television, most of the time, is just doing what television finds easiest to do. I think every profession does that for the most part. I think that print journalism does what's easiest most of the time, too. Except by tradition, it's suppose to put more facts in, it's longer. But television finds the easiest point of

resistance is to do short, quick pieces. Slam, bam, thank you ma'am and out. That's true about the news and just about anything it covers.

It's at its best and worst when it has a very powerful image of pain or disaster or joy or elation, and it shows that, and bing, it's out again. And it has your emotions on a hook, and it's got you. And whether they're doing the movie of the week or covering the news, that's often true.

I think television fails more often than print. I think print journalism has a lot to answer for, but I think on balance the batting average of print journalism is higher than television. What makes that even more troublesome is the burden is going to fall on television, at least on electronic technology, which will appear in some form visually because newspapers are in a declining period.

Because of technologies, because of the economics of newspapers, and a lot of other reasons, we have entered the era where newspapers are not going to be family owned and family run, but be owned by a large corporation, many that have nothing to do with communication. They will run it like a business. It will become more and more important for television to do a better job with the news.

On the surface, it sounds like we're going to have more all-news stations. But we've got to have an expenditure of money, I want to see if it happens, to do in-depth pieces, and to be courageous. I do not see that with television, certainly not the networks. The most recent evidence is that the networks caved faster than newspapers to corporate threats to sue for libel. The latest one is the CBS "60 Minutes" episode.[7] There was no good legal reason for them to not run an interview with a former senior cigarette company executive.

I see CBS's cave-in as a very serious matter. It's happened before at other networks, but this is a very serious one on a very important news program. I think it will embolden corporations, not just cigarette companies, to make these threats with a view to silencing. That's what libel suits are mostly about, they want to silence the press.

I'm worried about television because I don't see it getting better. I see it getting more popular, making itself more popular. I think that is something journalists should never aspire to be — popular. The moment you want to be popular is the moment you stop doing your job. You got to be willing to be all alone out there. You say, all I can tell you is, yes, I can be wrong, and I've made mistakes before, and I've admitted them. But I believe that I'm right, and as long as I feel that my information is correct, I have to put it out there. You're going to see a lot less of that if people are caving in. You can't be popular and do a good job as a journalist.

What advice do you have to a young person who wants to be a reporter?

The advice is to go and write. I don't care if it's for a small paper that nobody in the big city has ever heard of. Try to go from there. They can try to do it in the big cities.

It's what keeps me from losing my optimism because I see a lot of young people willing to fight for the integrity of their stories, to get information out.

It's going to get harder. As more and more journalism companies are taken over by business companies, the odds are that the quality of the journalism becomes less important and the bottom line becomes the only determining factor. Why didn't the journalist at CBS, "60 Minutes," stand up and raise holy hell? That tells you something.

I say go and do it and raise hell, if it excites you. If it scares you, that's par for the course. I think it scares all of us. I say go do it. I think it's great.

If it really excites you, really thrills you, then go out there and say, after a week on a story, that I'm really beginning to understand something. This is exciting, the learning process. Now I can tell somebody else, the reader, the viewer, the listener. If you're excited by that, stay with it.

You won't make a lot of money. Oh, you might. You might sell a book that will make you millions or whatever. But the odds are you won't make a lot of money, but you'll have a very good life. It's not going to be without tears and pain. I say, do it!

Notes

1. Sydney H. Schanberg, *The Death and Life of Dith Pran*. Elisabeth Sifton Books and Penguin Books (New York: 1985). Most of the book was published in the *New York Times Sunday Magazine*, January 20, 1980.

2. The United States was involved in the Vietnam War from the late 1950s until it withdrew its troops in 1972. In 1970, U.S. and South Vietnamese troops entered Cambodia in hopes of closing down suspected enemy sanctuaries. This action pushed Cambodia into the conflict with disastrous results.

3. Put Sophan was a soundman/expediter for CBS News in Phnom Penh, Cambodia. The interviewer worked with Sophan for a number of years. Sophan and his family disappeared after the fall of Phnom Penh.

4. Prince Norodom Sihanouk was elected king of Cambodia in 1941. After World War II, he attempted to establish a quasi-democratic government in his country. He tried to balance the demands of the forces fighting the United States and South Vietnam for free passage and sanctuary while trying to keep Cambodia out of the war. His government fell during the April 1970 incursion, and he was replaced by a military government headed by General Lon Nol.

5. Daniel Patrick Moynihan, the senior senator for New York state, grew up in the West Side district known as "Hell's Kitchen," and felt strongly that Westway would rejuvenate the area.

6. Robert Moses played a larger role in shaping the physical environment in New York state than any other figure in the twentieth century.

7. The CBS program "60 Minutes" pulled a story on tobacco scheduled for November 9, 1995. For an in-depth analysis of the controversy, see "CBS, 60 Minutes, and the Unseen Interview," by Lawrence K. Grossman, *Columbia Journalism Review* (January-February 1996). Later, "60 Minutes" broadcast parts of the suppressed interview of a former tobacco industry official.

7

David Burnham
Investigating Bureaucracies

> I talk to a lot of people, but I don't use the expression "network of sources." It's dangerous for investigative reporters to rely on that sort of thing. You get conned so often. To protect yourself, you name sources as much as you can.

For almost three decades, David Burnham has been investigating America's most powerful bureaucracies and exposing corruption and malfeasance at the highest levels of federal and state government, from the New York Police Department to the Internal Revenue Service. His most recent book, *Above the Law: Secret Deals, Political Fixes, and Other Misadventures of the U.S. Justice Department*,[1] was published in the winter of 1996 and investigated the U.S. Justice Department's record on civil rights, national security, and drug enforcement.

Pulitzer Prize–winning investigative journalist Seymour Hersh wrote that *Above the Law* "tells us that far too often the Justice Department represents not the people but politicians, corporations, and other entrenched private interests. … David Burnham once again shows why his investigative reporting is a national asset."[2]

Burnham began his journalism career in 1958 as a writer for the "Walter Cronkite Evening News" on the CBS television network and as a reporter for *Newsweek* magazine, United Press International, and the Monroe News Bureau. From 1965 to 1967, he served as assistant director of the President's Commission on Law Enforcement and Administration of Justice before going on to work as a reporter for the *New York Times*. While at the *Times*, he built his professional reputation writing stories about the Frank Serpico police corruption case, which led to the formation of the Knapp Commission, and covering regulatory issues affecting communications, occupational health, and nuclear energy.[3]

From 1980 to 1982, Burnham served as a fellow at the Aspen Institute Program on Communications and Society, where he researched and wrote *The Rise of the Computer State*, a book that investigates the impact of communications technology on privacy, freedom, and representative democracy.[4] He returned to the *New York Times* in 1986 to work as a reporter in the newspaper's Washington Bureau and then left again to research and write *A Law Unto Itself: Power, Politics and the IRS*.[5]

The journalism organization Investigative Reporters and Editors selected *Law Unto Itself* as the best investigative book of 1989. Burnham has won numerous other journalism awards, including the Golden Typewriter Award from the New York Press Club (1977), an Alicia Patterson Foundation fellowship (1987), and a Rockefeller Foundation fellowship (1992).

When not investigating bureaucracies, Burnham serves as codirector of the Transactional Records Clearinghouse (TRAC). Founded in 1989 at Syracuse University, TRAC collects, organizes, and makes available information of such federal agencies as the Internal Revenue Service (IRS), the U.S. Justice Department, the Environmental Protection Agency (EPA), and the Nuclear Regulatory Commission (NRC) and provides research and consulting services. As co-director, Burnham has given numerous seminars to a wide variety of organizations, including the Freedom Forum, the Union of Concerned Scientists, the American Bar Association, and the U.S. Justice House and Senate Committees.

The journalist feels strongly that investigations reporting on the performance of large institutions are among the most important investigations any news organization can undertake. His investigative books and articles and his work at TRAC, Burnham told the authors, focus on the big question: What is it that prevents large bureaucracies from working as they claim to work?

* * *

Let's start off with your latest book, Above the Law, *which is an investigation of the U.S. Justice Department. Could you tell us how it came about?*

I've been thinking about doing a book on the U.S. Justice Department for twenty-five years.

[Laughs.] That sounds exhausting.

[Laughs.] No, it was great fun. In nineteen sixty, I was on the staff of the President's Commission on Law Enforcement and Administration of Justice, sometimes known as the Crime Commission, and when I left there, I got hired by the *New York Times* to cover criminal justice. I came to realize I was covering the wrong thing. Yes, police are important, but they are a pretty easy target and changing them is pretty easy. A lot has been written about judges, but it's all out in the open and part of the public record.

What I had covered, though, were the prosecutors, and they intrigued me. They had all the power. I don't think journalists do enough investigation of large bureaucracies like the U.S. Justice Department.

Which is your specialty?

Yes, it's my hobbyhorse. It seems to me that if you go after the New York

Police Department, or the IRS, or the Justice Department, or the hospital system, or the school system, you will have a much greater impact because those agencies deal with millions of people.

Why do you think investigative journalists shy away from covering large bureaucracies? Is it because the institutions are too complex?
    Well, they take time to investigate. There are very few newspapers or broadcasting systems that will give a reporter enough time to become knowledgeable about large bureaucracies. To cover a large bureaucracy, a journalist has to have time to prepare, think, and analyze. Very few journalists can leap into a project that investigates a large institution and understand the nuances and dynamics, which is what we have to do as journalists.

How long did it take you to complete the actual research and writing of the book on the U.S. Justice Department?
    The research involved a major effort. I am co-director of TRAC and that takes up a lot of my time. I have been raising money for TRAC and doing research and putting out reports on the Nuclear Regulatory Commission, the U.S. Justice Department, and a variety of other subjects. So I worked years on the book while spending a lot of time on TRAC, but my work with TRAC contributed enormously to the book.

In what ways?
    Well, the data we collected at TRAC showed the huge discretion the U.S. Justice Department has to do things. West Virginia has the country's most active drug-prosecuting U.S. attorney general's office, while Nevada does nothing in comparative terms. The Nashville office does nothing. The San Francisco office does nothing. Los Angeles does very little.
    What's going on? It doesn't hit you over the head right away, but then you say, "Four or five U.S. attorneys have told me that drugs are the country's number one problem. They claim they are going to do this and that, but why all the variation?" That leads you to conclude that the U.S. attorney general has never really supervised what the agency does.
    The other thing the data showed me — and I sort of knew this — is that what an agency doesn't do is often more important than what an agency does do, and often what they do is a political decision. It has been that way for years. It's interesting to learn that ninety-five percent of the civil rights cases that the FBI recommends for prosecution were never prosecuted. It becomes more interesting when you learn the percentage of cases prosecuted is a lot higher for drug matters than for official corruption.

So did you have a thesis when you started researching Above the Law *or did you allow your research to lead to conclusions?*
    I didn't really have a thesis.

I mean, were you trying to prove that the U.S. Justice Department was corrupt and inefficient? Was that your thesis?

No, that was my hunch. I went to see Allan Morrison, then the number one lawyer for Ralph Nader. He's a very thoughtful guy who's been around. I asked Allan if there was a thesis. That was really early on in my research. He said, "The thing about the Justice Department is that it has nothing to do with justice." I went away from that interview not impressed with that thought. Looking back at that interview, however, I can see Allan is a very smart guy. The Justice Department is not about justice. The public may think it is. It's about winning the case, no matter what. It's about advancing one's political agenda.

In other words, bureaucracy protecting bureaucracy?

Yes, they don't achieve their stated goals. People say that's a cynical and negative view — no large bureaucracy ever achieving its stated goal. I don't think it's a cynical view. I think it's skeptical. There is an important difference. Cynicism is the absolutely worst thing an investigative reporter can have.

But isn't it easy for investigative journalists to become cynical about the American way of life? After all, exposing corruption and wrongdoing is a way of life for investigative reporters.

Yeah, but you have to realize that all federal institutions, despite all their failings, do kind of function. My IRS book was easier to write than my book on the Justice Department because it was clear the IRS was successful in the sense that it collects eighty-five to ninety percent of all taxes due. That's an outstanding record. There have been times that it has been politically corrupt and that's bad, but the IRS does function.

Now it's harder to measure the effectiveness of the Justice Department and argue that it works. With regard to the drug problem, it clearly doesn't work. I'm not sure its white collar crime program works. So you have to remain skeptical.

So what is the difference between cynicism and skepticism? At the time I covered the New York City Police Department, the police used to say to me, "Hey kid, nothing is on the level." If nothing is on the level, I thought, then that means you are not on the level. That's cynicism, and it can destroy you. Skepticism, on the other hand, means examining and looking closely at everything.

In examining and looking closely at everything, have some of your investigations made a difference?

Yes, I know they have.

Led to change?

Yes, but it depends. I don't know if my investigation of the IRS led to change. I thought the New York Police Department was powerful, but the IRS is a much more powerful institution and it's tough to mess with.

In reading Above the Law, *I was impressed with all that data you collected. It was an incredible amount of material. Do you have a system for organizing all that stuff, one that works for you in keeping track of it all?*

[Laughs.] I really don't have a system.

For example, do you use computer-assisted journalism techniques like spreadsheets and databases?

Oh, yeah. TRAC at the present time has the equivalent of ten thousand reels of tape, which report on the individual enforcement activities of the IRS, Justice Department, NRC, and the EPA. There is a lot of data, and I have to access it.

With regard to my Justice Department investigation, we decided to look at a number of areas. For example, we pulled data on narcotics enforcement over the past fifteen years and saw there was a great increase in narcotics enforcement, but it was uneven. We took a look at environmental crimes and found out that the U.S. attorney in San Diego brought many times more cases to trial than his counterparts in other cities. We had to ask: what's going on? So I followed up and went to interview him. That was interesting.

The U.S. Justice Department's allocation system is just nutty. We looked at it on a per capita basis and were just astonished. It's so crazy, in fact, that we put out a report about it, and a congressional committee asked us to testify, which led [Attorney General Janet Reno] to undertake a study to develop what she called "a principled objective way of allocating resources." That's an example of research by myself and Susan Long, my colleague at TRAC, which actually had an effect before the book came out.

So you use researchers on your investigative projects?

My colleague Susan Long, who, among other things, has researched the IRS for the past twenty-five years and is an enormously sophisticated investigator — I guess you can call her a statistician — has been very helpful in checking out things. I use other researchers occasionally. For example, in researching *Above the Law*, I used a young man with a master's degree in history for a couple of months to find out the names of all the attorney generals in U.S. history.

You said you've done some computer-assisted journalism. How have you been using it?

I've used it in both my IRS and Justice Department investigations. If you look in the back of my IRS book, you'll see a bunch of tables. We got the information for the book kind of late in the game, so the data is not as well integrated into that book as it is in my Justice Department book. In using data generated by computer-assisted journalism, I think it's important that the journalist incorporate it in such a way that it doesn't overwhelm the reader. If you do an investigation with just data and no anecdotes, it makes for dull reading and doesn't work. You've got to integrate the data and think of the dynamics of the investigation.

How long have you been doing data analysis?
Since the late nineteen hundred and sixties when I was covering the New York [City] Police Department.

With computers?
Yes. One time I got the police department to give me a random data sample for a couple of hundred murder cases from the previous year — the age, race, and sex of the victim. I then went to the courts and looked up the cases and got the age, sex, and race of the victims. I took this information over to the business office of the *New York Times* and got them to run a simple little program that gave the percentage for whites killing whites, whites killing blacks, and blacks killing blacks. [Laughs.] I could have done it by hand actually, but they were willing to do it on a business computer for me. The results revealed that half of the murders in New York involved blacks killing blacks, but more importantly, it showed that little cross-racial murdering was going on. I thought that was interesting. I did the same thing for robberies.

Another interesting thing I did using computers — New York City in the late sixties had about sixty or seventy precincts, and I got the reported crime figures by precinct. But the reported crime figures alone don't mean anything. One district may have twice as many people as another and twice as many crimes, but that doesn't mean very much.

The New York City police didn't have figures on how many people lived in each precinct or their racial breakdown. I took a map of the precincts and overlaid it on the census tracts. I had the Rand [Corporation], which is a big research institute in California, do a run for me. I then took statistics for every precinct in the city — racial breakdown, age breakdown, number of toilets, the usual census stuff — and I married them with crime.

Now, surprise, surprise [laughs]. My research showed that poor neighborhoods had more crime. In fact, it was overwhelming. That was the story. It made the front page of the [New York] *Times*. The story included a whole page of tabular material about every precinct. My story was widely read. Everybody was interested in their precinct.

Is it easier today to do that kind of investigative journalism because computers are more sophisticated?
I don't think that computers, when they're used in an investigation, are the key thing. It's not a technical problem; it's a thinking problem.

The human element?
It's figuring out what kind of investigation you want to do and using the data you uncover in a clever way. For example, we have nineteen hundred ninety-four data from the [U.S.] Justice Department that shows there were fifty-two thousand indictments in all. We have Republicans going around charging that the U.S. is going after business and how terrible it is and what a burden it's

putting on business. Guess what percentage of all those indictments involve occupational safety and health crimes and consumer product crimes? Well, it's less than one-half of one percent. It's two hundred fifty out of fifty-two thousand. That's nothing. It's baloney. So why haven't the newspapers questioned the National Association of Manufacturers? It's because they haven't done their homework. They haven't investigated. I think the American press is incredibly passive and lazy, and they depend too much on handouts. The media is full of high price stenographers.

So is there much serious investigative journalism going on today?
It's difficult to say, but let's look at investigative journalism historically, which I've thought about a lot. There was a lot of serious investigative journalism before World War I — the so-called muckraker era. In fact, my grandfather was an investigative journalist in Boston, and he investigated bad housing. In those days, they would investigate the Senate, and it was wonderful stuff. Then that tradition died out, beginning with World War I.

Why did that happen?
Some writers say it's because corporate America went after investigative journalists and sued them. They went after the few magazines that were publishing investigative journalism. In fact, as I recall it, the business interests started a magazine called *Collier's* to take business away from the muckraking magazines. It was a front for business.

Then comes World War One, and a hold is put on all that investigative journalism. We then slide into the nineteen twenties and nobody is serious about anything, and little investigative reporting is going on. The nineteen thirties come, and again there's not very much. World War Two breaks out, and we're all patriots. We don't do much in the nineteen fifties because we are afraid of the Commies and everybody is walking the same line.

But something happens in the nineteen fifties and nineteen sixties. My theory is that the civil rights demonstrations got a lot of people thinking, "What the hell's going on in our society?" Reporters started to become more skeptical.

That frame of mind became more and more active, and then, of course, came the Vietnam War, followed by Watergate, when we had this second period of quite active investigative reporting. Although I haven't done or seen a quantitative analysis, I don't think the investigative journalism was near the quantity and brashness of the early muckraking period. A lot of investigative books and articles during the Watergate period involved leaks. It bugs me that a lot of investigative journalists have become our heroes because of leaks. They don't explain who is leaking and what their motives are.

You mean the use of unnamed sources?
Yes, unnamed sources and stories where people have axes to grind, a fact that is not made clear. I'm a great admirer of Seymour Hersh. He's done an

enormous amount of good stuff, but you look at his piece on the CIA. It turned out to be right, but what was going on there? Well, one wing of the CIA was trying to destroy another wing. Read his writing on the topic, and you don't realize it. I'm not sure Sy knew it. Without knowing the source, of course, you wouldn't know it. And we have Woodward and Bernstein — the great heroes of investigative journalism — who don't use footnotes. We just don't know.

You mean we have to trust them?

We have to trust them, but I'm sorry, I don't have trust for anybody. There is a historian at Wisconsin named Kutler who did a book on Watergate.[6] His theory is that Woodward and Bernstein were getting their leaks out of the FBI and there was a power struggle going on at the time. That's interesting and affects what we know.

I don't like unsourced stories, especially those involving prosecutors. There are too many prosecutors who have made their careers on the backs of people they can't bring charges against. It's outrageous. That's often called investigative journalism, but I don't see it that way.

A lot of investigative journalists would argue that without those leaks we couldn't get at corruption and they wouldn't be able to do the big investigations. How do you answer that?

It's always a problem, sure, but we cave in too easily to the pressure to keep sources anonymous. There are a lot of reporters who are cracked up to be big-time investigative journalists but are nothing more than mouthpieces for prosecutors.

But a lot of investigative journalists say they need a network of anonymous sources to keep them informed about what's going on.

I talk to a lot of people, but I don't use the expression "network of sources." It's dangerous for investigative reporters to rely on that sort of thing. You get conned so often. To protect yourself, you name sources as much as you can.

But often they don't want to go on the record. I'm sure that's happened to you. What do you try to do? Do you try to talk them out of it?

Yes, I do, or I try to find other sources. But almost all scandals can be found in public records. When my book on the Justice Department was in the galley stage, the publisher sent it to "60 Minutes" for consideration, and one of the show's associate producers, whose name I can't remember, thank God, said, "Well, David, you have to give Mike Wallace six or seven of your best Deep Throats." I didn't say anything, but it stunned me. I called "60 Minutes" the next day and said, "Hey, you have to read my book. It's not Deep Throat stuff. It's public records stuff that I've put together. If you don't think that's important, that's your problem. Deep Throats don't know much anyway."

There are occasional exceptions. When Sy Hersh was investigating the CIA, the then head of the CIA was in a power struggle with James Angleton. So the head of the CIA gave Sy a lot of stuff, which, fortunately, turned out to be more or less true. We didn't know that battle was going on though.

I remember once going to talk to Woodward. It was after Watergate, and he was accusing the IRS of all kinds of misdeeds. I was researching the IRS and knew he was using the IRS's criminal division for sources. The old-line guys in the division were pissed off at the IRS commissioner because he was trying to cut back on their freewheeling style. So they leaked a lot of stuff. Some of the criminal investigators told me they went to Woodward and he got the story. I asked Woodward, "Did you ever question the motives of your sources?" He got really pissed off and defensive. I don't think he should have. Investigative journalists have to be very questioning of their sources and what their motives are. But we usually aren't.

In *Above the Law*, I wrote how the *New York Times* was used by a prosecutor to advance his political career. Prosecutors do that all the time. U.S. attorneys have the gossip, and reporters end up being interested in the gossip and don't investigate what those attorneys are not covering. They don't look at their performance, period.

It sounds as if you're suggesting that the period is a sorry one for investigative journalism as compared, say, to the period before World War One.

I don't think as much is going on as there was back then. I don't think the quality is as high either as it was in the muckraking period. I am really interested in finding out why that period of skepticism ended. There is a story there.

As for today, we have to be more critical, more aggressive, and more questioning than we are. That's why I'm devoting half of my time to TRAC. We want to make sure journalists have hard data to allow them to look at the performance of government and see if it's achieving its stated goals.

Are there any investigative journalists out there whom you admire; that is, analyzing the public record and doing their homework?

Yes, there are. For example, a team of *Cleveland Plain Dealer* reporters did a wonderful story that investigated how the NRC regulated nuclear material. Various members of the *Miami Herald* have done a terrific job on different investigations. Their data person is terrific. The *Raleigh News and Observer* staff have done some good stuff.

A few nights ago the *New York Times* published a piece on the record of public and private hospitals in treating their patients. Its investigation found that the care for patients in public hospitals was much worse than in private hospitals. The *Times* then tried to adjust for the fact that people coming to private hospitals are wealthier and in better health. The *Times* did a complicated but sophisticated analysis, and the point it made was important and interesting.

I can give you a lot of other examples. Newspapers are doing good investigative reporting compared to what's being done in book publishing and broadcasting. The record there is pathetic. Ben Bagdikian has written a lot of stuff that shows the concentration of the media is undermining serious reporting.[7] It makes sense to me, but I haven't done my own reporting on it.

Overall, though, the press is very, very passive. As I said before, much too much of it is high-priced stenography. Sure, we have to know what Bill Clinton and the mayor said yesterday, but the media needs to spend more time looking at our institutions to see how they are performing. Too few in the media are doing that.

I'm not an admirer of Ben Bradlee, who is also such a great hero of investigative journalism.[8] He didn't do anything on the Kennedys; he was totally in bed with them. I go into considerable detail in my book on the U.S. Justice Department. Sure, Ben Bradlee went after Watergate, but there are a lot of things he hasn't done, which he should be held accountable for.

The *Post* is so superficial. It has never covered the IRS. The reporter who is supposed to instead spends all of his time covering tax bills and legislation. Woodward will say, "Where is the crime?" Well, a lot of things are not crimes. If the big institutions of society write the laws, then they are very careful that certain things don't get defined as crimes. The insurance industry — one can argue it's a total crime. But the way the law is written you can't indict them.

It seems as if you are not optimistic about the future of your profession: investigative journalism.

Well, as I said, we've had these two great periods of investigative journalism, and they ended. Maybe we can learn something if we find out why.

What do you mean by that?

I want to teach reporters how to do investigative reporting. TRAC's purpose is to provide data to newspapers and other media to help them with their investigative reporting, but not many are picking up on it.

Why is that?

I really don't know. We made a proposal to Syracuse University last summer to set up a training program, the goal of which is to create a cadre of reporters from all over the country who can do statistical analysis. It turned out to be a little too rich for Syracuse's blood. Now I've sent the proposal to a couple of foundations.

How will the training program work?

Does distance learning ring a bell?

Yes, it's big in education.

We think we've worked out a way for a reporter, say, in South Carolina and a reporter in Texas to participate in a very extensive four-month training program from their newsrooms. It's complicated, but we hope to start doing it.

We are also writing a proposal to examine the possibility of creating what we call the wire service of the twenty-first century. The Associated Press grew out of the telegraph line. It was a co-op. We're thinking about trying to start a co-op that on a continuing basis will put out data from all the federal regulatory agencies, sort it out, and make it available to co-op members.

If, for example, another Three Mile Island happened, a reporter would be able to get access to all the investigative reports and all of the findings about the violations. A reporter would be able to compare the violations of utilities gone bad with all the similar reactors in the country. So right now we are trying to institutionalize the type of investigative reporting that looks at the performance of bureaucracies.

It sounds like you are not going to have too much time to write books.
I'll be doing this for a couple of years, but in the meantime, I'm sure I'll come up with a good topic to investigate.

Notes

1. David Burnham, *Above the Law: Secret Deals, Political Fixes, and Other Misadventures of the U.S. Justice Department* (New York: Simon and Schuster, 1996).
2. Seymour Hersh first broke into investigative journalism in a big way with his investigation of the My Lai massacre during the Vietnam War.
3. The Knapp Commission is one of several so-called "crime commissions" that have been organized over the years to investigate corruption in New York City.
4. David Burnham, *The Rise of the Computer State* (London: Weidenfeld and Nicolson, 1983).
5. David Burnham, *A Law Unto Itself: Power, Politics and the IRS* (New York: Vintage Books, 1989).
6. Stanley I. Kutler, *Wars of Watergate: The Last Crusade of Richard Nixon* (New York: W. W. Norton, 1990).
7. Ben Bagdikian, *The Media Monopoly* (Boston: Beacon, 1995).
8. Ben Bradlee was the *Washington Post* executive under whose direction Woodward and Bernstein conducted their Watergate investigation.

8

Byron Acohido
Covering the Company in a Company Town

> Be prepared to work hard and do your homework. It's all about research. It's all about having the right questions to ask. It's all about getting a knowledge base to where you can figure out what the story is and probe elements of it that you know would be important to your readers, if they knew about it in the right context. This would apply to any issue, whether it be government or big business, local politics or whatever.

The U.S. Air Boeing 737 was on approach for Pittsburgh in clear weather. The 132 passengers and crew were preparing for landing, most anticipating the end of another work week. Something happened. The aircraft made several unexplained maneuvers, then dived straight into the ground from 5,000 feet.[1] *Seattle Times* aerospace reporter Byron Acohido was at home when the paper called with the news. He was to go to Pittsburgh. Major crashes involving Boeing products are big news in Seattle.

Acohido stopped by the *Times* on his way to the airport. He pulled up his files on the 737 and started writing. The story detailed all the similar crashes, the problems being looked at, an overview of the aircraft's history, all based on his earlier reporting. More than 2,200 Boeing 737s are in service today, the workhorse of the world's airline fleet, and problems with this aircraft would have major implications for both Boeing and the airlines.

The *Seattle Times* ran the facts-based story in its next edition, and it was picked up by the wires for national distribution. Years before, the editors at the *Times* decided they needed someone to spend most of their time following Boeing, one of the driving economic forces in the Northwest. They turned to Byron Acohido, a business and investigative reporter with an interest in aerospace.

Acohido was born and raised in Hawaii, attended the Christian Brothers parochial school, and worked on the yearbook and high school newspaper. He quickly discovered a fondness for reporting and writing. At the University of Oregon, he chucked the idea of a career in law when he joined the school newspaper, and he switched to journalism.

After joining the Everett, Washington, newspaper, Acohido served a basic reporter's apprenticeship, covering city council, police, fires before moving up to issue-related beats such as criminal justice. The last two years in Everett focused on business reporting, which led to a job at the *Dallas Times-Herald* writing for the Dallas magazine.

Acohido describes the period after the *Times-Mirror* sold the paper as being aboard a sinking ship, but he did wind up managing the magazine, which he describes as a valuable experience. He returned to Washington and Seattle when he joined the *Seattle Times*, anticipating a move into editing and management. When the aerospace beat became a reality, however, he took the job and remained a reporter and writer.

Acohido embraces the West Coast casual look, in dramatic contrast to the buttoned-down world of the Boeing culture. He makes it clear from the start that in many ways he respects the company but feels there is a need for an outsider to follow their activities and developments, to keep their feet to the fire. He received a Pulitzer Prize in 1997 for his coverage of Boeing.

Our interview took place at a Seattle restaurant on the waterfront. The conversation was punctuated by various Boeing aircraft passing over, heading into nearby Boeing Field.

* * *

You're an investigative reporter with a beat. Do you enjoy covering the aerospace industry?

It's a great beat because the company is at a fascinating juncture in its role in corporate America, industrial America, and in aviation. All of those three things now are at a breaking point. They are trying all these strategies, business strategies, technical strategies. They've got Airbus breathing down their necks. For the first time, ever, they've got real competition. They've got this plan which Wall Street is sold on, buys into. Lots of analysts have torn apart the plan and buy into it.

Tracking the Boeing story has evolved. You try and pursue the really fundamental elements, which is to try and give the readers a balanced, accurate account they can use rather than an account the corporation is going to put out. It's not a different journalism from what other people practice or have practiced for a long time, but it is just such a fascinating point in its history. It's a wonderful opportunity in journalism.

You're talking about a very complex story here, aren't you?

I see it as a "big picture" story. I'm just trying to knock off elements of it, trying to pick off the best, highest payoff parts. Actually, the parts that mean the most in the current time frame. That's not hard to do. Selling airplanes, commercial market slash sales, this kinda default. The air safety stuff developed because you couldn't ignore it. It's an element of the story.

Byron Acohido. Photo by Haney Howell.

Do you consider yourself an investigative reporter?

Yeah, a lot of the time I do. I'm trying to flesh something out all the time, and what I'm trying to flesh out is a balanced story that is well researched and deeply researched and filtered in a way that results in something that is accessible and useful to my newspaper audience.

How important is Boeing to this area?

I don't think you can overstate it. It used to have about one hundred sixty thousand jobs, direct jobs. Now it's down to eighty-nine or ninety thousand and that's where it wants to be. It wants to streamline and put out the product on a lower cost basis. Most people figure there's a multiplier effect of about three jobs for every one Boeing job, other jobs in the region. You can't go anywhere without knowing someone who works for Boeing or holds Boeing stock, or — it's actually wider than that — the supply community is very wide. A lot of guys need Boeing, start up a company, supply parts. They're doing even more of that. Most of it they're shoving overseas, but still there is a real wide supply chain. The Japanese have set up plants here to build galleys and lavatories right near their plant. It's a big operation, and the Europeans have plants like that, that do composites work and so forth.

Do you consider your relationship with Boeing adversarial?

I consider my relationship with them straightforward; it may have evolved into an adversarial. I think I can argue that it's not anything I've done because I've been very consistent. I always say, look, here's what I'm working on, and here's what I want to talk to you about. There's no reason for me not to tell them.

But what has happened and has fallen into a real consistent pattern is that they respond to that in a certain way. It's hard to describe. I don't think it's much different than how other Fortune Five Hundred companies respond, especially to the hometown newspaper. If you look how corporations and their PR structures work, they're geared toward what they perceive as their highest impact, exposure deal. The *Wall Street Journal*, *Fortune* magazine, are at the top, and the trade magazines are right below that. Their whole mechanism is set up to feed into that.

It also reflects senior management's understanding of how the media works. This is a real generalization, but a lot of corporations have senior executives who have the view that this is somehow something that they can control, or they want to. That's their goal, they want to control the flow of information to fit their overall strategy, which you can argue is their responsibility to the shareholders. Whether it is realistic or not is another thing.

The hometown newspaper, even though we're a major newspaper, falls somewhere off the table. They deal with us when they have to, on a crisis basis. It's real consistent. How they view us is different from how we view ourselves. We view ourselves as: "We're here, you impact the community, and we're here to serve the community, and you need to talk to the community because you don't operate in a vacuum. Those questions that arise about the strategic steps you are taking or the problems with the products, the public has a right to know." Your classic approach. But their focus is not there. It's not to give access so we can tell our story. They think, "Do we have to do this right now? We've got the *Wall Street Journal* set up for next quarter and we'll give them a story." That's kinda my perception of it.

Are you comfortable with your role?
I guess it used to bother me, early on, when I would get frustrated. It's easy to get frustrated, not getting access, but it's so consistent that I've got to do it. The only other choice is to say this is too much of a bother, that we won't even do it. So, it's either you've got to do the stories, keep your ears out for the stories and go after them, and realize that you are going to get a certain level of response, a certain type of response, and then devise ways to work around that. That's what I'm doing. Actually, it's a challenge, trying to keep them in the loop. The challenge is a balanced, comprehensive story, and if the focus of the story is not playing along with you, it's just a challenge to get the information.

How do you develop your sources?
It depends on the story. I'm lucky in a way because they are a public company, one of the biggest and most actively traded stocks, so Wall Street swarms all over them. There are a lot of financial analysts out there, there's lots of institutional investors, there's a lot of people on the periphery of the airline business who track the financial part. There are guys in Europe who do this, track the price of these airplanes, financing trends. The whole game has gotten more complicated, more complex, since deregulation.

After a while you figure out who is who. You have the people who do the work, and the rest just go along for the ride, following the pack. Pretty soon you pick out the people that you can see are on the inside. I try not to use the same people all of the time. I'm constantly looking for people who have fresh insights, who show me they do their homework. But if they don't, I'll know right away in one or two conversations, this guy is spouting what everyone else is spouting. There is access to all of this information. All the ten-Ks, all the press lists that are put out, all the stories done by the business press are accessible to anybody. Even the airlines plug into that, and a consensus tends to grow, and they all say the same thing.

We try to look for the contrarians in the industry. Those guys have contacts to the other levels because that's what they've developed, fresher insights. I try and find those guys. There's a handful of them. It's interesting to see them work because they always move around in their viewpoint — bullish, bearish, bullish, bearish. How I can tell they've got good stuff is by their reasoning and analysis not being based on the pack consensus.

You can also talk to competitors. I've been over to a couple or three different airshows, and I've been to the Airbus plant in Germany twice, Toulouse once, and I've interviewed their top executives several times. It's interesting. Now they call me. But you have to realize why they're calling me.

Really, the job is collecting and filtering, and in that sense I guess it's investigating because you have to go out and accurately get it and then filter it.

You cite a lot of FAA, NTSB and other documents in your writing.[2] Do you do computer research, database research? How do you go about that?

You just try and stay current with what everybody else is doing. Just try and use enterprise. The air safety stuff is a little different. That's more classic investigative. You have a crash. You have evidence that they knew about a major design flaw that caused the crash. I'm speaking in general terms, but I can name five crashes that fit this.

There's a crash. After the crash, there's a suspect cause that has to do with a design flaw. You look a little deeper, and there is evidence that this design flaw was known about for a long period of time. In fact, there was probably another crash or indices strongly hinting that unless they do something proactive and in a tight time frame, it would lead to killing people. You just go from there.

You try to track those documents, track those people who are around those documents. Find people who were involved, find other supporting evidence, to the point where I know what all the databases are now, how they work, and what they've got.

For instance, the FAA has a couple of big databases that I use all of the time. In fact, I'm using them right now; service difficulty reports and accident and incident database. There is a law which says to the airlines, we want to track problems as they happen. If anything causes a problem at a certain level, you are to file this one-page report.

I did a story in eighty-eight that showed how massive that database was. But also how useless it was because it was kinda off to the side. The reporting level was all over the map, whether they reported or whether they looked at it. It was just sitting there. The other database is kinda like that, too. But nonetheless, that is one level of data.

In this case, I used it for rudders, and in September I used it again because I had watched a couple — after Colorado Springs, I said, whoops — I didn't do any stories about it, but other people did. It was another classic case of just what I told you, a design flaw with a track record of failure. The question was, Are they moving quickly enough to avoid another disaster?

When they had another one in Pittsburgh, in tracking all this, all these stories that other people had been doing and other airplane crashes, I made sure the paper published a story every time there was a crash of a 737. I did some reporting every time there was a crash. There were five or six others — Thailand, Korea, China — all with the same profile. You do one or two stories, and they go away. They go away because they're on foreign soil.

We tracked all those things and saw that they all had the same basic factors involved. You knew that when one happened in the Western world, in the right place, then all that would dovetail. Unfortunately, it happened in Pittsburgh, with a full plane of families and business people and everything. I'm not saying that I solved the problems at all.

So you saw that crash coming.

Right. When that crash happened, I was already home. I got the call, and I've got to go to Pittsburgh because I've covered these before. I know that the "go team" for the NTSB will go there, they will set up, and very flatly start giving out statements with no context for people to jump all over them — exploding watches, birds, whatever. This one they saw with no help at all. Later on they're crying about how irresponsible the press is.

Are you concerned about how the NTSB and the FAA handles these investigations?

I try not to look at it that way because I don't want to lose my objectivity or lose my credibility and be open to charges that I have an agenda. The way I look at it, and again, I try to look at it quite straightforwardly, is to try to understand why the dynamic is like that. People have written books about it, Congress has looked at the FAA, people have written about it, but not too many people have written about the NTSB.

When you follow them over a period of time, you see that the system was set up in the thirties and forties, I think, because aviation was fledgling and because we had to support it, to nurture it, to make sure it got off the ground and it became viable. Well, that investigation system, by and large, has not changed. But the world of aviation, the business of aviation, the business of selling airplanes, the business of flying passengers, of course has changed vastly, considerably vastly since deregulation in nineteen seventy-eight. Then over the eighties and nineties.

My reading of all the material that is out there is that the balance is such that industry naturally takes advantage of that. The fact that you have an FAA with a dual mandate to serve as a watchdog for the public and maintain safe skies and promote aviation safety. If you look at the top couple of guys at the FAA, it's like a revolving door back and forth. They serve in top-level jobs at the FAA, oversee all these safety issues, and then when they reach retirement age they turn up in industry with six-figure jobs.

The NTSB is sort of the balancing force, but they have no enforcement powers. You kinda see over the years where it does reflect political appointments and the political times. Even in the short time I've watched it, from 1988 on, I can point to evidence that the aggressiveness of NTSB, as being an element of promoting safety, shifting from aggressive to less aggressive. You could make a case that they're being less aggressive now versus how they handled, for instance, the Lauda Air crash in Thailand nine years ago.[3] The chairman was putting out all kinds of recommendations right after that. You could argue that you have a comparable problem, that there is more evidence with the 737 rudders, yet there seems to be, they seem to have softer kid gloves in handling it. Of course, they would disagree with that, but I think if you go on and take your own look at it...

I don't write about that. I write about the facts of the case. They come out and say we've looked at the evidence. I just returned from a briefing in Washington. It all revolves around this valve jamming. The valves jam all the time, and if they jam, the rudder moves. It can move hard over, and it's being signaled all the time. So it seems to me that it's really obvious that it's impossible to figure out how the thing jams. And I've already talked to guys who say if you talk to general mechanical engineering, that there are all kinds of studies on how that thing can jam. It is susceptible to jamming, and you know what the result is.

The NTSB concluded that there is no evidence of a jam on the Colorado Springs airplane or the Pittsburgh airplane.[4] If you break down their analysis, it's kinda a narrow analysis. You could take a broader analysis or look harder. Maybe they'll never figure out whether it jammed to their satisfaction. It's like you have to prove beyond a shadow of a doubt that there's solid evidence that this thing jammed or we're going to look somewhere else. They've now come up with some wake vortex studies that show that some sort of weird, sustained stall happened, that wake vortex four miles ahead, that the rudder moved it or something else. There is nothing else known, so they are going to do these studies that show a sustained crab caused by the vortex.

But you see, they use different levels of logic. If you demand that circumstantial evidence is not enough to show that this valve jammed, that was probably the cause, there is no evidence [they say]. You see, Boeing is involved in this. They're going to go and develop this study, and who knows what they're going to do with that. Are they going to say that the airplane went into a new phase called sustained yaw when it hit this vortex from four miles ahead? That the rudder was not involved and that probably caused it? Well, there's no evidence of that either.

Is anyone outside of Boeing, the manufacturers, testing these products?

That's the amazing thing. That's what I'm saying. It's a system that was set up in the thirties, still is in place. I just asked Bernard Loeb, who's director of the NTSB office of engineering, what's the deal here? How do you make the argument that it's OK to have the principals involved with the culpability potential drive your investigation? That's what they do, they drive the investigation.

Their argument is that it has to be that way. Their first argument is that the system has worked. We've got the best safety record, so therefore, it's good. The second argument is that it has to be them because they're the only guys who know the system as well as they do. Well, what about the fact that their asses are on the line too? If they're going to look at a set of facts and say there is no evidence. Here, let's look at the rudder unit this way. See, aha, no evidence, let's look somewhere else.

Take anything — thrust reversers, lock sectors on the cargo doors, fuse pins that hold engines up, let's look at it this way — aha! This level of safety, let's take this much time to do it, and that's sufficient. So they buy into it because there is no evidence. It's nothing original — people know this — they call it the Tombstone Safety Regulations. You have to have a certain number of deaths before you track it.

It would seem to me that overlying this is the fact that every once in a while you have a Pittsburgh, you have a mess on a hillside. That is an element that doesn't exist in most other industries. Is that an element to your story as well?

Yeah. Windows 95, if it crashes, isn't going to kill one hundred thirty-two people violently. But it's always a business story. It's not only trying to go to the next generation 737 to finish out this current line at about three thousand aircraft, and then move to the next version of the airplane. The image of the airplane has to be kept up. They can't have an airplane with a public perception of people questioning whether to get on it. This is the story that I'm developing right now. I've heard that the rudder system and the rudder, the rudder actuator and the rudder, on the new 737 that's coming out next year, is going to be completely different. The yaw damper is going to be completely different. Obviously, I would anticipate Boeing saying "that's progress." That's fine.

But as a journalist, what I'm interested in — knowing as much as I know about the company, thinking about giving my readers useful information, that gives them a broader context to make their own decisions — is the fact that Boeing always uses the same thing over and over. They never change things unless they have to. They keep systems in place, which fits with their current strategy, to streamline and stuff. If they're changing a system like the rudder — I don't know if they are or not, they haven't gotten to the point yet where they have to tell the FAA — to a split rudder with dual actuators, why are they doing that? Does that imply anything about the old version of the fleet and the single dual concentric rudders with huge rudder slab that's on there, and the potential for this valve to get a little hydraulic contamination and jam?

That's kinda like my overview. Whether I have a chance to write that or not or a story. But I won't write that until I have a news story to write that in the context of. But I'm thinking like that, and it's always one big story. And that's going to affect the sale of the 737s. And what is this element of risk, and who gets to play with the risk?

Because the public doesn't really know, they just take for granted that flying is safe, and it is. Statistically, very safe. The whole point is that if there is a mistake, and they know there is a built-in mistake that can happen under certain circumstances, and there's a way to get rid of it but it would cost a lot of money, not to mention the public perception that could get out of hand if they went in to fix it. Yet you've got a bunch of people dying violently. You're talking about coming down from thirty-five thousand feet or six thousand feet in a two hundred thousand pound aircraft.

That's what makes the 737 so fascinating. It's got all of those elements plus the technology. Pushing the whole technology.

Are we moving toward a totally new type of aircraft?

Yeah, represented by the Triple Seven [Boeing 777].[5] It looks like any other aircraft, but it's the step aircraft of fiber optics. It's the farthest reaching fiber optic aircraft out there, even more so than any military aircraft. The military has to deal with all the instability, but they don't have to deal with air conditioning systems and entertainment systems and everything else that's on that airplane.

The fascinating part about covering Boeing—I admire Boeing as a company in many ways—is that they are using their core. Their core competency, they call it, the core competency to be conservative about financing and engineering, but move forward and dominate the market. They take advantage of the fact that their installed base is so big, they know all these things. Good ole boys come to the airlines that they know. They've done a fabulous job with their support. Nobody can support their airplanes like they do, and they do.

But they are now being forced to overreach with the technology and where is that all going to end up? Are they right? Can they push the technology that far with their old system? Fly by the seat of their pants? That's what they do, that's what they've done historically. They call it a sporty game. They get to a certain point in a project, like the 747 or the 707, and there's no sensible way that they can finish out and stay on schedule, yet they do, by working extra hard, by crunching the engineering.

But it's all been mechanical primarily to date. This is the first one where all that stuff is coming to a head, one hundred percent electronic at the core of what is running the system.

They seemed to put the entire company on the line behind the aircraft. You say for the first time they really have competition for the airplanes and that Airbus initiated the "fly by wire" with the 320. Has Boeing been playing catch-up? Or have they taken it to another level?

Both. They were forced to play catch-up, and because they were late, they felt they had to take it to another level. They went with a new data buss, went with this new system of shared resource management. It's a next generation that people are just talking about. They'd even agreed upon the electronic community standard for it. They went out and did it. That's interesting, another part of the story.

You've talked to Airbus[6] and the other companies. Are they a lot different from Boeing?

They're completely different in terms of their nature and their structure. But they're the same in that they share the same goals. They want to get to the top of the market and dominate it. They're going to try and get exposure and public perception geared to their advantage, so they're both the same that way. They want the same thing, and they're both going to do whatever it takes to get there.

But behind that, they're completely different. Airbus is a consortium of European countries. It's a bunch of Frenchmen, Germans, and Englishmen who hate each other.

What fascinates me is that you're covering the company in a company town. Are you comfortable with that, and what type of support do you get from the paper?

I'm comfortable with it. The paper has been real supportive, and I think that's why they asked me to get on the beat seven years ago. They asked me if I would cover Boeing and aerospace. They really didn't tell me how to cover that, just cover it. I started covering it and starting doing stories approaching it from the viewpoint of trying to get more aggressive about wider context to whatever the news event was. Instead of saying, "Boeing says this is the issue, and here's what they're doing about it."

The paper had a legacy prior to my getting there of being kinda an extension of the Boeing PR department. They had a guy there, I think he was called aviation editor, and he's legendary. I've had to live down his legend. He played poker with the Boeing guys. He'd go on all of their delivery flights, he'd have their press releases in advance. If anything negative came up about the company, he'd marshal it to where there would be no story, or it would be downplayed.

I would look back in the clips to find history and stuff, and I'd see stuff in stories like, "It's premature to say… It's too early too tell…" That's straight-out Boeing lingo, and it's here in a news story about an issue that should be more aggressively covered. In this day and age, people would laugh and say why weren't you more aggressive? Issues like labor contracts or accidents.

I think the paper wanted to move away from that. No one has ever told me this, but it's what I gather. And as I'm on the beat, they've been real supportive, and that's how I'm drawing this conclusion, but they've gotten behind me.

It's been interesting because Boeing has gone through different levels of responding to me. It's almost like, "It's a small-town paper and we don't have to pay attention to them." But if I make some noise that bothers them, get a story out on the wires that gets some response. It doesn't even have to be that. It only has to be something in a story that bugs a senior-level executive, that seems to be the hot button. It's often something inconsequential. Then they'll put their machine to work to try and impose their weight, to let you know that this is a company town and that they're the biggest company and the sacred cow, and how dare you let a newspaper not treat us the way we should be treated. I've got letters in my file that say exactly that.

So you've had a lot of support from the paper?
Yeah, because there's been a lot of pressure from Boeing. To actually pull me off the beat, I think.

Any examples of stories you've broken based on your research?
The cargo door pins on the 747.[7] [A United Airline's Boeing 747 lost a cargo door over the ocean off New Zealand. Nine people died. It was found that the door pins had failed, causing the crash. The initial reports claimed that a maintenance technician had failed to properly lock the doors.] I was the first and only guy to hook up with sources that were saying that it couldn't have been the guy on the ground closing the door, that it doesn't make any sense. It makes more sense if you examine the documents, that the electrical short back-drove the weak locks. Eventually, we wound up doing a magazine story, and we timed it right before we knew they were going to hold another hearing after digging the door out. They reversed the ruling and confirmed our story. I had it right.

After that, the freeze pin, the two engines that came off the 747 which slammed into that housing project in the Netherlands.[8] That was another case where I knew that was a problem because I saw that eighteen months earlier when the two engines fell off the China Airlines [plane] in Taiwan and it slammed into the cliff trying to turn back to the airport. I saw that.

I said, isn't that unusual that two engines would fall off? I made a couple of calls and talked to some experts who said that is crazy, that is totally wild that two engines would fall off. So I did a story saying that they were looking for these engines, and I started keeping a file on it. So when the one went down in Amsterdam, I just went back and did a database search and found that it had happened on 707 and just started doing the cycle again. Then it got to a point where they were downplaying everything by saying, oh, why would two engines fall off? No one came up with a reason that two engines would fall off.

Then a reader called me. That's another big thing about what I'm reporting, the thing that I've found that is a breakthrough, that could only happen on this beat. Our audience is very aviation-savvy and real technology-savvy. I think as I've built my reputation, done stories, built my body of work, what's happened is this thing that has pushed me to higher and higher levels. It has nothing to do with me. What it is, is readers calling up after they've read something, after I've tried something, they'll call me up and say, "Well, you think that's bad ..."

Do you have a quota? Do they expect a certain amount out of you?

There's a normal production pressure. I keep real busy. I always have ideas going, I'm always updating. So they've been real supportive. They still make me do daily stuff, you know. I don't mind that. I like to be a team player. But by and large, I just chip in on the business desk.

You describe yourself as a business reporter. How do you see your job?

I think the bulk of it is trying to develop story ideas. The Triple Seven story, I developed that over five years. I did stories all along. Like right now, I have a big story in mind on this 737 flaw. Weave back to the legal story and why. Explain the motivation, who benefits by keeping it unknown and stretching out the probable cause several more months, more than a year past the last accident. But along the way, I'm doing these other stories.

It seems like I'm always aiming toward a big story, but trying to do breaking stories. By the time I get to the big story, I can refer to what I broke about the story along the way.

So the corporate loyalty is very high? You haven't found a "deep throat"?

No, I haven't found one yet. I'd love to have one. On the technical side, that's the case. I've never really thought about that, but there's probably a reason. I think it probably has to do with the corporate culture over there and the mind-set. There's a certain Boeing mind-set, and some people have called it arrogance. It's like this "If it ain't built in Seattle it ain't no good" mind-set. Engineers, too. Engineers tend to be control freaks, they think they can analyze everything and control it. Everything should happen in a certain way. It meshes in their mind. I think that's part of it.

I know that you're on the Internet. How have you used it as a tool?

Talking to guys, contacting pilots, contacting mechanics. I have contacted Boeing engineers but haven't gotten very far. E-mailing them back and forth, bouncing things off of there. It's a real interesting phenomenon because the top level FAA guy, Anthony Broderick, is one of these guys who hangs out on it. It's like this big fishbowl, you've got to learn the ethics.

Here's this top-level FAA guy that I normally have to jump through hoops to talk to, if he says something—we talk back and forth. I've never asked him something official for a story, and I'm waiting to see how that evolves and how to approach it. There's that whole arena. It's fast moving, too. People will be generally aware of something going on, but I'll have the latest, most comprehensive chunk of information. I'll float it out there. Or they'll respond.

How do you check your information?

Another important part of what I do is develop sort of aces in the hole, key sources in the right spot who are so valuable to me that I'll never quote them in a story, even rarely attribute to what they say. And most often they're most useful as a sounding board. Or they'll give me some primary information that allows me to ask pointed questions. And that's the whole game right there.

If you go in with general questions, or just a general sense, without doing your homework, Boeing — not just Boeing but any big business — will chew you up alive, especially engineers. You have to have very specific questions. In fact, you have to know the answers before you go in. Leveraging. That's it. Give them a little bit, and let them hang themselves. I mean, getting that first little bit is the key, and I think this is common in all good investigative reporters. I've developed through these various ways, just being around long enough, essentially, kinda a core group of aces in the holes. They're deep throat–type sources, well placed. They know who I am, they know what I'm doing. I know who they are, and I guess they respect what I'm doing, otherwise they wouldn't agree to help me out in that way because they're all helpful. I bounce stuff off of them, or they'll feed me stuff. Most often, I bounce stuff off of them. I'll say, is this the right direction? What are the questions I should be asking, or is this off-base? Invariably, they'll feed me a whole branch of other roads I didn't even know about, to take me to the next level of the story. Then I can go back and check with them again. You've got to keep those checks and balances, and the more complex the material you're dealing with, the more you have to have a certain level of confidence.

What I write in my stories represents perhaps a fraction, maybe one-tenth, of the reporting and research I've done in order to understand it. What I essentially do is I filter and boil down to simple concepts, and almost every sentence is very carefully worded. And I can defend it.

What would be your advice to a young person who wants to be an investigative reporter? What would you tell them.

I'd say be prepared to work hard and do your homework. It's all about research, it's all about having the right questions to ask, it's all about getting a knowledge base to where you can figure out what the story is and probe elements of it that you know would be important to your readers, if they knew about it in the right context. I guess that would apply to any issue, whether it be government or big business, local politics or whatever that might be.

Do you find conversational writing important? For the guy in the back of the plane who knows nothing about flying. How important is the writing versus the research?

They're both equally important because you have to make the story accessible to draw the reader in and keep them with the story to the end. He needs a sense of why it is important to him and gets something out of that. And to do that, you've got to do all of the research to develop the material firsthand. I just went to a Poynter seminar and it was all about getting back to writing stories and getting the "what next" element in there.[9] I'm sold. It makes sense to me. Now the problem is selling editors on it. There's a lot of work that goes into that, and again that gets back to doing your homework.

You've really got to understand it before you make a conversational, generalized statement, especially about a technical subject. Or it could be a political issue, you've got to know the material. To be an investigative reporter, this is not original, but I think it is true. You have to have a real sensitive "bullshit meter," but not necessarily come across as the cynical skeptic. But you have to challenge things in your own mind. Does it make sense what that person is saying, where did he get that information from, why is he saying it? That is the most important question.

What would you like to do in the future?
I want to stay with this a little longer. I'm thinking about some books. Got a lot of good material for new novels. [Laughs.]

Notes

1. The *Seattle Times*, August 9, 1994.
2. The FAA is the Federal Aviation Administration, the government agency responsible for setting guidelines for aircraft standards and operation. The NTSB is the National Transportation Safety Board, the agency responsible for investigating aircraft accidents.
3. *Seattle Times*, "Lauda Air 767-300 Crashes in Thailand," May 27, 1991.
4. *Seattle Times*, "U.S. Air Crash: The Clues Are In," January 29, 1995.
5. *Seattle Times*, "Computer with Wings — Boeing's Ultracomplex 777 Flies Into Debate Over Technology Hazards." Byron Acohido, June 5, 1995.
6. Airbus is the European competitor to Boeing in the world aircraft industry. Airbus pushed technology when they developed the first "fly-by-wire" airliner, which depends on computers for all controls.
7. Byron Acohido, "Flight 811 Lost a Cargo Door and Nine Lives — Boeing Is Still Wrestling with Solutions and Settlements." *Seattle Times*, January 5, 1992. The cargo door pins are devices that secure the access door to the cargo area and prevent it from opening in flight. The doors opened on Flight 811.
8. Byron Acohido, "El Al 747-200 Crashes in Amsterdam," *Seattle Times*, October 5, 1992. Two engines fell off the El Al 747 cargo aircraft moments after takeoff, and it crashed into a ten-story apartment complex. Six crewmembers and at least 50 people on the ground died in the crash.
9. The Poynter Institute for Media Studies is located in St. Petersburg, Florida. The institute offers seminars and fellowships for journalists.

9

Dan Moldea
Investigating Organized Crime

> I think this country is run by three elements: corrupt politicians, corrupt media, and organized crime. Through my investigation of organized crime, I've learned about every institution in America because whether it's business, religion, politics, sports — organized crime touches every institution in this country.

Dan Moldea, investigative journalist, is proud that he has never been sued over the content of any of his five books. But Moldea sued, and it almost destroyed his journalism career. Moldea sued the *New York Times* after its book reviewer, Gerald Eskenazi, accused him of "sloppy journalism" in his book *Interference*, which investigated "how organized crime influences professional football."[1] The review upset Moldea, who thought it was a blatantly inaccurate description of his book. The investigative journalist had been the target of negative book reviews before, but this was the *New York Times*, the country's most powerful newspaper, and he feared the review could irreparably damage his journalism career.

Moldea demanded a retraction from the *Times*; the newspaper refused. Moldea went to court, and his suit ended up in the U.S. Supreme Court, which refused to hear the case. Some from the journalism fraternity viewed Moldea's lawsuit as an act of courage, one that performed a valuable service by drawing attention to the lack of accountability in the arts sections of major newspapers like the *Times*. Others shook their heads and said Moldea's lawsuit was a foolhardy move that would make it difficult for him to get another major book contract and might even get him blacklisted among major publishers.

After losing in court, Moldea wondered, too, about his career in publishing. Was he through as a major investigative journalist? Moldea sent out eleven different book proposals to publishers. All were turned down. The investigative journalist regrouped and decided to give it the best shot he had with the best project he could find. He came up with a proposal to write a book that investigated the assassination of Robert F. Kennedy in 1968. His thesis: Sirhan Sirhan did not shoot Kennedy.

W. W. Norton Publishers gave Moldea a good advance of $75,000 to research and write the book. The investigation went well, and he nearly had the book completed when he reached the inescapable conclusion that would be stated in the end of his book on the Kennedy assassination: "Sirhan Bishara Sirhan consciously and knowingly murdered senator Robert F. Kennedy, and he acted alone."

Moldea showed intestinal fortitude again, rejecting the temptation to go with the conspiracy theory, which in today's book market would have, most likely, meant big sales. He rewrote the twenty-seven chapters he had submitted to Norton and made his case. The book came out in early 1995, and Moldea anxiously waited for the reviews to be published.[2]

Thankfully, they were good, even the one from his nemesis, the *New York Times*. In the May 25, 1995, edition of the *Times*, reviewer Lehmann-Haupt praised *The Killing of Robert F. Kennedy* as "carefully reasoned ... ultimately persuasive ... dramatic" and said, Moldea's book "should be read, not so much for the irrefutability of its conclusions as for the way the author has brought order out of a chaotic tale and turned an appalling tatter of history into an emblem of our misshapen times."[3]

Dan Moldea is back, wiser from his tangle with the *New York Times*, but he is the first to tell you that he would do it again. It would be in character, for during his long journalism career, Moldea has shown a willingness to take chances and be controversial. Working on the edge has made him one of the country's top investigative journalists.

Born on 1950 in Akron, Ohio, Moldea graduated from the University of Akron with a bachelor of arts degree in English and history in 1973. Since 1974, Moldea has worked as a freelance journalist specializing in organized crime investigations.

Moldea's first book, the *Hoffa Wars*, which chronicled the rise and fall of former Teamsters general president Jimmy Hoffa, included excerpts from his exclusive interviews with men the FBI identified as Hoffa's killers.[3] The book was a best-seller, and newspapers syndicated excerpts worldwide.

Other investigations of organized crime followed. In 1983, *The Hunting of Caine* dug deep into the police investigation of the 1980 contract murder of company executive Constantine "Dean" Milo, in Bath, Ohio.[4] Moldea's third book, *Dark Victory,* charged that Ronald Reagan, through his talent agency, MCA, maintained ties to major organized crime figures.[5] Moldea followed those successes with the controversial *Interference* and *The Killing of Robert F. Kennedy.*

Moldea's base of operation is Washington, D.C. It was evident from our interview that working more than two decades as an investigative journalist has not dimmed his passionate commitment to the profession. He talked candidly about the *New York Times* case, his many investigations, and the craft.

* * *

Let's start off with your book about Robert Kennedy, which you published recently. It was well received by the critics. I guess a lot was riding on that book.

My career was riding on that book [laughs]. A lot of people think I walk through life with a broken beer bottle in my hand. They are probably right about that [laughs].

Because of the stakes, did you spend more time on that book than you normally would have?
    Yeah, I had eighteen months to finish the book. For *Interference*, I had eight months. For *The Hunting of Caine*, I had six months and I had six months, too, for the *Hoffa Wars*. That's from the time I got the contract to the time the book was due. Until I got the contract for the Kennedy book, I never had much time to write a book. This time I did, and it paid off.

The reviewers said it was your best book, writing-wise. I would agree with that. Was the fact that you had eighteen months to do the Kennedy book the result of the high stakes at hand?
    Yeah, but I still came in three to four months early with the book.

Why did you decide to investigate this particular subject?
    First, as you pointed out, the stakes were high for me. I was coming back from the *New York Times* review. Everyone who was close to me knew everything was on the line this time because if the book had gotten trounced in the reviews, it would have finished me once and for all, even though I have never been sued over one of my books. I consider myself a team player when I deal with editors. It was just that I had the reputation of being a troublemaker, whether I deserved that tag or not. I just don't like to be fucked with, and when I am, I strike back.

You must have had some weird thoughts when you discovered that your thesis for the Kennedy book — Sirhan Sirhan did not kill Kennedy — was wrong.[6]
    It was as if somebody hit me with a straight right hand. I believed a second gun had gone off in the room where Robert Kennedy was killed, whether intentionally or accidentally. I suspected another man of killing Kennedy, and I spent a lot of time with him.
    When I polygraphed that man, he passed with flying colors. Then I went to Sirhan Sirhan, who wanted to talk to me. I took full advantage of it. I went into the first interview and patted Sirhan's hand while getting all that background. Prior to the third interview, I rode to the prison with Sirhan Sirhan's brother, a real fine person, and I said to him, "I'm going to climb all over your brother today. So get ready." I went at Sirhan like a rifle shot for five or six hours. It was contentious interview, to say the least. Then it dawned on me that he had done it.

So you were almost through with the book.
    Yeah, I was almost through. The editor said, "Well, I read twenty-seven or twenty-eight chapters, and I'm convinced there was a second gun in the room.

Maybe the mob did it" [laughs].[7] I said, "Gee, listen man" [laughs]. The editor said, "Oh, no. You better make this work." I said, "The only way to make it work is to tell the truth." So I had to reshuffle the book.

Did you have to go back over the material you researched?
  I had to go back over everything. I had to resolve all the questions I had raised myself about my own investigation. People said to me: "You are going to get killed. You should leave the question of who killed Kennedy hanging." But I had a responsibility to go back over the evidence and explain why the evidence appeared in the room. I decided I had a responsibility to set the record straight, even if I did have to admit I was wrong. I don't think there was one person at my publishers who didn't think I was going to get killed.

Did anyone try to talk you out of changing your original thesis?
  No, my editor said this is the way Dan wrote it and this is the way we will publish it. In fact, the publisher had invited me to speak at their annual sales conference in December. I was the one author they asked. I went and made my pitch for the Bobby Kennedy book on the basis of what I found. Everyone liked what I said, but thought I would be an easy mark for critics. They thought that, coming off the *Times* case, I had a credibility problem.
  I got good reviews from the trades (*Publishers Weekly, Kirkus, Booklist,* and *Library Journal*) when they came out, but I never thought I would be reviewed by the *New York Times*, especially by Christopher Lehmann-Haupt.
  I have a lot of friends on the news side of *Times*, but I don't get along as well with the book review side [laughs]. One of my friends from the *Times* called and said Lehmann-Haupt is reviewing your book tomorrow in Thursday's paper. I said, "What's he going to say?" He said, "Nobody knows, but everyone is talking about it and they are keeping it a big secret."
  The night before the review came out, I was like a condemned man waiting for his execution. I knew everything was on the line. I couldn't eat, I could not sleep. Finally, at six in the morning I gave up, got in my car and went down to the 7-Eleven convenience store. I got there just after the *Times* paper-boy had delivered the paper. I picked up a copy of the *Times* and read the review.

What were your feelings?
  I was thrilled. I thought Lehmann-Haupt had reviewed my book fairly. I wrote him a letter that said it was a classy thing for him to have done. A couple of weeks later, the *Times* gave me a review in the Sunday paper, which was even better.

So how difficult was the Kennedy book to sell?
  Before my book on *Interference*, anytime I pitched something to New York publishing, at least one of the publishers always offered me something for it.

Sometimes I didn't take it because the advance was too low. But I always got something. After the *Times* review, I couldn't sell anything. I went through eleven different proposals on many subjects. So I decided to come out with the best proposal I could do, which was the Kennedy book.

But twelve publishers turned it down. Then W. W. Norton offered me seventy-five thousand dollars for it, which tied the best advance I ever got for a book. I received seventy-five thousand dollars for *Dark Victory* almost eight years earlier. The money, of course, is important, but it's always the work that has most interested me. I figured if I work hard on a book it would do well, and I would be rewarded for all the hard work I put into it.

I thought the NFL book would do well, so I took just a fifty-thousand dollar advance for it. When I sent the book proposal in, I had no evidence of fixed games, but when I sent the book in, I had evidence of ten fixed games. I thought that would carry the day for me.

Then politics kicked in. I had a confrontation with the NFL. But the book was moving and had gone through three editions when the *New York Times* review came out. The book was stopped dead in its tracks.

You had been the target of negative reviews before. Why didn't you let this one slide?
I can take bad reviews, and I certainly had my share of them, especially from the *Times*. But the irony is the *New York Times* made me. In nineteen seventy-eight when the *Hoffa Wars* came out, I was with a small company called the New Republic Book Company, which publishes the magazine the *New Republic*. They gave me a five thousand five-hundred dollar advance for *The Hoffa Wars*. At that time, I had worked four years on the book. So I took the five thousand five-hundred dollar advance, wrote the book, and turned in a large chunk of it. All but three chapters.

Even though New Republic Books publishes its own books, it has an exclusive distribution contract with Simon and Schuster. An article comes out, which says everybody is looking at a book on the Teamsters by Steve Brill, which Simon and Schuster is going to publish, but the book they should be looking at is this book by Dan Moldea called *The Hoffa Wars* because Moldea got the only interview with the alleged killers, that is, those identified by the FBI.[8] So Dick Snyder, the head of Simon and Schuster, calls Martin Peretz, the owner of New Republic Books, and says, "Sorry, guys. We aren't going to distribute Moldea's book." I call my lawyers. In the end, it costs me thirty thousand dollars.

To Peretz's credit, he lets me out of the contract, and I got a new publisher, Paddington Press, a small but aggressive British publisher. Paddington decides to come out with my book at the same time that Brill's book was to come out. We literally came out the same day. My war with Brill began.

The *New York Times* picked up on the war when Herbert Mitgang of the *Times* called me up and asked, "What's going on?" I told him what had happened. It was June twenty-ninth, nineteen seventy-eight. The *New York Times* bought the U.S. syndicate rights to the book. The *London Observer* bought worldwide syndicate rights. My agent called and said *Playboy* bought a twenty thousand word excerpt from the book, which I believe is one of the longest excerpts the magazine has ever run. The Book of the Month Club picked up the book. That all happened in one day — a spectacular day. So the *New York Times* made me and broke me.

I know at the time a lot of writers thought you were crazy to take on the New York Times.

I just went out with a buddy from the *New York Times*. We hadn't seen each other since I lost the case. I said to him, "Dave, I had a righteous case." I think he knew it. Most reasonable people who knew the details of my case knew it was righteous. I wasn't off the wall. I had to do something. When the *New York Times* says something about a book, it's a lot different than when the *Milwaukee Journal* does.

But by taking on the New York Times, *you brought attention to yourself. Would not it have been better if you would have let the whole thing slide?*

That review was hurting me. Everybody in publishing was blacklisting me. Nobody remembers that it was a hack reporter who reviewed the book. They remember it was the *New York Times* that reviewed the book. For a reporter, credibility is everything. I had to try and get a retraction or the tag that I was an "irresponsible" reporter would have stuck to me. The *New York Times* did not expect to do anything about it, but my lawyers went after them.

And it became war?

Yes, that's pretty much the way it went.

Did you seek the opinion of other investigative reporters?

Oh, yeah, god, everybody.

What was their opinion about what you were doing?

It was pretty much divided. It ranged from, "Dan, everybody is going to blacklist you" to "Gee, Dan, you take on the Teamsters, you take on the Mafia. You take on big business. You've taken on pro-football. And now you're taking on the *New York Times*. Wow!"

Would you do it again?

There is no question in my mind that I would do it again, given the set of circumstances. I had no choice. Remember, I couldn't sell anything for a long time after that *Times* review. To this day I believe I would have been out of business if I had not sued. I would be selling shoes somewhere.

When we filed the appeal, we thought we were going to win the case. It was an incredible experience to go before the U.S. Court of Appeals. The tension that ran through the court was unbelievable. It was high drama. The best I had ever seen. My attorneys performed marvelously. The judge was very respectful towards my attorneys and very aggressive towards the *Times* attorneys.

I told a friend who was sitting in the back of the court with me, "I think these guys are on my side [laughs]." The debate was heated and contentious, and we thought we would come out of the whole thing a winner. Five or six months passed and I got a call from my attorneys. They said we don't know what happened, but we think the court has ruled in our favor. And they did.

But there was no celebration. We knew real power was going to come at us like a rifle shot because when we sat down and looked at the opinion we realized the judge had gone far beyond what we had asked him to do. And, of course, the court reversed itself, and then the [U.S.] Supreme Court decided against reviewing the case.

You lost the case, but, as a journalist, what lessons did you learn from the experience?

I have no regrets. I don't have a family, I don't have any responsibilities to any other human beings other than those I make contracts with. If I had a family, if I was putting children through college, if I was taking care of sick parents, if I was anything other than the lone wolf I am, I couldn't have done this. It would have been stupid. I would have had to turn the other cheek.

Was that the only lawsuit you were involved with as an investigative journalist?

I was involved with one other one. A guy had asked me to write a book for him. I was under the clear impression that he had never tried to sell it before. After I had spent months on the book for nothing because he wasn't paying anything for writing the book proposal, I found the idea had been pitched all over New York. I had never been told about it. I sued him for breach of contract. I confronted him and he fired me. I got him for breach of contract.

Someone listening to this conversation might ask: why does Dan Moldea want to be an investigative journalist, with all the frustration, uncertainty, living from one book to the next, never knowing how much money you are going to get.

Well, let me tell you how it all started. It was nineteen seventy, and I was at the University of Akron. At that time, I was just a beer-drinking, ass-grabbing fraternity guy.

Were you writing?

No, although I did have a term paper business. I had a staff of four working for me. I later got elected student body president. But back in nineteen seventy before that happened, all I cared about was me.

What changed your attitude?

My girl was attending Kent State University, and I went to see her on a Friday, the first month of spring. Things were going nuts. There was a lot of vandalism, but it certainly wasn't political then. The following Saturday it became political. A lot of kids were antiwar, but I was neutral on it. My dad was an officer in the air force, and my position was that if I got called to go to Vietnam, I would go because the country had given me a good life for twenty years.

Saturday night the ROTC building burned down and the National Guard came on campus. The following day there was a menacing atmosphere in the air at Kent. I said to my girlfriend, "Let's go back to Akron." We did, and then we heard what had happened at Kent State: four students dead and I believe thirty-three wounded.[9]

The initial reports said the students had shot at the guards. I was working as a bouncer at a bar then. The owner saw that I was troubled, and so he told me to take the night off and go to the [University of Akron] campus to see what was happening. People were at a podium speaking to a crowd, including my friend, the editor of the campus newspaper. He saw the pain I was in and said, "Why don't you come up here and say something." I was just a sophomore at the time, but I did go to the podium and said something incoherent. I can't remember what. But it was a defining moment for me. The week that followed became my radicalizing week. By the end of the week, I had gone from a self-serving asshole to a guy who didn't think he was the center of the universe anymore and who became a society-serving person.

What did you do after graduating from university?

I traveled for a quarter and then went back to graduate school at Kent State. I fell short on my master's degree. I worked at an antipoverty agency, where an embezzlement scandal broke out. I caught the boss cooking the books [laughs]. He wasn't very creative about it. He would make a check out to ACE Construction Company in his own name. So I confronted him and suggested he go to the prosecutor and cut a deal for himself. He fired me. I protested, but I needed another job, so I went to work as a columnist for a newspaper called the *Reporter*, which serves the black community in northeastern Illinois. I was their token white guy who writes a column. I did that for six or seven months.

I also ran for the state legislature in nineteen seventy-three but got my ass kicked pretty good. I ran as a Republican because the Democrats were kind of stodgy and they had this pecking order. The Republicans were in so much trouble with Nixon, Watergate, and so forth that I thought they would be looking for new blood. But I was a pariah. I was pro-bussing and pro-choice. I was beaten in the primary.

How did you get interested in the Teamsters Union?

I got to meet a bunch of Teamsters who were part of the rank and file of the reform movement in the party. I was working for the *Reporter*. They started to tell me horror stories about the Teamsters Union, and so I wrote an eight-part series about the union, its pension fund, and the Mafia.

But no one cared about the Teamsters at that time. I got to know Jonathan Kwitney, who was at the *Wall Street Journal* at the time, and he was working on a three-part series on the Teamsters and I helped him out a little bit.[10] A week after that series came out, Jimmy Hoffa disappears. Now we have all this interest in the Teamsters, and here I am now one of the experts on them. I end up doing research on the Teamsters for NBC, the *Detroit Free Press*, and Jack Anderson.[11] I didn't get a byline though. Then I published my own book.

So how did the book about the Teamsters originate?
Frankly, I didn't have a clue about how to write a book. I had always been a researcher for others. The first time I had my own byline on something I wrote other than what I wrote for the *Reporter* was my book on Hoffa and the Teamsters.

My friends were skeptical that I could do it, though. After all, it took four years to do it, and they kept waiting and waiting. But then suddenly the book does come out. I'm on "Good Morning, America," and my book is selected for the Book of the Month Club. Reporters are writing articles about me. I am an author.

Since the first book came out, you've concentrated on investigating organized crime. Why is that?
It's what I'm good at; it's what I know. I think this country is run by three elements: corrupt politicians, corrupt media, and organized crime. Through my investigation of organized crime, I've learned about every institution in America because whether it's business, religion, politics, sports — organized crime touches every institution in this country.

I'm sure over the years a lot of people have approached you with ideas for investigations. How do you decide if a topic is worth investigating?
There are five levels that an investigation has to go through. The first level involves investigating the public record and seeing what you can find on a particular subject. This is usually the very unglamorous part of investigative reporting. Going to a public official's office and looking through grantee and granter files is boring work to most people, but exhilarating work for those of us who like to do it. I can't think of anything I'd rather do than go into an office and sift through a bunch of documents I'm interested in.

Do you like to do that better than the writing?
It's one and the same to me. I love the work — research and writing — but hate the business: going out and trying to sell it. If that makes any sense.

So what are the other levels?
Go to the friendly sources — the people whom you worked with before and whom you trust. The third level is to go to the neutral sources. You don't know

where their loyalties lie and whether they are going to help you or hurt you. Level four — go to dangerous sources — those people who can hurt and mislead you. Finally, the fifth level — go to the targets and do the confrontational interview. If the story has all the elements, then it's a good one. And if I have plenty of research materials relating to the story, I feel I can write the book.

So what are some of the qualities that an investigative journalist needs to be successful?

First, you've got to stay honest. You have to learn how to keep a secret. That's a real close second. When someone tells you something and asks that you don't repeat it, you shouldn't repeat it. Number three — you've got to have some self-discipline. You have to sit down and examine the evidence honestly, even if it goes contrary to the evidence you collected. You have to be able to see that there is a bigger issue here, whatever the topic you are dealing with. You got to ask yourself: where does this piece fit into big picture? Finally, you've got to have the equipment. Nowadays, you've got to have a computer. You have to use databases, and, to do that, you have to be technically hip and know how to merge all the information. I have a three-eighty-six computer, which in nineteen ninety-one was almost state of the art. Now I feel I'm in the Dark Ages. I don't have a four-eighty-six. I'm not on the Internet.

You don't use spreadsheets or technical things like that?

I have my own databases which I create on my word processor software. My job would be a whole lot harder if I didn't have all that stuff at my fingertips. I wrote my first book on a manual typewriter. My second book on a IBM Selectric. My third book on a KPRO TWO CPM computer. My fourth book on a IBM model thirty with twenty megabytes hard disk. Now I have something with one hundred twenty megs. It's still the Dark Ages, and I have to upgrade my equipment.

Is there a problem with being too modernized, so to speak?

You've got to weed out the bad information, and, believe me, there is lot of it.

In researching your books, you gather a lot of data. Is organizing that data the hard part of your job?

Absolutely! Getting organized is the key.

Do you have any special techniques in doing it?

I keep chronologies on everything. I do them early in the project. Then I can go to the investigation I'm working on — whether it's the Hoffa wars or the Kennedy book — and pinpoint what I was doing on a particular day. For me, organization is everything. Keeping good paper files is everything. If you need a document, you have to know where to find it.

Have you used researchers?
  I've used them on the *Hoffa Wars*, *Dark Victory*, and *Interference*.

Why?
  The researchers were people who had good information. For the *Hoffa Wars*, I hired a person who had gathered a tremendous amount of information on the Kennedy and Nixon administrations. He was excellent. I paid him a flat fee and ten percent of the profits from the book. For *Dark Victory*, I used a friend who was an excellent researcher. I paid him a flat fee and ten percent of the profits from the book. With *Interference*, I have a friend, a producer for "Frontline," the PBS series, and he had done a segment on the NFL. He came to me and said: "Why don't you sell this as a book. I will give you everything I have." I paid him a flat fee and a percentage of the book. I didn't use a researcher on the Bobby Kennedy book because I wanted to do all the interviews myself. No one in the country knew more about the case than myself.

You mentioned equipment. What about tape recorders?
  Yes, they are very important.

Do you tape everything?
  Not everything, but a lot. I like to hook up a tape recorder to my phone. It frees me up to concentrate on asking questions, to think and comment on the answers, and to guide the direction of the interview, as opposed to scribbling and taking notes. Also, it's a permanent record in case someone ever tries to sue you or take back what they said. That's happened a couple of times. But I feel it's my responsibility to call back my sources and read back their quotes. Everybody in the Kennedy book, including Sirhan Sirhan, had the opportunity to amend or amplify their quotes. I've done that for my last four books — since *The Hunting of Caine*.

We talked a little about sources. Do you have a network of sources you go back to again and again?
  It depends. I have a lot of Mafia and law enforcement contacts who weren't much use to me on my Kennedy book, but I do try to stay in touch with them. I don't deal with mob characters who are flat-out bad guys. I deal with a network of mob guys who are in the Federal Witness Protection Program. They are the guys who were not caught, and they did not plea bargain. They are guys that wanted to change their lives. Those are guys I respect.

Why do sources talk?
  You just have to know how to push their buttons. I don't go up to a mob guy and say, "Why did you knock off so and so?" I go up to him and talk to him about a subject he wants to talk about.

Do you have special techniques that you use to get sources to talk?

Pissing them off is one way. Get them angry enough, and they are apt to say anything. I do a lot of things a prosecutor does. I get between two sources with opposing points of view and jump right in the middle of it. I go back and forth saying, "Here's what the other guy said." This is the way war starts. But that's my job as a reporter. It's part of the job.

Can your job be dangerous?

I've almost got clipped a half dozen times because of decisions I've made. Some of the stupid decisions I made. I've had a gun rammed down my throat.

How did that happen?

I was in a room with the secretary treasurer of the Teamsters, interviewing him. Then it struck him [laughs]. What am I doing in this room with this kid. Maybe the kid is setting me up [laughs]. He couldn't figure me out. He pulled his gun out and said to me to open my mouth. Then he rammed his gun down it. It was a terrifying experience [laughs].

[Laughs.] What else has happened?

Two guys kicked the shit out of me and laid me up for two weeks. It's a long story. Here's the gist of it. I was told I could get some good information if I went to this bar north of Chicago. It was broad daylight, four o'clock in the afternoon. I heard a couple of doors slam behind me. I didn't even have time to turn around. I don't remember much about what happened. I just got my ass kicked, and I had blood coming out of my mouth. I peed in my pants. I was laid up for a while.

Then there was this time when one of my sources called and informed me that someone had accepted one thousand five hundred dollars to kill me. I was offended [laughs]. I thought my life was worth at least fifty thousand dollars and finding out that my life was only worth one thousand five hundred dollars was embarrassing. I taped the conversation and took the tape to my friends in the FBI and said, "Listen to this." The FBI said, "Gee, Dan, what are you going to do?" [Laughs.] I said: "What am I going to do? What are you going to do?" They said, "What can we do? No one has committed a crime." I said, "You don't understand. For a crime to be committed I have to be dead. That's why I've contacted you." They said, "All we can do is advise you to move to a neutral city." I said, "What's a neutral city?" They said, "A neutral city is where no one particular Mafia family owns a town." I said, "What cities are those?" They said, "Try Las Vegas, Miami, Washington, D.C." I have friends in D.C., so I moved here. I ended up saving my ass.

Did you ever think about finding another line of work [laughs]?

The publishing industry sometimes makes me think about that. But the threat of violence emboldens me to keep going. If people are reacting to me that way, I think I'm on to something. Why would they bother me?

Looking back over your long career, is there one investigation that are you particularly proud of?

The Hoffa project is certainly one of my favorites because it was the first one. As for *The Hunting of Caine*, I played an important role in helping to solve the murder. *Dark Victory* was the book I'm known best for on the West Coast. I was under heavy pressure for that one because I was in competition with a writer I was afraid of — a Pulitzer Prize–winner from the *New York Times*, who was doing a similar book. I ended up doing the book a lot faster than I wanted to, but I still think I'm dead right on the mark. The Bobby Kennedy investigation is also close to my heart because I made a tough decision. I have to give myself credit for going 180 degrees on that one. There may be diehards out there that would dispute my findings, but I solved the case. But the book I'm most proud of is *Interference*. I put my heart and soul into that one, and I was right on the money.

Is the book still in print?

No, it was supposed to come out in trade paperback in September nineteen ninety-five, which would have been a great time, given all the turbulence in the NFL with the Cleveland Browns.

Maybe you can update your book.

I did. I have a whole new postscript. I have an afterword which deals with my dispute with the *New York Times*. Then the publisher got in some financial trouble and ended up canceling its fall list. *Interference* has had a rough history, but it's one heck of an investigative book.

On the subject of the NFL — have I told you the story about Jack Kent Cooke and *Washingtonian* magazine?[12]

No, go ahead.

The *Washingtonian* published an article about Jack Kent Cooke, which was written by his chauffeur Harry Turner, whom Cooke had let go. In the article there were things like how Cooke had got a traffic ticket, but because of his friendship with Marion Barry, the traffic ticket was fixed. Secondly, after Jimmy the Greek Synder revealed his views on race and lost his job at CBS, Cooke sent him a sign of support. Thirdly, there was a caption with Harry's picture that said something like "Cooke asked me if I bet on NFL games and he said, 'Don't because sometimes they are fixed.'" So Cooke ends up slapping the *Washingtonian* with a thirty million dollar lawsuit. The lawyer for the *Washingtonian* asks me if I can come aboard as an expert witness because they knew I knew a lot about game fixing. I said to them, "Look, the editor of the *Washingtonian* has owed me a phone call for four months. I had pitched a story about the black Mafia in D.C. to him. I took offense to that. You tell him to get back to me and pay respect and I'll think about participating in this lawsuit."

I didn't hear anything for nine months and then the executive editor of *Washingtonian* asked me out to lunch to discuss being an expert witness. He was so polite I knew something was up. I called some friends and asked them to find out how much trouble the *Washingtonian* was in. About twenty minutes later, I got a call back from one of my friends, who was laughing his head off. He tells me that Harry Turner had been deposed for several days by Cooke's attorneys. He was asked about the period of time, a few years ago, which he couldn't account for. Under oath, during this deposition, the sole source for the article said he had been kidnapped by space aliens and taken to another planet [laughs].

My lawyers work out a nice deal whereby I would be called in as an expert witness, but the *Washingtonian* decides to settle and publishes a full-page retraction, apologizing for everything, including the game-fixing statement. And they give Cooke fifty thousand. I was horrified and called the *Washingtonian* writer who had ghosted the story for Turner and asked "What's this about a settlement?" He said, "I don't know. I just got fired. I was a part of the settlement." I said, "Why did you agree to the settlement if you were going to get fired?" He said, "I didn't sign the settlement." I said, "You are the defendant in the case and you didn't sign off on the settlement?" He said, "No," and I said, "If you didn't sign off on the settlement, there is no settlement."

The writer goes back to the bosses and reminds them that he has not signed off on the settlement. But instead of going to war, he decides this is a way for him to make some money. He goes in and talks with the bosses and makes a large cash settlement [laughs].

Then the following week, the publisher and executive editor of the magazine are seen in Jack Kent Cooke's box at the Redskins home opener. That's journalism in the nineteen nineties. That would have been unheard of in the nineteen eighties when we had the great ones like Sy Hersh, Woodward and Bernstein, and I. F. Stone, and David Burnham.[13]

So is the craft of investigative journalism in trouble?

Investigative journalism today is viewed in terms of Kitty Kelley, Geraldo Rivera, and "A Current Affair."[14] Investigative journalism is about the sex lives of celebrities and lurid tabloid garbage. That's replaced serious investigative journalism. Just look at the best-sellers list today and who is on it. That's what I have to deal with today.

Notes

1. Dan Moldea, *Interference: How Organized Crime Influences Professional Football* (New York: William Morrow, 1989).

2. Dan Moldea, *The Killing of Robert F. Kennedy: An Investigation of Motives, Means and Opportunity* (New York: W. W. Norton, 1995).

3. Dan Moldea, *The Hoffa Wars: Teamsters, Rebels, Politicians and the Mob* (London: Paddington, 1978). James Hoffa (1913-1975) was an American labor leader who headed the International Brotherhood of Teamsters. Reportedly, he was seeking to regain his position in the Teamsters when he disappeared on July 30, 1975, and presumably was murdered.

4. Dan Moldea, *The Hunting of Caine: A True Story of Money, Greed and Fratricide* (New York: Viking, 1986).

5. Dan Moldea, *Dark Victory: Ronald Reagan, MCA and the Mob* (New York: Viking, 1986).

6. Sirhan Bishara Sirhan (1944-) assassinated Robert F. Kennedy on June 5, 1968, because he disliked the senator's support of Israel. In 1969 he was convicted of murder and five counts of assault in the wounding of five other persons. He was sentenced to death, but in 1972 that sentence was reduced to life in prison.

7. In *The Hoffa Wars*, Moldea revealed new details about the CIA-Mafia plots to murder Cuban premier Fidel Castro.

8. Steven Brill, *The Teamsters* (New York: Simon and Schuster, 1978).

9. Four college students at Kent State University in Ohio were shot and killed by National Guardsmen on May 4, 1970. The shootings sparked a wave of student protests across the country that touched more than 530 universities.

10. Jonathan Kwitney is an investigative journalist and author of such books as *Acceptable Risks, Crimes of Patriots: A True Story of Dope, Dirty Money and the CIA* and *Endless Enemies: The Making of an Unfriendly World*.

11. Jack Anderson is a well-known Washington, D.C.–based investigative journalist who has covered the national scene since 1947.

12. Millionaire Jack Kent Cooke is the owner of the Washington Redskins pro-football team.

13. I. F. Stone edited the famous newsletter *I. F. Stone Weekly* and is one of the most celebrated investigative journalists of all time. An interview with David Burnham appears in this book.

14. Kitty Kelley has published best-selling books on such personalities as Frank Sinatra. Geraldo Rivera is a television personality and host of the "Geraldo Rivera Show," who bills himself as an investigative journalist. "A Current Affair" is a popular television tabloid show.

10

Eileen Welsome
Always Check the Footnotes

> Even though I never met any of those people, and many of them had been dead for a long time, I felt their stories had to be told.

In her Academy Award–winning performance as a textile worker named Norma Rae, actress Sally Field stood defiantly atop a loom and rallied the workers to her cause. The 1979 movie *Norma Rae* exposed unsafe conditions in a North Carolina mill and the uncaring management that valued profits more than people. Sally Field portrayed the petite employee who, despite a usually subdued temperament, eventually teamed with a labor union organizer to lead a strike aimed at gaining better working conditions.

Eileen Welsome, who bears a striking resemblance to Sally Field, is soft-spoken and petite, and she, like Norma Rae, summoned forth the courage to do battle with a giant foe. In Eileen Welsome's case, however, the enemy was the American government.[1]

The term "cold war," coined by American financier Bernard Baruch in 1946, and the image, used that same year by Winston Churchill, of an "Iron Curtain," produced a siege mentality that came perilously close to paranoia in America. We perceived our way of life to be under attack from the Soviet Union and believed that to triumph against our adversary, which gained access to atomic weapons in 1949, required a total commitment of our country's resources. Ironically, this total commitment did not stop with material goods; it included unwitting citizens who would become guinea pigs in medical experiments involving plutonium.

Eileen Welsome won the Pulitzer Prize in 1994 for her reporting of our government's manipulation of the lives of the experiments' participants. In the following interview, Welsome tells us of the horror which swept over her when she discovered that documents listing livestock tested by the government actually hid the truth: that citizens — not animals — had received doses of radioactive substances.

Welsome has been a reporter for the *Albuquerque Tribune* since 1987. Like other investigative journalists interviewed in this book, she considers her mission to include righting past wrongs. In her judgment, stories such as the revelations of the plutonium experiments make us a stronger country because reporting the truth — even when it shows painful flaws in our system — is in the finest tradition of the muckrakers who used the protection of the First Amendment so effectively early this century.

* * *

Could you describe your emotions when you learned that you had received a Pulitzer? That is the top journalism award. What went through your head and what did you think about when you received notification?

I guess the expectations were so great from people at the paper and my friends and acquaintances that I had a sense of relief. It was only in the following months and even now that I'm beginning to digest and think about what happened. I obviously was thrilled at that moment, but my overwhelming feeling was just one of relief.

So it took months to really sink in that you won the top award in your profession.

I feel very honored to have won. I think that a lot of it was hard work, but a lot of it was being in the right place at the right time.

So you would say there was some luck involved in it.

Yes, I would. I would say that definitely there was an element of luck to it. This was a story that might have gone unnoticed had not the energy secretary, Hazel O'Leary, mentioned it during a press conference a month after it appeared in our paper. She acknowledged that the Department of Energy had conducted numerous radiation experiments and that they were going to get to the bottom of them. That was a break with history. Prior to that time, there was an obstructionist attitude within the Department of Energy. I was not there, and I do not know what led to her decision to do this. Certainly, the cold war was over. The people in the Clinton administration had no political interest in keeping this hidden. One of Clinton's promises was to be a more open president, to get some control over all these documents that were classified, to make the government more responsible to the people, and so I think this fit into that agenda.

How did you first get interested in journalism?

Well, it's an interesting story. I was looking for a job and I walked into a bookstore because I love books. There was a really nice person in the bookstore, and he told me there might be an opening for a printer or a person in the back shop down at the newspaper. I went down and applied for that job. So essentially my first experience in the newspaper business was working in the back shop where we had a copy camera that photographed the pages and made the halftones and burned the plates and did the color separations. I did that for a while, and I knew almost immediately, within months, I wanted to be a reporter.

So you saw that side of the business, which I think is unusual.

Yeah, it was very unusual. You know, I walked into the newspaper building, and I had never been in that kind of environment. I can't describe my feeling — it was, well, this is my home, this is where I belong.

So you felt at ease.

I felt it was where I wanted to be, instantly, and I'd never had such a strong feeling prior to that time.

And you haven't had second thoughts since then?

Well, I've had fifteen years' experience reporting. I've worked

Eileen Welsome. Courtesy of Eileen Welsome.

at large papers and small papers and weeklies, and I've covered every beat I think there is to cover. I've been very frustrated in my job, particularly in the last few years because it was … I don't know if it is the age I am now, or just that a person gets to this point in a career. But I began to think that the frustrations weren't worth it.[2]

And there seem to be some major changes going on right now in print journalism.

Right. There are so many changes going on in our business. It's becoming harder and harder to just be a reporter and do your job. Sometimes editors don't want controversial stories; certainly they don't want investigative stories where they are putting their newspaper and the newspaper company on the line. You need a lot of courage to dig into controversial topics in your town. And then, when you do get hold of the dragon's tail, you have to have every fact nailed down; otherwise, you and your newspaper will be sued. So, it's a very stressful and treacherous kind of business.

And it has become a business in many ways, has it not?

I've never felt in the years I've worked in the business any commercial pressure or that you should or would not do this story because of X, Y, or Z advertiser. Obviously, our business is changing and newspapers are struggling for survival, but I've never felt any kind of economic pressure, either to do a story, or not to do a story and I would never, ever bow to that kind of pressure. I don't think that's what we journalists are. You know, a good editor will protect his reporter from those kinds of pressures. That's not our problem to worry about.

Let me ask you, how do you feel about the label "investigative journalist"? Is that a label that you're comfortable with or would you rather call yourself just "journalist" or "reporter." How do you perceive what you do?

I was never comfortable with the label "investigative reporter." I think it's somewhat pretentious, although I have accepted that I am an investigative reporter, and so I will at times describe myself as an investigative reporter.

I think that the techniques we use in investigative reporting apply to all reporting. If you're writing a story about the mayor, one of the things you might want to do is go down and look up his tax records. Investigative reporters probe more deeply into the news events and into the people they are writing about. But the techniques that we use should be part of every reporter's arsenal.

Were there any investigative journalists whom you would consider to be role models?

I guess, because I met him recently, I'd have to say Seymour Hersh.[3]

Bob Woodward, perhaps?

I don't know him, but certainly I think the two reporters who have inspired or made investigative journalism were Woodward and Bernstein.[4]

Does gender matter in the newspaper business?

Gender has never made a difference, either in getting a job or in getting a newspaper story. I'm a very petite woman and I have a soft voice, so I think that people may misjudge the kind of work that I do or the tenacity that I have. But gender has never been an issue.

Am I correct in saying that most investigative reporting comes from folks on the political left? Is that a correct assessment or am I being too general?

I can't answer that question. I never gave it any thought, and I don't know enough about the backgrounds of other investigative reporters to say whether they're on the left or on the right.[5]

How do you go about selecting a topic to research or investigate? Do people come forward and say, " Well, Ms. Welsome, we ought to look into this," or do you choose the topic?

I would say that it's a combination of the two; sometimes it'll be a phone call that will initiate a story, and other times I'll be working on a story and get a lead that I'll follow. I think of them as leads, but I also think of them as strings that I pull on.

Oh, I like that image.

I also think of investigative reporting as a way to see more deeply into the world. You know there is so much about the dynamics of our world that is unseen but is available through a paper trail. Paper can help a reporter discover the motivating factors, say, behind a candidate's race for governor or a senator's position on a bill.

When you choose a topic, how do you handle resistance when perhaps you find that people are not being cooperative, that people have something to hide, that they don't want to tell you the truth?
I rack my brain and look for another avenue. I'll use an example: Several years ago I was researching a utility company's diversified investments. I talked to the officials who were involved with their company's holdings and asked them how much money they were worth and what these investments were. Eventually I just went to bankruptcy court, and I went through eighty volumes of bankruptcy records. Even that was not enough. I got depositions in the case, and by the time I had read all those depositions and had read the bankruptcy records, I learned about their diversified interests. They were so complex that nobody had put it together. I don't think even if one of these officials had the information at their fingertips they could have just reeled it off. They would have needed a map also.

So if somebody is uncooperative or doesn't have the information or does not want to provide me with the information, I'll look for another avenue. Is there another person who could be interviewed? Is there a neighbor that I overlooked? Where else could this information be found?

So, when you find out that you're not getting the answers, do you step back and look for another avenue?
I rarely give up. I mean there's a point in time when you know you've shaken every tree and so that's it, the chase is over, but usually, I'll do a lot of thinking. Where else might this information be located? There have got to be other avenues to get it; there's paper out there somewhere. You know our world is full of paper, and a lot of it's public. And then, when I've exhausted all those avenues and if I've not come up with what I'm looking for, then I drop the story. It's not there.

I tell my history students that they have to be detectives. And a detective checks under every stone before he or she decides that there's nothing there. And I guess that's what you're saying there.
Right. I think that a problem with young reporters is that they lack the tenacity. In other words, a door shuts in their face and they say fine. That's the end of my story. You have to be willing to have the door shut in your face fifty to a hundred times. A lot of it is intuition. If your intuition tells you there is a story, that this is a real event, then I will do everything I can to find out about it. If I don't find anything, I'll put it aside. Maybe something will develop later, and I can go back to it.

That's what I do with projects I'm working on, I use old-fashioned files and I keep them and I keep little scraps of paper and phone numbers and then I go back to them from time to time, trying to finish up a story and I guess in a way that's what you do.

Right. In the plutonium experiment, I started out with a footnote that I found in a scientific report at Kirtland Air Force Base. At the time I was researching radioactive waste dumps, and I was just curious about what they had done to these animals and what kinds of animals were in these dumps.

I went over to the Air Force Weapons Laboratory. The archivist brought me out a stack of reports about a foot high. I didn't understand any of them, but I continued to thumb through them. And I remember this quite vividly. I remember their smell. They were very old and musty like they hadn't been opened in fifty years. I thumbed through one report after another and, you know, it was late in the day. I think it was a Friday, and I thought, well, I can't just walk out of here after I went through all this effort to get these reports. So I kept thumbing through them. One thing I've always done is look at footnotes. It's an intuitive habit because in financial reports a lot of caveats are contained in the footnotes. The story is in the footnotes.

Always check the footnotes.

Always check the footnotes. So I was looking. I had looked through a report and had gone to the back, skimming the footnotes. There was a footnote referencing an experiment in which eighteen people were injected with plutonium. I was stunned. You have to keep in mind that at the time all I knew is that they were using animals for these experiments and that they were giving them radioactive isotopes and all kinds of things. So to find human beings in this context was shocking to me. I jotted that reference down and went to the library that weekend, the university library, and started my research efforts. It was that footnote that got me going, but there were a lot of points at which the story could have died.

The first moment was when I went in the following Monday. I was very excited about this story. I was a little foolish in that I thought it had never been reported before. I knew it was fifty years old so I was going to have a little problem selling it. When I went in and I said "I've got this fantastic story; eighteen people were injected with plutonium during the Manhattan Project," the city editor said to me, "Well, that's a great story but you're the neighborhood writer."[6] So, I sort of shrugged and walked off.

That's the first place I could have stopped. I continued to gather this data on my own time, and then I did a Nexus search through the computers to find out if anything had been written. This was nineteen eighty-seven. I still have the print-out. Sure enough, it had been in the papers. That was even more discouraging to me, because it told me that I wasn't going to be breaking off this new-slash-old story. I looked at those stories. I still felt that there was a story that hadn't been told. Yes, it had been reported in the scientific media and in the popular media that eighteen people had been injected with plutonium. Yes, the story was fifty years old. But my intuition told me that there was more. So I kept going.

When you approach technical subjects like that, that maybe are out of your field, do you have a rolodex that you use to call people and ask them to explain things so that you can understand and know which direction to go with research?

Well, what I do, what works for me is, I immerse myself in the documents and it seems like somehow during that process I understand or develop a general understanding of the technical issues. During the course of reporting and writing the story, I work on those issues. I call up people and say, what is a "microgram"? What is "strontium 89"? I'm never afraid to ask.

It's valuable to have experts in the community who will help you, but I don't have a group that I rely on. I rely on the people who are involved in the story, whether it's a regulator or a member of the attorney general's office or a scientist in the government. I'll call anybody and ask them anything.

You're saying that you're not going to be discouraged. You're always going to continue and try to develop leads and try to see the story to its conclusion. I think that's what's made you a success.

I think that reporting is very difficult work. It's adversarial, and it's full of stress. People don't want to tell you embarrassing things, people don't want to tell you, "Oh, yes, I pulled out a million dollars in bonuses from this company before it bellied-up." So those kinds of stories are the great stories, and they just don't get volunteered. In the real world, people don't call up reporters and tell them that, certainly not reliable people. The best stories always take a lot of digging and a lot of work. Nothing comes easy in this world, you know, and you put one foot in front of the other and you've walked a mile.

Do you use a tape recorder when you conduct research?

Oh, yes, I use a tape recorder, and I use a computer. Right now I'm using a database system for my book. I'm not extremely knowledgeable about computers, but I view them as another tool that can be useful.

How do you verify what sources tell you?

I try to learn about the subject, immerse myself in the subject, understand it, talk to as many people as I can on both sides of the issue. The documents are one of the strongest things that I rely on because they're there in black and white and they're a defense to libel. They're generally truthful, and so I rely heavily on the written documentation. But I also contact people on both sides of the issue.

If a document says something like "so-and-so received two hundred fifty thousand dollars on X date" and then three months later a company bellied-up, then I can call that person and say, "Well how was it that you received this money, and how do you explain the fact that the company bellied-up and was there anything inappropriate in what you did?" The best check is fairness. If you are fair and honestly seeking the truth, then I think you'll get an approximation of that.

Do you enjoy researching more than writing or do you like them both?

Actually that's a very opportune question because I've just finished my research on this book. I have seven filing cabinets of documents and over one thousand one hundred entries in my computer database. Now I'm in the writing phase. I still call people for little details I don't understand, but I guess the pleasurable part comes during the writing phase.

Well, you write clearly. When I was conducting my research in preparation for this interview, I was struck by that. You can deal with things that perhaps are technical but you can make them clear to a wide readership, and I guess that's what the Pulitzer committee was impressed with: how clearly you write. Do you enjoy writing?

Well, yeah, but writing is very painful for me. It doesn't come easy.

But you do it well.

Let me just put it this way, it feels good when I'm done. Right now it feels terrible. I'm racked with doubt and a lot of anxiety about whether I am going in the right direction. In every story that I write, I can't tell you the kind of mental anguish that I go through. These are the kinds of questions that I ask myself: Do I have it right? Are these facts accurate? Am I saying too much?

When I was writing the plutonium experiment, for example, my butt was on the line. I identified five people who had been injected with plutonium, and I had no confirmation from the federal government that these, in fact, were five of the eighteen people who had been injected in a top-secret experiment. In other words, these were my conclusions, my identification of these individuals. I made that decision. I was constantly going back to these people in my mind and saying, "Why do I think Albert Stevens is Cal One?" I would actually write out the reasons that this was Cal One. Then I'd say to myself, "What are the chances that this could be somebody else?" There was no chance.

I'd do these gut checks. I did that up until the day my story was published. And I do that with any story, with my book right now. You know, what's really difficult about some of these stories is that as the writer, I have to be cognizant of the fact that I'm only seeing a certain portion of the documentation that's available. So I'm constantly asking myself and reminding myself that there's more out there. That this could change radically.

Do you conduct the research yourself or do you ever have anyone at the paper, maybe a trusted friend who helps?

I generally do it all myself. I also do my own fact checking. Usually so much is on the line. I have to go over this material over and over again to make sure that it's accurate, to make sure that it's not overstated and not understated. So I'm very painstaking about reporting. That does not make writing easy when you're dealing with specific facts and you have to strike a certain tone and balance. It doesn't leave a lot of leeway to be imaginative and creative in the writing process. I think it's very difficult to write a story that's investigative and readable.

When you got to the end of the plutonium story, what did you look back on and like the best about the process? I know you had to have a sense of satisfaction because you were telling a story that needed to be told.

Even though I never met many of these people, and many of them had been dead for a long time, I felt that those stories needed to be told. You know what I felt? I felt that there'd been some justice done for these long-dead people; that they had been so abused during their lifetimes and treated so inhumanely that it just was not fair.

So, justice delayed, but it finally came.

Exactly.

Well, let me ask you then, when you look back on something like that story, is there anything there that you feel like maybe I could have done it differently, or maybe I should have gone further?

Oh, yes, I do. There is a whole archive of material that's being produced at this moment in Washington, D.C. There's a whole forty years of history that's really never been delved into in this area of human experimentation; I've seen all kinds of documents that weren't available when I wrote the story. I found relatives of scientists, I found relatives of patients, and I've always thought, well, maybe I could have dug a little harder and found it prior to when I went to press. But the fact of the matter is that at the time this story went to press, the Department of Energy was still stonewalling us and the paper had spent thousands of dollars in legal fees trying to get a Freedom of Information Act request answered. The federal government was dragging its feet.

That brings up an interesting thing. Have you ever been sued for libel?

I've been threatened. I've never been sued. It's something I'm aware of. I took a course in college about things to look for, the things that were privileged, the things we could write with comfort about and that's helped me for years. There've been some people who indicated that they might sue, but the lawsuits have never materialized. Nobody in the plutonium experiment approached the paper and said that they were going to file a lawsuit.

If you were going to present a guest lecture at a journalism school, what advice would you give to young people wanting to get into the profession?

I would tell them: Number one, never give up. Number two, there are great stories in every city, and I would tell them Number three: they should always follow their intuition. If they have a story they are enamored with or that they care about, they should pursue it in their spare time and they should take what an editor says with a grain of salt.

What are you working on now? I know you're finishing up your book.

I'm on Chapter Six. It's a story that sprang out of the plutonium experiment, and it's about this particular aspect of the Cold War that's not been reported.

What do you think your investigation of the plutonium experiments tells us about our government?

It confirms for me that governments are like people. They have their strengths and weaknesses. It tells me that we, as reporters, need to be ever-vigilant, particularly when it comes to covering parts of our government that are allowed to have a great deal of secrecy, such as the Department of Energy, the CIA, and other organizations. That we owe it to the public to probe as deep as we can to make sure that our money is being spent in wise ways and to make sure there are no abuses going on.

I think the press was duped during the cold war. They were out-and-out lied to about things by very smart individuals, and those smart individuals are still around today. The thing that we as reporters need to do is to not let these people get by with the things they've gotten by with in the past.

I'll give you an example of that: The director of Los Alamos National Laboratories said recently in connection with the federal budget cutting, " Well, Los Alamos exports science and technology." A good editor should have asked that reporter, What does he mean by "science and technology." Ask him for specifics. In other words, that does an injustice to our whole country when you let somebody get by with a blanket statement like that. They are entitled to make those statements, but they also should be required to concretely explain them. For example, in the nineteen seventies, when somebody was saying, "We need to improve our stockpile," I think that the reporter should have explained that "stockpile" meant we've got to build bigger and better bombs. That is a code word. And in these very difficult areas, we should translate those words.

I think so, too. I was thinking last week, George Romney died and I remember when he was running for president in nineteen sixty-eight and he said that he's been "brainwashed" about Vietnam and that was the word he used. It destroyed any chance that he would get the Republican nomination. I think many people were brainwashed and you use word "duped," and I think many people were duped; that reminded me of that.

I don't think there's any way of calculating the kind of money that went into these laboratories and these weapons that were produced or the kind of problems which arose. Those problems are still with us, and that is why the media is so valuable. That's why I get frustrated when people take the media down. Every day we are out there asking those questions, and some days we do a better job than others. But I don't know anybody else who's down at City Hall going through tax records or up at Los Alamos going through scientific reports. You don't find members of the public doing that very often.

I'm reminded of a masthead that I saw once in a Chicago newspaper in the nineteen twenties that they were to comfort the afflicted and afflict the comfortable.[7] I think that's what you do as a journalist. You help those who have been treated unfairly, and you focus attention and the light of the truth upon the people who have taken advantage of them.

Right. And that's certainly the case of these plutonium people. They were treated unfairly. And that's an understatement. They were tracked, many of them were tracked by the federal government for decades. They had their body parts removed. They were lied to about what was done to them at the time. And they were lied to back in the nineteen seventies when they were brought back into the hospitals.

What impact do you think that you have had on the profession of investigative journalism?

I don't know what impact I've had on investigative journalism, but I would like to think that my story is an inspiring one for young journalists. I think there are a lot of lessons here about the kinds of obstacles that we face every day and how we can overcome them.

Notes

1. Eileen Welsome's battle with the federal government was aided by Secretary of Energy Hazel O'Leary's decision in 1993 to open research files on the cold war plutonium experiments. Welsome's reporting earned her numerous awards in addition to the Pulitzer, including the George Polk Award, Managing Editors' Public Service Award, and the Heywood Brown Award. For a complete list, consult *Who's Who of American Women 1995-1996*.

2. Welsome's résumé includes a bachelor of journalism degree with honors from the University of Texas (1980) and positions with the *San Antonio Light*, *San Antonio Express-News* as well as her Pulitzer Prize–winning stint at the *Albuquerque Tribune*. See *Who's Who of American Women 1995-1996*, 19th edition, for a complete vitae.

3. As an investigative reporter, Seymour Hersh exposed the March 1968 My Lai massacre in which over 200 Vietnamese were murdered by American soldiers. Twenty-five army officers were charged, but only one, Lieutenant William Calley, was convicted and he was later paroled by President Richard Nixon.

4. The June 1972 break-in at the Democratic Party headquarters and the cover-up which followed were reported by *Washington Post* reporters Carl Bernstein and Bob Woodward; this "Watergate Scandal" climaxed with President Nixon's August 1974 resignation.

5. See the *American Spectator* (January 1994) and the Brock interview in this book.

6. The top secret Manhattan Project produced the atomic bombs which were dropped on the Japanese cities of Hiroshima and Nagasaki in August 1945.

7. *Chicago Tribune*, circa 1920.

11

David Brock

Investigations from the Right

> I think our job is to get the stories, check them out, and do as thorough a job as possible in putting the information out there. I think you'll find a lot of liberals now making the argument that journalism has become tabloid. That's because now some of the guns have been turned on liberals. But we're doing the same kind of journalism that has been going on for years.

Strategically located on a hill in Arlington, Virginia, the offices of the *American Spectator* stand as a shining citadel protecting the country's right flank. As one enters the fortress, framed covers spanning three decades of the publication's history line the walls. The Nixon and Reagan years are glorified, and the covers document a steady assault on the remnants of Lyndon Johnson's Great Society and the current occupants of the White House. Soldiers of the conservative movement are everywhere and, on this June day, they are energetically preparing yet another edition of the *American Spectator*.[1]

One of the knights guarding this fortress is David Brock, the magazine's chief investigative reporter, a title of which he is proud. Brock is a decorated veteran of the cause, and he earned his stripes by firing a blistering salvo from the right wing in his 1993 best-selling book, *The Real Anita Hill: The Untold Story*.[2]

Two years earlier Anita Hill's allegations that her former supervisor, Clarence Thomas, had sexually harassed her while the two worked together in the Reagan administration had captivated the nation. Stereotypes — racial and sexual — paraded across front pages and television screens as Thomas was nominated in 1991 to succeed retiring Supreme Court justice Thurgood Marshall.[3]

In his still controversial book, Brock zeroes in on Hill's veracity and suggests that Hill became increasingly disturbed over the years as she realized that she had less and less influence with her former boss, Clarence Thomas. Brock argues that sexual harassment was not proved by Hill, and the spectacle of the sensationalistic confirmation hearings allowed "passion and politics" to "displace reasoned analysis." Brock adds that "an innocent person's reputation can all too easily be ruined."[4]

David Brock. Courtesy of David Brock.

Politically incorrect and seemingly proud of it, Brock says that feminist organizations used Anita Hill to promote their own agendas, which had little to do with whether or not sexual harassment had occurred in the Hill-Thomas relationship. In biting commentary, Brock writes that Hill was "canonized as the Rosa Parks of sexual harassment, [while] Thomas, who had the not inconsiderable consolation of serving on the Supreme Court, continued to be demoralized."[5]

On this summer morning, Brock and I sit in the *American Spectator*'s conference room to discuss Anita Hill, President Bill Clinton, and the craft of investigative journalism.

* * *

We had Edna Buchanan on our list of journalists to interview, but she said, "I'm a crime reporter, not an investigative reporter."[6] *Do you perceive yourself as an investigative reporter?*

Yes, I do.

How would you characterize investigative journalism?

First of all, investigative journalism pieces involve articles that are usually not written on a daily or a weekly deadline. They're usually done over the course of several weeks of reporting. Often it involves not only interviewing many sources, live sources, but also leaves of documents but lots of official or unofficial written records.

I think that's basically it. It goes beyond what your run-of-the-mill, everyday reporting does. In addition to just informing you of the day's news events, it goes on and brings a totally new factual material to light. At the *Spectator*, there is no expectation that I write an investigative article every month. If something doesn't check out, it may take several months to get a piece done. But that's the investigative nature of what I'm doing.

And the American Spectator *is very patient about that type thing? They're willing to allow you to take six months perhaps?*

Yeah, they're working on it [laughs]. It takes some time, I think. The *Spectator* hadn't done all that much reporting. It's almost thirty years old now, and

I think for the first twenty-five years or so it did much more commentary than it did reporting. But they've been moving in a direction of doing more reporting, trying to fill a niche, as they see it, of what the more established press is not covering. And so, over time, they have adjusted to the idea that often a lead does not check out; often we spend time and money running down some trails and you don't go anywhere and it doesn't produce anything.[7]

How did you first get interested in journalism? Were you a newspaper editor in college or high school?

I was in both, in high school and in college at the University of California in Berkeley. So as far back as I can remember, journalism always interested me. When I got out of school, I came to Washington to work for the *Washington Times* and had several different jobs there working on their magazine, which is called *Insight Magazine*. Of course, I didn't like school too much, and this is something you can do without too much education [laughs].

I edited my college newspaper, and I almost got kicked out. It was a church-related school, and we had mandatory assembly. And it was just ridiculous. We had to go once a week, and I made fun of that one time. I said Jesus Christ was coming to be the assembly speaker, and He was going to perform miracles. Did you ever run into anything like that?[7]

Oh, yeah. I had a controversy where I wrote a column in the fall of 1983, a signed column, expressing my own view on the Grenada invasion.[8] I was at Berkeley. I was in favor of the invasion, and I seemed to be the only one in Berkeley who held that view. I wrote from that point of view and created controversy.

There was an effort to recall me from my job, but it didn't succeed because it was an independent corporation run off campus and the by-laws of the corporation did not permit recall of editors. So I was saved by the skin of my teeth. But, yeah, it was a big controversy, and what struck me then was that no one really argued with what was said in the column, it was just that since this was a progressive newspaper with a long liberal tradition, then it was unacceptable to have one of the editors, you know, saying something like that. So everything I did after that was seen as some kind of conservative plot.

Who are your role models?

Well, let's see. In journalism I would probably say somebody like Bob Woodward or Seymour Hersh, who are not necessarily considered to be politically in line with the view the *American Spectator* takes on a lot of issues, but they do the kinds of things that I would like to do. As far as conservative writers and journalists, I would say Bill Safire or Bob Novak because they bring new facts to light as well as unearth new material.[9] They are also able to put their own political point of view, their own ideological take on things. So, as a columnist I find them more interesting than simply the pundits who stay in the library and don't go out and talk to people. I would list them in that manner.

Does Bob Woodward maybe trouble you a little bit with sources that may not exist or ...

Well, yeah, sure. He's had his problems as far as that is concerned, but, on the other hand, I'd probably tend to defend Woodward more than criticize him, knowing that a lot of times when you're hitting your targets you're going to be, as an investigative reporter, you're going to be attacked in various ways. So I'd be uncomfortable saying he was wrong about anything without looking into it myself because I know how politicians will often react against things. His most recent book I thought was pretty compelling —*Agenda.*

Howard Kurtz had an article in the Washington Post *about a month ago in which he said that only five percent of journalists were conservative. Is that a fair assessment that only five percent are conservative?*[10]

That's probably right. It doesn't seem that way because there are conservative columnists and commentators on the television talk shows. I think conservatives are pretty well represented in television, but as far as in newsrooms and print journals, I would say that sounds right to me. There are very few people doing reporting who also accept the label of "conservative." I can't think of too many besides me. So, yeah, I think that is probably right.

Why is that, do you think?

I think they self-select out and do something else, like go to law school because there are no clear paths to success in journalism. You know that major news weeklies, the big prestigious newspapers, and the main networks are all dominated by liberals and so where're the jobs? I think that's the reason; I think that those who've been successful and also conservative in journalism like Dennis DeSousa have found success through the writing of books or being at the *American Spectator*. It's not through some kind of a mainline job like working your way up through *Time* magazine, being a reporter, then an editor, then an assistant managing editor. You don't see many conservatives in those kinds of career paths; it's always something of a fluke is what I would say. And then there are a few editorial pages to work on. There are the *Wall Street Journal* and a couple of the regional newspapers that have conservative editorial pages, but again, it's editorial writing, not news reporting.

So I think it's sort of self-reinforcing if you look around, and everybody you look at in journalism that you might want to emulate is of a different political point of view. So you decide to do something else.

I guess the 1960s may have something to do with that and Watergate and the fact that the press, since about the time of Watergate has been seen as an adversarial institution and conservatives, on the other hand, are generally more defenders of institutions like the presidency and are not as comfortable generally in that kind of investigative role. Conservatives in general don't like journalism that much. They see it as tearing down society's institutions. So the crusading aspect of journalism from the seventies on, I think, probably accounts for a little bit of the temperament that a reporter needs, but is not always found among conservatives.

Did you find your research for The Real Anita Hill *to be particularly difficult?*
To be honest with you, no, it wasn't particularly difficult. And the reason for that is that almost everybody that I can think of, and I'm very familiar with the journals that came out at the time. We weren't really interested in the aspects of the story that I deal with in my book.

For example, how did — and this has nothing to do with whether you believed Anita Hill or not — how did her charge surface publicly? And there's a clear line of events that you can trace from the day that Thomas was nominated in July up until the time that Nina Totenburg broke that story in October.[11] And a lot of events are going on behind the scenes where Anita Hill's story was being coaxed out of her by the Senate staffers and then in the form of a written statement. So that's fascinating to me and that was virtually unreported at the time. There were a lot of aspects of the story I was able to go after, and I, in a sense, had the field to myself. For example, I found a lot of unmined public documentation. Take the transcripts of the hearings. If you went back and really read the transcripts and really analyzed them, you would see a lot of things in there had bearing on whether Anita Hill was a truthful witness or not. But people just glossed over it. There are a variety of reasons for that but basically, Anita Hill got a free ride from the press at the time. So going back and looking with a more skeptical eye at her story wasn't terribly difficult.

Did you expect the book to do so well?
No, I didn't actually. Basically, my expectations for the book were that it would get a modest kind of sales. I also thought that those who did not believe Anita Hill would like the book, that it would be well read among some political conservatives.

But I didn't really expect it to break through and really sell the way it did. This is the way I view this, that the attacks were proportionate to how well the book was doing, and so the more the book succeeded commercially and also in some reviews, which I might mention, the more that the defenders of Anita Hill, or critics of Clarence Thomas, or feminists, or whomever you want to say, the more they had to try to discredit the book. I didn't expect it to become that kind of phenomenon because I didn't expect the book to get that much notice.

But what happened was it did get a very good review in the daily *New York Times* by Christopher Lehmann-Haupt very early on. And the power of the *Times* being what it is, that really gave it a push onto the best-seller list, and so at that point you had the *New Yorker* review and then you had several columnists who I believe just read the *New Yorker* review rather than the book and ran with it that way. So, it was unexpected.

So you developed a thick skin.

Oh, yeah, I've always had a thick skin. When I first read the Anthony Lewis column, I had a knot in my stomach, and I was upset by it. My publisher was delighted, 'cause [as] he said, "It will move from a six to three on the list," because you know, once you get noticed, it kind of doesn't matter. I mean it matters to you, but as far as the success of the book, and if you look at the bell curve—once you're on the radar screen it doesn't matter whether they are raving or screaming, as long as they are doing something. I think basically it means you're doing something right. That's my view of it. I was on to something. That's why I got that kind of response. If I wasn't, if this was just a bunch of fabrications, as is said, then why deal with it? Why bother with it?

Are people willing to talk with you? Take the time you went to Little Rock and did the article, which is one of my favorite articles that you have done, "His Cheating Heart." Did the people in Little Rock talk to you?[12]

Yes, they did. Even now, and we're two and one-half years into the Clinton administration, all rocks have not been overturned in Arkansas, and I can still go down there, as I have the past few weeks, and find people willing to talk to me and find new information on that. But I'm not saying there's a huge scandal. This story developed a little differently in that I didn't really find those sources. They originally found me and they found the *L.A. Times.*

They came to both of us simultaneously and told their stories, and we both ended up publishing somewhat different stories within a few days of each other. We both published the troopers' allegations. We tried to corroborate those allegations, but originally they just sat down and told me their story. That was off the record, though, and there was a struggle to get the thing verified and get it on the record, which took about four months. The original impetus was that they were ready to talk to somebody, and it was just a question of whether it was going to be me or somebody else, what the ground rules were, and that kind of thing. So it was fun actually, and an exciting four months. [Laughs.] Cause I knew about it and nobody else did for four months.[13]

You kept it secret, which was very hard.

Yeah, very hard.

What do you consider to be the most rewarding part of your job?

I enjoy the reporting. Probably in time it will come that I'm fussier about my writing, but right now what I really like is the thrill of the chase, finding out all the information, tracking down leads, getting a list of leads and sources. I like the fact that you never know where it's going to lead. The writing of it does not excite me as much as ...

The research?

Yeah, cause once you're writing it, you've already got it figured out. I try to write it as clearly and as coherently as possible, but I don't agonize over the word choice and all that that much. I like imparting the information and I enjoy finding out what's going on before other people do, that kind of inside stuff. There are three investigations going on in Capitol Hill right now: Clinton's Whitewater, Waco, Travelgate and I just enjoy knowing who's being deposed today [laugh].

You have to be a detective?
Yeah, I would say so. That's the part that interests me more than the literary aspects of it, I guess. In the case of Anita Hill, a lot of my investigation was analysis of testimony from written documents. It wasn't so much detective work as it was like legal work. I enjoyed that too—like trying to poke a hole in my own case. Does everything fit? You want it as airtight as you can get it.

Did she ever respond? Call you?
She didn't, no. I made several attempts to get an interview with her, and what she ultimately did was refer me to her lawyer who had represented her during the hearings, a professor at Harvard, Charles Oglestreet. I did fly up to Boston and interview him. Subsequently, I couldn't get any communication after the book was published.

Do you tape record your interviews?
Yeah, but it depends. I don't tape record them all. I don't have an ironclad rule about it. Sometimes it's just a judgment call. I did an interview recently where I felt that the presence of a tape recorder was going to make the source nervous, so I did a two-hour interview without the tape recorder. Now I'm going to go down this week, which is two weeks later, and record it and go over the same material on tape because I'd like to have it on tape. I wanted the source to cough up what they gave me in our first meeting when I didn't have a tape recorder.

If it's someone like a senator who's not put off by the tape recorder, I will record. So I guess the general rule is record as much as possible, but when you've got sources who are skittish, I think you have to be a little more careful. It's good to have a tape recorder when the story is complex. That's true if you're dealing with material, say, about arms control policy or something technical where you may have to listen to it more than once to get it right. If it's some general political profile, it's probably less important to have it on tape because you're kind of picking and choosing what you're going to use as you go through the interview.

What did the Little Rock folks prefer? Notes or the tape recorder?
It probably took about a month to get them on tape, but there was no question in my mind that that story was not going anywhere without getting it on tape [laughs]. So I wanted to make sure that there was no embellishment of the story they told me. I interviewed them over the same material

several times. I taped the interviews, and I transcribed the tapes when I came back to Washington. Three weeks later, I went back and did the same interview and came back and transcribed it to see if things changed; how they quoted Clinton, was it the same or was it different. That was the only way I felt that I could assess the credibility of the story. If it was changing, if it was getting better as time went on or if it was just getting different, then I would have been uncomfortable with it. So that's why I needed all that on tape.

Then I broke them up. I had a group of troopers, and I divided them up in different ways. Sometimes I had just one-on-one, sometimes I had two or three in the room, that kind of thing. So, I was very careful to, as best I could, to make sure these guys weren't pulling the wool over my eyes. It definitely involved taping, handwritten notes wouldn't have been good enough there.

Howard Kurtz's book Media Circus *came out in 1993.[14] Do you think maybe investigative journalism is somehow to blame for becoming a media circus? You know, I see in my students a certain cynicism. For example, they don't want to serve in government as people once, say thirty years ago.*

Oh, that's something I don't give that much thought to. I would probably err on the side of let's have too much information out there than not enough.

Thomas Jefferson would have agreed with that, would he not have?[15]

Yeah. As a voter, how important are Clinton's multiple infidelities? Personally it might not be that high, but I don't think that's my judgment to make for readers. For some voters, that's an important issue. It might be a deciding factor in an election. I think if a story like that had been published before the election, Clinton probably would not have been elected. So I don't think it's up to me to exercise any kind of censorship and say, well, this story is not as important to me as his position on Bosnia, so I'm not going to write it.

I think our job is to get the stories, check them out, and do as thorough a job as possible in putting the information out there. I think you'll find a lot of liberals now making the argument that journalism has become too tabloid. That's because now some of the guns have been turned on liberals. But we're doing the same kind of journalism that has been going on for years. It's just that almost always that kind of journalism has been targeted at Republicans. Now, however, the targets are a little different, and people are more uncomfortable with it. You are getting a lot of lectures about "journalistic standards," and you've got a lot of hand-wringing over Paula Jones that you didn't get over Anita Hill, for example.

If a story is wrong, if it doesn't hold water, it never rises onto a level where people are paying attention to it. I'm not one who wants to go back to the days when reporters protected President Kennedy because they were close to him, and when four or five editors in Washington and New York decided everything that got into print.

I do think Jefferson was right; I think we need to have an open press. In a free press, the government interest should be sacrificed.

I agree. And it's a market-driven thing, too. If people really believe that some of the stories are irrelevant, they won't believe them and that fact will drive it out of the marketplace.

Mayer and Abramson reviewed your book. I thought that was very interesting because they had to be working on the book at the same time. That's not the way that's usually done. You said that. That was very rare.

No, they did say they were conducting some kind of research or that they had conducted research. They didn't say they were writing a complete book. It was an odd assignment choice because clearly they had an interest. They were not just dispassionate reviewers.

I would say that historians do the same thing. We look at the evidence and we interpret it differently. We often come to radically different conclusions.

Speaking for myself, I tried to strip away racial politics, the sexual harassment issue — all those things that were driving the Anita Hill confrontation — and boil it down as much as possible to the question of which of the two was more credible. And there's some room for interpretation there obviously, and someone could take the same material and reach some different conclusions.

But I don't think Mayer and Abramson — we're not working from the same factual base. Their approach is more ideological. When there was evidence that didn't really fit, they did not deal with it effectively in the book. I would like to have seen the material that I presented rebutted or to have seen a competent attempt at rebutting it, but what they tended to do was when they got into a difficult area for Anita Hill, they glossed over it and they didn't actually deal with the facts. So, that's really how the books are different, as I see it.

So you didn't use their approach?

Right. People find that hard to believe. I remember watching the hearings at the *Washington Times* in my office and eight or nine reporters came in and we were all gathered around it for the first day of testimony. I was certainly on the fence then. I didn't know Clarence Thomas. I didn't know anybody who knew him, and I didn't think he was the greatest witness in the first round of hearings. I thought he was hedging a bit, but I understood why he had to take that position. If he was really candid, then he would have come across like Bork.

But anyway, I was no big supporter of Clarence Thomas or defender. Anita Hill seemed to be a compelling witness. By the end of the week, though, I did not think her witnesses were that strong. I didn't think she'd proved the case at the end of the weekend, although, if I was asked my opinion, I would have said that something happened, or something like what she said happened. But since she didn't prove it, he shouldn't be denied confirmation. That probably would have been my personal view.

It wasn't until much later that I became convinced there was virtually no truth in the central allegations that she made on a number of fronts. I questioned her credibility. I knew I could find other witnesses or public documents that contradicted her various points, and when you finished with that, you had somebody who didn't have a high level of credibility.

On Thomas' side you couldn't really do that. You can't really find any discrepancies. You can't poke holes in his account the way you can in hers. You're talking about what happened or what was alleged to have happened between two people ten years ago with no witnesses. All you really got is the witness' credibility. I don't think any damage was done to Thomas in that sense.

What direction do you predict investigative journalism will go in the twenty-first century?

CNN has given so much coverage to breaking news that the print media is going to be less and less depended upon to give the public its first take on the news. I guess as far as political coverage goes, you'd have to predict that the "no holds barred approach" to journalism will still be around and everything will continue to be fair game. Reporters will continue to go to wherever the president is from and dig through events of his life thirty years ago. That's just a political reality now.

Notes

1. One of the most obvious examples of David Brock's thorough research occupies a place of honor along the wall of the *American Spectator*— the cover of the magazine's January 1994 edition, which features a tiptoeing Bill Clinton, shoes in hand, silhouetted by moonlight, accompanied by a tomcat, with the legend "His Cheatin' Heart, David Brock in Little Rock." Other covers criticize Iran-Contra special prosecutor Lawrence Walsh and the Clintons' tax returns.

2. David Brock, *The Real Anita Hill: The Untold Story* (New York: Free Press, 1993). This book was on the *New York Times* best seller list for three months and has been through seven printings.

3. President George Bush nominated Clarence Thomas, a federal court judge, to the U.S. Supreme Court in August 1991; Hill and Thomas had worked together a decade earlier at the Equal Employment Opportunity Commission.

4. Brock, *Anita Hill*, 386.

5. Brock, *Anita Hill*, 13; Brock's critics are many; among the most outspoken are Jane Mayer and Jill Abramson, who in 1994 published their own study of the confirmation battle, *Strange Justice*. Rosa Parks challenged segregation in Montgomery, Alabama, in 1954-1955 by helping to lead a boycott of the city's segregated bus system.

6. Edna Buchanan formerly reported for the *Miami Herald* newspaper.

7. See *Collegiate Journalist* 27, no. 2 (Fall 1990), "A College Newspaper's Encounter with Watergate."

8. In one of President Ronald Reagan's uses of military muscle against Marxist outposts in the Western Hemisphere, he authorized the invasion of the Caribbean island of Grenada in September 1983.

9. William Safire of the *New York Times* labeled First Lady Hillary Rodham Clinton "a congenital liar" in a January 1996 column; Robert Novak writes a conservative column with Robert Evans.

10. Howard Kurtz, the *Washington Post*'s media critic, wrote this column in May 1995.

11. Nina Totenburg of the Public Broadcasting System was one of Anita Hill's chief defenders.

12. *The American Spectator* (January 1994).

13. See the Douglas Frantz interview. Frantz was at the *L.A. Times* when Brock delved into President Clinton's philandering.

14. Howard Kurtz, *Media Circus* (New York: Times Books, 1993).

15. A recent examination of Jefferson's views on the press appears in Willard Sterne Randall, *Thomas Jefferson: A Life* (New York: Henry Holt, 1993).

12

Brian Ross
Big Stories from Simple Pictures

> I believe strongly that you must master production to be good in TV. It's not good enough just to have the story. If we haven't mastered the art of taping, editing, writing for television, of the production and pacing so it doesn't get boring, all those ingredients that make a story interesting, if you haven't mastered that, it does not really matter.

In the corner of the ABC Investigative Unit is the office of Brian Ross, the correspondent the unit is built around. It's simply furnished, sparse in fact, and his window faces the building across the street. After nearly two decades with NBC, Ross moved to ABC several years ago, and in doing so, gave up an office that looked down on the famous Rockefeller skating rink. Making the move wasn't easy for Ross, but now, the view seems to be the biggest thing he misses.

Yet the photographs and awards on the office walls give away the man and the nature of his job. Above the couch is a photograph of a younger Ross seated in an airliner, a tight smile upon his face. Next to it is a photograph from the next day, his face badly bruised but with a bigger smile. He'd been aboard a hijacked airliner in Honduras, and his reporter status almost cost him his life.[1]

Another photograph shows an aging American standing outside a Cuban villa. Ross and his crew had found the elusive financier and reputed drug king Robert Vesco, despite Fidel Castro's claims that he wasn't in the country.[2] Getting the film was one thing; getting out of Cuba was yet another adventure.

His achievements and adventures are a stark contrast to Brian Ross the person. Handsome and soft spoken, Ross can disappear into a New York City crowd as another successful banker or businessman, although his midwestern roots show in his manner and his voice. He has established himself, however, as one of the country's most feared and respected investigative reporters, using television as his medium and the telling pictures as his proof.

Ross was born and raised in Highland Park, Illinois, a suburb of Chicago. He started in radio while in high school and soon got a taste of the thrills and pressures of investigative reporting. He got his degree from the University of Iowa, although he admits he was more interested in reporting than in the studies.

His first television job came in Waterloo, Iowa, and he quickly moved up to Miami, Cleveland, and finally to NBC. It was his investigative reporting that got him his network break in 1976, and he's remained at that level ever since.

Ross has won every major award, including the DuPont, George Polk, Sigma Delta Chi, and the National Headliner Awards. Yet he sees such honors as a team effort and quickly acknowledges the producers and photographers involved in each. His long association with NBC producer Ira Silverman ended only when Silverman retired and Ross moved to ABC. Ross credits Silverman with taking a young reporter and helping him to refine his skills and learn how to get a controversial story through the network bureaucracy and on the air.

His colleagues in the investigative unit are constantly working on a number of stories, for they serve many ABC programs, including "Day One," "Nightline," "PrimeTime Live," "20/20," and "World News Tonight with Peter Jennings." The multitude of outlets and the ability to craft long reports is one of the major reasons Ross joined ABC.

We settled in with cups of deli coffee in his office and talked briefly of current and former colleagues. He left the door open and warmly greeted each member of the unit as they arrived for work. It was obvious to the visitor that they were delighted to be part of the operation and that Ross was the key person to its success. After discussing his background, we started to explore the craft of the television investigative reporter.

* * *

When did you first say you were an investigative reporter?

I don't know that I've ever said that that's what I am. You can have an academic debate on whether that's a redundant term, and I think that probably what it means is that you are spending more time on more difficult topics. I think it's the same skills applied with greater intensity.

Do you feel that all reporting involves investigative work?

In some ways that's what we're really doing, we're asking questions. When you get into what has come to be known as investigative reporting, I think that's when you are in areas that are more difficult, can't be done quickly, require a commitment of time, extra energy. I guess it's more when the editor says we're going to give you the time to go after this, that's when you become one. If you're a reporter, you're a reporter, I think. I would cover any story the same way, essentially. I guess I'm known as an investigative reporter because I tend to go after stories that you've never heard of before, do original reporting, and take on wrongdoers. It's not really a feature thing.

When did you first start doing that?

I guess the first time I was fired. I'd just finished high school, and I was working for WEEF, the local radio station in Highland Park, Illinois, and I covered one of the local city council meetings. There was a councilman who just missed seven, eight meetings in a row. I got on the phone, this was radio, called him at home and he was in the middle of a barbecue. I had one of my stringers go to the meeting, to make sure he wasn't there, and we called him. He's at a barbecue. I grilled him on why he was at a barbecue instead of at the meeting.

Unfortunately, he owned a big chain of gas stations, was a big advertiser, and he pulled his advertising. I was fired; no ifs, ands, buts about it. I was rehired two months later because it

Brian Ross. Courtesy of Frank Micelotta/ABC.

seemed like they needed me. Again, it was quite a lesson on how things worked. It was also when I first realized that this was fun. This is great fun.

You have a lot of awards on your wall. Looking back, which stories did you like the most?

You know, that's very hard because I'll probably wind up saying the last one I did. Last night, I just finished a story on the failure of the FBI to investigate police brutality cases around the country. That was a terrific story. It took a lot of research, nobody wanted to talk about the FBI, and here I was doing a story that essentially attacked an organization that for years has been the principal source of stories for me. I've never hesitated to do that, but it was difficult. I knew going into this, that once this is broadcast, that may well be it for Tenth and Pennsylvania [the address of the FBI headquarters in Washington] for a while. I've gone through this with other federal agencies, and you just take them as they come. I can never tell you what's the best story.

One highlight would be the very first one I did in Cleveland as a local reporter. I was under contract to NBC News, which ran the news organization's local news divisions at that time — the farm teams, so to speak. That changed after I left there. We did a story in Cleveland about the local Teamster boss, Jackie Presser, who went on to become the national Teamster boss.[3] That local story won a DuPont Award, and I had the good fortune of doing that right at the time that Jimmy Hoffa was kidnapped and disappeared.[4]

And Dick Wald and others in New York at NBC said, "Is there anybody here who knows anything about the Teamsters?" Somebody said, there's this kid in Cleveland. I was twenty-five years old. I came in to receive the DuPont, and I met Julian Goodman and all of these people and was introduced to Dick Wald, Paul Friedman — those two men are now my bosses here at ABC — and Ira Silverman, who was a producer for "Nightly News."

They said, "We are going to try something that we've never, ever done before. We're going to try to do stories longer than a minute and a half on the Nightly News, and we might try to do two or three of them back to back. We want to borrow you for a couple of weeks to give Ira some of your background information."

That two weeks turned into a twenty-year career because I never went back to local reporting in Cleveland. In fact, I ended up being the on-air person for this five-part series that "Nightly News" called "Teamster Power," which won more DuPonts and a lot of other awards. That was my first appearance on the network, in a first-of-its-kind, five-part series. Now they have American Agenda, and everybody has that. It was invented by Wald and Friedman and Les Crystal back in nineteen hundred seventy-six, that idea of the longer forms.

In some ways, that was my favorite because that was such a launch for me. Five parts on the teamsters. I investigated the heck out of those guys. The more I did on Jackie Presser, the higher he went in the Teamster organization. Sort of like the dirtier he was made to appear, the more they liked him, which was consistent with the Teamsters, certainly in those days. That was a big highlight.

Then Ira and I were teamed up and did a lot of stories together. A big highlight. Other memorable ones include payola in the music industry. We did a long investigation, seven minutes on the "Nightly News," which is a lifetime when there's twenty-two minutes of content. We traced the Mafia involvement, and we essentially shut those guys down for six months, maybe much longer than that. That was a very big story.

We were in Colombia, South America, a lot during the height of the drug wars. We spent a lot of time in 1982 in Honduras.

You and Ira Silverman were a team for a long time. What was your relationship? How did you work together?

As two reporters. Two producers. We collaborated on everything, up to the point where someone had to narrate it.

What did he bring to the table and what did you bring to the table?

In the beginning, he brought everything to the table, I just brought energy. He's one of the smartest guys I've ever met or worked with in my life, a brilliant, terrific writer. Great story sense. He brought everything to the table. I was lucky enough to be teamed up with him. What he hadn't had at NBC was somebody who shared his passion. This is not a good job to work by yourself. It gets pretty lonely, people think you're crazy. Sometimes it's hard to defend when you're off working for six weeks or six months with no apparent results. When there are two of you, you at least have that to share. When you learn something, you want to share all that, bounce it off someone else. We had a great, great partnership.

He was already a "Nightly News" producer?

Yes. He knew the people; he had the rank. He knew what it took to make a fifteen-minute spot work or what it took to make a four-and-a-half-minute spot work. I didn't know any of that. I knew what it took to make a local piece work in Cleveland or Miami, which wasn't much, compared to what we had to know. I was very lucky to work with him.

I had one other little break right after the Teamster story. They did a little general assignment with me, and the next day there was a strike with NABET.[5] [This union] covered all the people on the desk, on the "Nightly News," the script editors and producers. So all of the bosses were suddenly on the rim. It was sink or swim then because they saw firsthand whether you were any good or not. It was fortunate for me that my work was given more scrutiny than ever by these bosses. Without Ira, I don't know if I would have broken in like that.

How did you wind up on a hijacked airplane?

I had been with some bail-bondsman in Miami. We'd done a series on bail bondsmen, and one of these guys called and said: "I've got a good story for you — what's going on with the Contras. I can get you in there, in their secret camps in Honduras, and you can go with them across the border into Nicaragua." No one had done that at that point.

I went down there with a cameraman, and we, in fact, went through the jungle and crossed the Coco River, watched booby traps and ambushes — that was supposed to be the dangerous part.[6] We get back out, and I'm with the tapes. I get on the plane in this little town in Honduras to go from Las Sava to San Pedro Sula, and from there by jet to New York. In fact, money passed hands to get me a seat on that plane. It was the last seat.

As it was landing in Las Sava, Honduras, after an hour flight, four guys jump up with dynamite and guns. The plane is hijacked. We were on there for three days and three nights. They took us to Tegucigalpa, the capital, and we sat on the runway there. They would fire off guns. One passenger had a heart attack. They separated the Americans from the Latins, the Norte Americanos up here and the rest back there. They were getting ready to blow the plane up.

The negotiations back and forth had gone awry. The U.S. government was putting pressure on the Hondurans not to negotiate. In principle, probably the right position, but I thought they could start their principle after I got off. It was very tough at the time because I thought I was going to die for some principle that didn't matter and I was convinced we were going to die.

On the third night, I made a last ditch suggestion to them. I said, "Those two Learjets out there are from NBC News, where I work." The issue was fifty thousand dollars, if you can imagine that. The Hondurans said you can't pay fifty thousand dollars in this country. I said you let everybody go, and you take this plane and fly me to Cuba. I can guarantee you that people from NBC will follow and bring fifty thousand dollars. If not, shoot me.

They went to the very back of the plane. It was the first time that they had left us unguarded. I decided that we had to get out of there. They'd shot so many holes in the plane that it would never take off.

We went out the windows. We got all but one of the Americans out. We went out, ran towards the terminal, I ran parallel with one of the wings. They started shooting, but didn't hit anybody. We got out.

How did you get on the Robert Vesco story? Did it take a long time to get it on the air?

It did. We got onto Vesco primarily because we started doing reporting on the Bahamas during the drug war. Corruption on the part of Lyndon Penland, who was then the prime minister. One of our favorite cameramen, Randy Fairborne, was in a helicopter that was covering some Haitian or Cuban refugees in the Bahamas. The Bahamians were forcing them back into the sea. They were shooting them from the air. When the crew tried to fly back to Miami, their plane, I believe, was shot down by Bahamian Defense Forces or by drug dealers. I believe they saw something.

After the plane disappeared, there was an announcement on Bahamian radio that they had found the wreckage. Then about four hours later, they said it was not true. That was it. The NBC crew was never seen or heard from again. We got information that they were shot down because they had seen a drug operation on an island involving the government. This launched us on a long, long search for the truth in the Bahamas. We uncovered the corruption in the Penland government, and I think this led to his eventually losing office.

The Royal Commission investigated and that led to Vesco. Vesco was one of the early people to pay off Penland for a safe haven, through a guy named Everett Bannister, who was the Penland bagman.

We got Bannister's son to talk to us, and we went there. After the first story, Penland's lawyer, F. Lee Bailey, warned me that we would be arrested for criminal libel if we ever set foot in the Bahamas again. I've not been back there since that story aired in nineteen eighty-two. I was burned in effigy.

That led us to Vesco. It became a passion to find this guy. Every two months we would have a report—he was here, he was there, the U.S. marshals almost captured him in an undercover sting. We were waiting in Tallahassee for two weeks for him to show up. They almost got him, but they missed him.

Then someone said they knew where Vesco was in Cuba. And a source drew a map for me on a piece of paper. He said when you get to Cuba, this is his house. Castro was sponsoring a conference urging all of the third world countries to renounce their debt to the United States, and he was encouraging news coverage. We arranged to get credentials to go into Cuba on that pretense.

By day, we would be at this conference. We rented one of the few cars you could find, over the objections of the other NBC people who were trying to cover the real conference. That was the big news, they were furious with us. They said, you're going to embarrass us, get us thrown out of the country. Most of the opposition came from the NBC people.

We had a driver named Israel. He was more than a driver, he was a watcher. He had just gotten back from Angola, was in the military. Ira would go off with Israel to shoot some shot of nothing, and I'd take the rental car with one of the people working with us, and we'd drive around and try to find this place. I took a wrong turn, and I realized that I was on the street. As I drove by, there was Vesco right in front of the house. I'd found him. No camera crew. Just my eyes. Drove around again, and by God, it was Vesco.

That night, we took Israel out for a blow-out dinner. Drank, drank, drank, big cigar, the whole thing. Then we said, Izzy, let's sleep in tomorrow. See you at noon at the hotel.

At four A.M., we rolled out in this little rental car. Cameraman Charlie Zacariah, soundman Bob Gonzolas, Ira, and me. Vesco's house faced an empty field; beyond that were houses. We went into this field, and set up in the weeds. We were there from four in the morning until noon. If you look at the picture over your head, that's the shot of Robert Vesco. That's the last time he's been seen publicly.

We got these shots, went back to the room, called New York and told them that we had material. They suggested that we should go back and interview him, go knock on his door. We said, "You know, Castro says he's not here, we're not in a friendly place, we're not going to do that." We had been warned that we could be arrested anytime and held.

We packed up and went to the airport. We had a private plane to take us back out. The next day the lead story on "Nightly News" was Robert Vesco in Cuba, despite Castro's denials. Castro went crazy, but it was a big, big story. Essentially, it came down to a minute and twenty seconds of videotape. In our reporting, that we knew where he was. Just to report it would have been one thing, but to have the pictures, to have the proof, was everything. It was very satisfying.

ABSCAM?[27]

That was the year I'd applied for, but did not get, the Neiman Fellowship. It was a big letdown. Thank God I didn't. At that time, I was still a fifty thousand dollars a year, very basic rate, correspondent. Money didn't matter, I was doing investigative stuff. We got a tip from two different sources that something big was coming down. They were stinging Congress. Then through a lot of hard work, and a lot of drinks, we got the address of the undercover house in Washington that the FBI had rented, where supposedly these Arabs lived. They were going to buy what they wanted from Congress. They'd been meeting congressmen there.

We set up with a Winnebago on cold February nights, night after night of shooting the comings and goings from this house. We're watching the FBI sting house. It was so cold that the orange juice we had froze up. But we got it. Now it came time for the thing to go on the air. The FBI was going to contact the congressmen and senators involved. That was the point at which we could go with our story. We had told then NBC president Bill Small about this on Thursday or Friday. He said, that doesn't sound right to me. Usually, when something like that happens, the Speaker goes up to the director and the story is killed, I don't think we should put too much into that. They didn't think the story could be ... like we were imagining this!

We kept working on it. That night, on the "Nightly News," they doubted the story. The FBI didn't doubt it. They were going crazy, chasing around for all these guys, and at one point they lost Pete Williams, the senator from New Jersey. That night the lead story was supposed to be a prison riot in Albuquerque. ABSCAM wasn't going to be the lead on NBC. They hadn't seen it on the wires, there was no talk of it. We hadn't told the Washington bureau chief anything about it because we felt that in Washington, they're all married to staff people. We brought camera crews from outside the city.

Sure enough, there was a problem in the transmission from Albuquerque, and the Frank Burkholtzer spot on the prison riot couldn't be fed. They were forced to lead with ABSCAM.

How about the Iraqi arms?[8]

Again, just good sources, people who we'd worked with on stories before. They said, "Would you be interested in this?" Indeed. Well, there's a place outside London that's the headquarters for this acquisition network. They're buying all of this nuclear stuff. We went to England for a long time, set up in this little house across from the pub on this little green and watched and watched the comings and goings. Then we got the word that the actual nuclear triggers were being shipped out of California on a particular day and date.

I flew to California, and we were able to figure out which box on which flight and to film this box going into the hold of the TWA jet for London. We shot that taking off. Then I caught the British Air flight about an hour behind it and chased it to London. The box went to the TWA freight place at Heathrow. They couldn't make the arrest until the people came to pick it up. Scotland Yard was all over the place. They didn't know we were there. We were watching them, waiting for the Iraqis to come pick it up. When they did come, we followed them.

Then I got a call from my source saying that they'd decided to back off the investigation for the moment. At that time a British nurse and a so-called British journalist, who was later hanged, were in custody in Baghdad. The English were afraid that if they went ahead with this case that they would definitely execute those people.

I flew back to New York with all of this terrific tape of everything that moved. Then two days later, they said there has been a mention of this on one of the other British networks. In fact, Pierre Salinger has done a forty-five-second standup on it for "Good Morning, America."[9] Well, the cat's out of the bag. Which is sometimes the best thing, to have the opposition take the bait.

We came on the "Nightly News" with everything.[10] The beginning, middle and end, chapter and verse. Here are the pictures. It was a huge, huge exclusive for us. Again, I couldn't help thinking of what we had. We had pictures of guys walking out of an office outside London, in a little suburb. Then we had a picture of a crate going up into an airplane, which by itself is nothing. But when you put it together without the pictures, it would not have been very effective, and without the words, the pictures would have been boring.

I've always thought there was the perfect example of what we do. An ordinary kind of shot, a guy at the airport takes a crate and puts it on the escalator and puts it on the plane. That's nothing. But when you know what you know about that, it's extremely dramatic.

Have you fought many battles with the networks to get your stories on the air?

I've fought many battles, none at ABC, but the day will probably come. A lot at NBC. When John DeLorean was arrested on cocaine charges in eighty-two, suddenly all they wanted on "Nightly News" were stories about cocaine, Hollywood, and so forth.[11] So we started working on a story.

We got a guy who had been a big drug dealer and drug user, who was in treatment and was persuaded that the best way for him to overcome his habit was to talk about it openly. He did. We sat down on camera, not in back light. He said yes, I used to deliver drugs. My rounds would first take me to Universal Studios, then over to what were called the Burbank Studios, Warner Brothers Studios, then to the NBC Commissary, in a concise, wonderful soundbite.

We put together the story, which ran four-and-a-half minutes. A great story. We send it in, and on the first pass the lawyers approve it and it's all set to go. Then somehow this word gets up higher. A call comes back. You know, I think all you have to do is clip out the thing about the NBC Commissary, and the story is all set. No, yes, no, yes. It was a big war back and forth.

Then word of this impasse reached the *Washington Post*, which ran a story about it. It wasn't leaked by Ira or me; somebody put it out. Rubin Frank, the president of NBC News at the time, was quoted as saying he felt that it was "incomplete journalism" and that what we should do is go off for three or four months and investigate it fully. There's more there to be told. I think that was a dodge. I don't think that. I know it. At the time that happened, I was furious with NBC. I talked all I could about it publicly, they still tried to kill it. In the end, the story ran as written, with the reference to NBC, they didn't touch the thing. But they were afraid of an FCC investigation of drug usage at NBC. I think they were afraid that some of their big, important stars who were rumored to be cocaine users would be implicated, and that may well have been true.

So Rubin Frank was under pressure from above?[12]

From [NBC president Bob] Mulholland. Very big pressure. He later apologized to me because at that same time [ABC president] Roone Arledge first came knocking at my door.[13] I was so unhappy. It was the first time I'd run into that sort of corporate nonsense. I think NBC would look good broadcasting a story like that. Obviously, everybody has got problems, it's not like NBC would be immune. Why would they be? They didn't see it that way at first.

Rubin Frank and I were at the University Club. I said we're going to work at ABC. Roone [Arledge] really put the heat on, and it was very down to the wire. In the end, Rubin invited me to the University Club for a drink, and I felt terrible. Here was a man I really admired in the business, one of the great men of television news. I was thinking, who was I to sit here and demand that Rubin Frank apologize? I thought, on the other hand, I'm right about this story, and I may only be thirty-one years old, but I think I know about this story, and I did not think that was wrong.

He apologized, I stayed, and infuriated Roone Arledge, but a decade later I made the move. That was one example, not the only one, of corporate interference.

Didn't you have a showdown over a WalMart story?

That story was produced by Rhonda Schwartz. We did a big story about Wal-Mart. Wal-Mart was selling clothes labeled "Made in the USA." They were actually made by bad plants overseas, particularly in Bangladesh, at a place where there had been a fire a few months earlier that had killed forty-two children.

We went in there with cameras, hidden and otherwise, and we saw eight, nine, ten-year-old children making clothes, and they're sewing in the Wal-Mart label right there. I couldn't believe it when I saw it.

We then arranged an interview with the chairman of Wal-Mart, David Glass, and Rhonda had been out to Arkansas to set it up. They treated her, and this was their mistake, like she was "just a woman." They ended up giving her to the secretary of the PR guy. He didn't have time to deal with such a low-life as Rhonda. Their mistake to underestimate Rhonda Schwartz. They never asked what the interview was about. They just assumed — it was around Christmas time — and we'd shot in their stores. We started by asking what makes you successful, about the "Made in the USA" ads, and I asked, "Is everything made in the USA?" He said, unless it says otherwise. Then I asked, what about this? What about this? What about these pictures? Here are the dead children.

At which point he walked out of the interview and went to his phone. He didn't call Michael Gardner, who was president of NBC News. He didn't call Bob Wright [president of NBC]. He called Bob Welch, chairman of General Electric. At which point, Bob Wright issues an order that the interview will be done again.

I thought that there were two ways to play this. I could fight this, the story would never get on, and I'd have to quit. So Rhonda and I strategized and decided we'd treat this as a continuation of the interview, that what we'd shot already we could use. I said to Glass, I know you're very busy. Let's just pick up with it where we were, and we got back to the interview. They were stuck with it. They hated it.

In the end, I will say, they ran the story. I was told by a top NBC news guy that Wal-Mart told Welch that if that story runs, all GE products come off the shelves the next day, one hundred seventy-five million dollars worth of products every year. They put it through the kind of checking you never get, but that was not a problem. The story ran as written. They had Rick Cotton, the general counsel to NBC, to come in and personally go over the story, word-by-word and line-by-line.

The only reason they did it was because they felt there was a threat to GE. No one else could demand that kind of scrutiny. If my story was about a small-time guy, it wouldn't happen. On the other hand, if the story is about a big corporation like Wal-Mart, it is certainly in NBC's interest to make sure that everything is there, that all i's are dotted and t's are crossed, and they were.

Production is obviously an important part of what you do. How do you balance the amount of time for research and reporting and getting the pictures in, putting the whole thing together?

I believe strongly that you must master production to be good in TV. It's not good enough just to have the story. If we haven't mastered the art of taping, editing, writing for television, of the production and pacing so it doesn't get boring, all those ingredients that make a story interesting, if you haven't mastered that, it doesn't really matter. I guess some stories would overcome that, but most stories wouldn't be as strong as you want them to be.

I always feel after I finish the reporting and shooting that it's really a heavy burden to write it and tell it right. In the telling is how it comes out. You can tell a story a hundred different ways, and no one of them is right, but you try to pick out the best one. I really feel that it's very, very important. I think that I'm fortunate to have a lot of experience in local news, just doing a lot of it and shooting myself, editing, working in radio, where I got a sense of audio, which is very important.

In newspapers, other people do the layout and the graphics. In television, you're doing all of it. I feel like we're setting the type and writing the headlines. We're laying out the front page when we do our stories. The reporter does all of that in television. In newspapers, you do the reporting and turn it in, and somebody else creates how it looks. If that paper looks boring, no one is going to read it. If you ignore production, it's at your peril.

Your advice to people who think they'd like to be an investigative reporter?

Don't be afraid of being fired. I guess that's where I started. Go after the biggest target you can and don't be afraid of losing your sources. That may be the most important thing. When you start out, and you have a friend at the police station or city hall, to do a negative story about their department or them, you figure you're cut off, that you'll never do another story on them. That's not true.

Over the years, your work comes to speak for itself. No sacred cows. There's that real practical thing as a reporter. If you're getting good leads from people, do you want to bite the hand that feeds you? And I guess I'd say yes. If the story is there. It is not your obligation to protect anybody.

How many stories are you working on now?
Ten or twelve.

How many assistants do you have?
I wouldn't call them assistants. Colleagues. There will never be another Ira, but there are four producers, two field producers, who work with me in this unit, and we're all working on stories. I'm the reporter on each of them, and they're honchoing the stories in some way. They've developed some of them from leads I've gotten. We try to work them together.

We try to clone the relationship Ira and I had, in terms of doing these magazine pieces. They take a lot more time, a lot more effort, but it's a much nicer place to do the work because we have the time on the air. Ira and I used to spend two or three months, and then we'd have two or three minutes on "Nightly News." Here you have twelve to fifteen minutes, or two-part stories, twenty-four to thirty minutes each. I like the longer format because there is more time to tell the story. The interesting details, all the things you learn that just won't fit in to two or three or seven minutes. That was the longest story we ever did on "Nightly News"—seven minutes. It was certainly one of the longest individual stories ever on "Nightly News," and yet a seven-minute story now to me is—you can't get going.

How important is writing?
Key. Very, very important. Simple, clean writing. Start simple, stay simple. Read *Elements of Style*.[14] I was lucky. I had Ira and a very, very tough editor at "Nightly News," Gil Milstein. Merciless! I used to come out of there soaked with sweat, literally. It was great. Tough editors. Don't take the easy way out. The path of least resistance is not a good path, I don't think.

They'll hate to hear this at NBC, but in a way I came here because I felt—not that I was getting lazy—but there weren't high expectations for the quality of work. I didn't find that at NBC. I didn't think my colleagues were as demanding and tough as I wanted them to be. I really wanted to be continually challenged. I thought this was no time to slack off and be comfortable. Then you are not doing your best work, I guarantee you. If you're floating through life, do something else.

I came here and it was tough. Fighting for airtime with Diane and Barbara and Peter—that's the big leagues, and that's where I wanted to play.[15] I think it is always best to go for the tough stuff.

In terms of real practical advice for this kind of work, it's all there. Every city has its own scandals right in front of you. Stick to principle. I was at local stations where it was very tough to do these stories. I did it. Avoid doing the fashion shows and the junk, which doesn't win you favors with a lot of news directors.

How important are the basics?
Very, very important. It's very simple. It's the ability to pick up the phone

and spend the day on the phone just asking questions. One person leads you to another and another. I don't think there's a magic too it. Persistence more than anything. You do the simple stuff again and again and again. You just don't stop.

So you didn't waste your time in Waterloo?
Not a waste at all. It's absolutely essential. Do you have to stay there for ten years? No. But you should be there. I think that if you haven't covered those local zoning board meetings and tried to figure out what that's all about, you probably haven't done enough work. I hate to see people start just at the network. There are two paths. You can start at the local stations and work your way up, or you can start at the network.

At ABC, they hire people from print. They hire them because people in print have done that basic work. You should forget about the so-called glamour and the large salaries that sometimes you can make in television because that will not sustain you. When you are sitting here at two in the morning trying to figure out how to rewrite this thing, they can't pay you enough to do that. You have to really love it.

Let's talk about the process of reporting. You really see it as all the same?
I really do. I see it as the most simple, but essential, thing. Pick up the phone and go see somebody and get the facts. Of course, you have to figure out the right questions to ask and the order in which you ask them. Sometimes you don't want to show your hand at first, exactly where you come from. You want to develop, have people be as forthcoming as possible. You are not there to get prepared statements, you are there to get information. But it's really pretty simple. You just keep asking questions. Don't give up. If you don't know, is there somebody else who does know? Sometimes it's like the fifth person, and the story might be ninety degrees off from what you thought it was going to be. But it's there. I can't tell you how many times that has happened.

I guess the other key thing is cultivating sources. As you get people who are reliable, stick with them, always be talking to them. Ira used to say, and he was right, contact these sources, talk to them when it's not prime time for them. So when your buddy is in the middle of the biggest Mafia investigation in history, everyone is calling him. That is not the time to cultivate that source. He can't do it. It's like, eight months before that when you had drinks and dinner with him, and nothing really hot is happening, but you are just interesting and you are talking — that's when you make that connection. Then he'll take your call and nobody else's call.

I think Ira and I were successful as a team because we would recognize that and stay with those sources. Because we weren't split up, I wouldn't go off and work with another producer, or Ira with another reporter. Sometimes that drops between the cracks. When you have teams like this, you keep working and working. The trigger story came off of sources from other stories that had nothing to do with that kind of thing.

Does it make a difference when you're on the phone to say you're Brian Ross of ABC News or NBC News? Does being at the network help?

A lot of times it can be a hindrance. People get their guard up. The network's calling! I used to think, when I was in Waterloo, Iowa, that if I could ever say Brian Ross, NBC News, the world would open. That's just not true. Sometimes you get more access, but very rarely. You can't live off that. That's not going to work.

The best reporters are the local reporters who are closest to the story. What works best is an understanding of what you're dealing with. In fact, I find that when you have been tough and hard on a story, that gets the attention of the FBI or the Justice Department more than if you're in there, you're their buddies. You almost want them to be a little afraid of you, respect you. Be a straight shooter. Don't be unfair. But if you have been fair and tough. That's what I've always thought. Tough and fair. That's what you want to be.

What does Brian Ross want in ten years?

Maybe to have a better view. I hope I'm doing the same thing. There's nothing else I want to do but keep doing these stories. I have the perfect setup here. As it's arranged here, we have a little unit that works together, and we do stories for "20/20" and "Primetime" and "Nightline" and "World News" and "Good Morning, America." It couldn't be a better arrangement. I don't want to anchor or that kind of stuff. I just want to do what I'm doing. If my legs hold out, you'll find me right here.

Notes

1. "NBC Nightly News," 1982.
2. "NBC Nightly News," 1982. Robert Vesco was an international financier who was reportedly involved in drugs and money laundering. During decades of economic sanctions by the United States, Castro gave people like Robert Vesco sanctuary in exchange for hard currency.
3. Jackie Pressler was one of the key Teamster Union bosses in Cleveland. He was one of Jimmy Hoffa's main rivals for the national leadership of the union.
4. Former Teamsters Union boss Jimmy Hoffa disappeared from a Detroit restaurant in 1975, and his body was never found.
5. NABET is the National Association of Broadcast Engineers and Technicians. The 1976 strike hit NBC hard because NABET also had jurisdiction over writers and editors. Management personnel took over those jobs until a settlement was reached.
6. The Coco River forms the border between Honduras and Nicaragua.
7. In 1980 the FBI established a sting operation to trap corrupt members of the U.S. Congress. Undercover agents posed as wealthy Arab businessmen and set up the deals and payoffs, thus the name "ABSCAM."
8. In 1990, Ross reported that Iraq was attempting to buy triggers for nuclear devices. This was only a few months before Iraq invaded Kuwait, which led to the Persian Gulf War and the eventual liberation of Kuwait by an international military force led by the United States.

9. Pierre Salinger was press secretary for President John F. Kennedy and later became a correspondent for ABC News based in Paris.

10. "NBC Nightly News," 1990.

11. John DeLorean was a top automotive industry figure who before his arrest and trial had created and marketed a luxury sports car that bore his name. His case gained national attention when videotapes from a hidden camera showed him receiving cocaine from undercover agents. DeLorean was acquitted on the charges after a high-profile trial.

12. Rubin Frank was then president of NBC News. Frank is highly respected for his integrity and journalistic skills.

13. Roone Arledge is credited with turning ABC around and developing a top-flight news department. Many of the top ABC correspondents and producers were hired from other networks.

14. Strunk and White, *The Elements of Style*. New York: Macmillan, 1959.

15. Diane Sawyer, Barbara Walters, and Peter Jennings. All are high profile reporters and anchors for ABC News.

Selected Bibliography

Books

Adams, James Ring, and Douglas Frantz. *A Full Service Bank*. New York: Pocket Books, 1992.
Bernstein, Carl, and Bob Woodward. *All the President's Men*. New York: Random House, 1974.
Brock, David. *The Real Anita Hill: The Untold Story*. New York: Free Press, 1993.
Burnham, David. *Above the Law: Secret Diaries, Political Fixes, and Other Misadventures of the U.S. Department of Justice*. New York: Scribner's, 1996.
_____. *A Law Unto Itself: Power, Politics, and the I.R.S.* New York: Random House, 1990.
_____. *The Rise of the Computer State*. New York: Random House, 1990.
Carter, Jimmy. *Keeping Faith*. New York: Bantam Books, 1982.
Clifford, Clark, and Richard Holbrooke. *Counsel to the President*. New York: Random House, 1991.
Clurman, Richard M. *Beyond Malice: The Media's Years of Reckoning*. New York: New American Library, 1990.
Contemporary Authors, Susan Trotsky, ed. Vol. 126. Detroit, Mich.: Gale Research, 1989.
D'Souza, Dinesh. *Illiberal Education*. New York: Free Press, 1991.
Filler, Louis. *Crusaders for American Liberalism*. New York: Harcourt, Brace, 1939.
Frantz, Douglas, and David McKean. *Friends in High Places: The Rise and Fall of Clark Clifford*. Boston: Little, Brown, 1995.
Gaines, William. *Investigative Reporting for Print and Broadcast*. Chicago: Nelson-Hall, 1994.
Garment, Suzanne. *Scandal: The Crisis of Mistrust in American Politics*. New York: Times Books, 1991.
Greenfield, Jeff. *Playing to Win: An Insider's Guide to Politics*. New York: Simon and Schuster, 1980.
Halberstam, David. *The Best and the Brightest*. New York: Random House, 1970.
Hersh, Seymour. *The Price of Power: Kissinger in the Nixon White House*. New York: Summit Books, 1983.
Hess, Stephen. *The Ultimate Insiders: U.S. Senators in the National Media*. Washington: The Brooking Institution, 1986.
Isaacson, Walter, and Evan Thomas. *The Wise Men: Six Men and the World They Made*. New York: Simon and Schuster, 1986.
Jameson, Kathleen Hall. *Dirty Politics: Deception, Distraction, and Democracy*. New York: Oxford University Press, 1992.
Karnow, Stanley. *Vietnam: A History*. New York: Viking, 1983.
Kessler, Ronald. *Inside the White House*. New York: Pocket Books, 1995.
Kurtz, Howard. *Media Circus*. New York: Times Books, 1993.
Kutler, Stanley I. *The Wars of Watergate*. New York: W. W. Norton, 1990.
Manchester, William. *The Glory and the Dream: A Narrative History of America, 1932–1972*. Boston: Little, Brown, 1974.

Matthews, Christopher. *Hardball: How Politics Is Played*. New York: Simon and Schuster, 1988.
Mayer, Jill, and Jane Abramson. *Strange Justice*. New York: Random House, 1995.
Mayer, Martin. *Making News*. Garden City, N.J.: Doubleday, 1987.
Moldea, Dan. *Dark Victory: Ronald Reagan, MCA and the Mob*. New York: Viking, 1986.
____. *Interference: How Organized Crime Influences Professional Football*. New York: William Morrow, 1989.
____. *The Hoffa Wars: The Rise and Fall of Jimmy Hoffa*. New York: S.P.I. Books, 1983.
____. *The Hunting of Cain: A True Story of Money, Greed, and Fratricide*. New York: Atheneum, 1983.
____. *The Killing of Robert F. Kennedy: An Investigation of Motive, Means, and Opportunity*. New York: W. W. Norton, 1995.
Murphy, Bruce Allen. *Fortay: The Rise and Ruin of a Supreme Court Justice*. New York: William Morrow, 1988.
Neustadt, Richard E. *Presidential Power and the Modern Presidents*. New York: MacMillan, 1990.
Peck, Janice. *The Gods of Televangelism*. New Jersey: Hampton Press, 1993.
Posner, Gerald. *The Bio-Assassins*. New York: McGraw-Hill, 1988.
____. *Case Closed: Lee Harvey Oswald and the Assassination of J.F.K.* New York: Random House, 1993.
____. *Hitler's Children: Sons and Daughters of Leaders of the Third Reich Talk About Their Fathers and Themselves*. New York: Random House, 1991.
____. *Warlords of Crime: Chinese Secret Societies — The New Mafia* (New York: McGraw Hill, 1988).
Ramsey, Austin. *Channels of Power: The Impact of Television on American Politics*. New York: Banic Books, 1983.
Randall, William Sterne. *Thomas Jefferson: A Life*. New York: Henry Holt, 1993.
Rather, Dan, and Gary Gates. *The Palace Guard*. New York: Harper and Row, 1974.
Roberts, Chalmers. *First Rough Draft: A Journalist's Journal of Our Times*. New York: Praeger, 1973.
Roosevelt, Theodore. *Presidential Addresses and State Papers*. New York: Review of Reviews Company, 1910.
Ross, Shelley. *Fall from Grace: Sex, Scandal, and Corruption in American Politics*. New York: Ballantine, 1988.
Sabato, Larry J. *Feeding Frenzy: How Attack Journalism Has Transformed American Politics*. New York: Free Press, 1991.
Safire, William. *Before the Fall: An Inside View of the Pre-Watergate White House*. Garden City, N.Y.: Doubleday, 1975.
____. *Safire's Political Dictionary*. New York: Random House, 1978.
Schanberg, Sydney H. *The Death and Life of Dith Pran*. New York: Elisabeth Sifton Books and Penguin Books, 1985.
Schlesinger, Arthur M., Jr., ed. *The Almanac of American History*. New York: G. P. Putnam's Sons, 1983.
____. *The Cycles of American History*. Boston: Houghton Mifflin, 1986.
Smith, Page. *Killing the Spirit: Higher Education in America*. New York: Viking, 1990.
Solomon, Robert, and Jon Solomon. *Up the University: Re-Creating Higher Education in America*. Reading, Mass.: Addison-Wesley, 1993.
Steffens, Lincoln. *Autobiography of Lincoln Steffens*. New York: Harcourt, Brace, 1931.
Ullman, John, and Jan Colbert. *The Reporter's Handbook: An Investigator's Guide to Documents and Techniques*. New York: St. Martin's Press, 1990.
Weiner, Tim. *The Blank Check: The Pentagon's Black Budget*. New York: Warner Books, 1990.

Wilson, Harold S. *McClure's Magazine and the Muckrakers*. Princeton: Princeton University Press, 1970.

Magazine and Newspaper Articles

Acohido, Byron. "Computer With Wings — Boeing's Ultracomplex 777 Flies into Debate Over Technology Hazards." *Seattle Times*, June 5, 1995.
____. "El Al 747-200 Crashes in Amsterdam." *Seattle Times*, October 5, 1992.
____. "Flight 811 Lost a Cargo Door and Nine Lives — Boeing Is Still Wrestling with Solutions and Settlements." *Seattle Times*, January 5, 1992.
____. "Lauda Air 767-300 Crashes in Thailand." *Seattle Times*, May 27, 1991.
____. "U.S. Air Crash: The Clues Are In." *Seattle Times*, January 29, 1995.
Anonymous. "The Death of a President." *Economist*, October 9, 1993, p. 95.
Case, Tony. "Investigative Reporting: Have Cost Cuts Killed It?" *Editor and Publisher*, December 26, 1992.
Farwell, John Aloysius. "Dan Moldea's Lonely Beat." *Boston Globe*, August 31, 1995, pp. 57–58.
Frank, Jeffrey A. "Who Shot J.F.K.? The 30-Year Mystery." *Washington Post*, October 31, 1993, p. 4.
Grossman, Lawrence K. "CBS, 60 Minutes, and the Unseen Interview." *Columbia Journalism Review* (January/February, 1996).
Halverson, Guy. "The Case for a Lone Gunman in J.F.K. Killing." *Christian Science Monitor*, September 28, 1993, p. 13.
Lundstrom, Marjie. "Clayton College." *Denver Monthly Magazine* (March, 1981).
____. "Diary of a Teen-aged Prostitute." *Denver Monthly Magazine* (November 1989).
____ and Rochelle Sharpe. "Getting Away with Murder." Four-part series. Gannet News Service Broadsheet, 1990.
McHegan, David. "The Author Dares to Claim There Was No Conspiracy." *Boston Globe*, November 2, 1993, p. 61.
McManus, James J. "Book Closed on J.F.K. Murder." *Atlanta Journal and Constitution*, October 17, 1993, p. 10.
Parshell, Gerald. "The Man with a Deadly Smirk." *U.S. News and World Report*, August 30, 1993, pp. 62–98.
Radolf, Andrew. "Inquirer Upheld." April 16, 1988, pp. 9–10.
Ross, Kathy. "Still an Unthinkable Thought." *New York Times Book Review*, November 21, 1993, p. 18.
Schanberg, Sydney H. "The Death and Life of Dith Pran." *New York Times Magazine*, January 20, 1980.

Index

ABC Television 157–158, 169–170
ABSCAM 164
ACE Construction Company 124
Adams, James Ring 64
African Americans 129
Agency France Press 80
Airplane safety 66, 70, 107–109
Alabama 33
Albuquerque Tribune 133, 145–147
Alfred K. Lowenstein Award 75
Altman, Robert 67
American Bar Association 92
American Spectator 147
Anderson, John 5, 125
Angleton, James 98
Angola 163
Argentina 51
Arledge, Roone 165–166
Army Times 12
Aspen Institute Program 91
Associated Press 100–101
Atlanta Constitution 33

Bagdikian, Ben 99, 102
Bagladesh 76
Bahamas 162
Bailey, F. Lee 162
Bank of Commerce and Credit International *see* BCCI
Barry, Marion 129
Baruch, Barnard 133
Baton Rouge, Louisiana 21–23, 28–29, 32
Bay of Pigs 32
BCCI 63–64
Benard, Sherman 27, 33, 98, 136
Berkowitz, Mark 51
Bernstein, Carl 3
Bernstein, Pam 54

Blumenthol, Ralph 66
Boeing Corporation 103–104, 110–115
Book of the Month Club 122
Boston, Massachusetts 22
Botsky, Ivan 64
Bradlee, Ben 100
Brandeis, Louis D. 3
Brill, Steve 121
Brock, David 3, 70
Bundy, Ted 35
Bunyan, John 3
Bureaucracies 93–94
Burkholtzer, Frank 164
Bush, George 12, 67

Cable News Network *see* CNN
Cambodia 75, 77–81
Camden, New Jersey 7
Carter, Jimmy 12
Casey, William 33
Castro, Fidel 157, 163
CBS Television 88, 91, 129
Centers for Disease Control 43
Central America 32
Central Intelligence Agency *see* CIA
Champion Insurance Company 27
Chicago Tribune 69, 72
Chico, California 21
Child abuse 41–44
China 77
Churchill, Winston 133
CIA 5, 15, 17, 49, 52, 60, 98, 99
Civil rights 97
Clayton College for Boys 38
Cleveland, Ohio 159
Cleveland Browns 129
Cleveland Plain Dealer 99
Clifford, Clark 3, 63–64, 67, 71–72

177

Index

Clinton, Bill 52, 54, 69–71, 99, 146, 150
CNN 154
Cocaine 165
Coffee, Shelby 70
Cold war 141
Collier's 97
Colombia 52, 160
Columbia University Journalism School 5
Committee to Protect Journalists 52
Communications 91
Communism 97
Computers 91, 96
Conservatives 148
Contras 161
Cooke, Jack Kent 129–130
Cotton, Rick 167
Crime commission 92
Criminal justice 92, 104
Cronkite, Walter 80
Cuba 49, 162
Current Affair 37

Dade County, Florida 22
Dallas Times-Herald 79, 104
Danner, Frederick 57
Dawalamie County, California 21
DEA 54
Death squads 16
Deep Throat 8, 98, 115, 125
DeLorean, John 165
Democrats 124
Denver, Colorado 35, 38–39, 41
Denver Monthly Magazine 37
Denver Post 40
DeSousa, Dennis 148
Detroit Free Press 125
Douglas, William O. 63
Drug trafficking 29
DuPont Award 159

Eisenhower, Dwight D. 12
El Salvador 16
Environmental Protection Agency *see* EPA
EPA 92
Eskenazi, Gerald 117
Ethics 16, 47, 63
Evans, Harold 58
Everett, Washington 104

FAA 107–110, 114
Faure, Gregory 40, 46–48
FBI 49, 60, 93, 128, 163–164
Federal Aviation Administration *see* FAA
Federal Witness Protection Program 127
First Amendment 2–3, 28, 134
Flaubert, Gustave 14
Fort Collins, Colorado 35–36
Fortas, Abe 32
Fortune 500 106
Frantz, David 3
Freedom Forum 92
Fortune Magazine 106
Freedom of Information Act 52, 141
Freelance journalism 58
Friedman, Paul 160
Fry, Don 48

Gambling 22
Gannett News Service 40, 43
Gardner, Michael 166
George Polk Memorial Award 75, 157
Gettysburg Address 8
Glass, David 166
Glenn, John 1
Golden Typewriter Award 92
Gonzales, Bob 163
Goodman, Julian 160
Gore, Al 67
Green, Doug 27
Grenada invasion 147
Guatemala 16
Gulf War 35, 67

Hammett, Dashiell 15
HBO 29
Helms, Richard 33
Heroin 50, 54, 60
Hersh, Seymour 3, 13, 57–58, 97–99, 130, 136, 147
Highland Park, Illinois 158
Hill, Anita 145–146, 152–153
Hitler, Adolf 50
Hoffa, Jimmy 118, 121, 125, 129
Honduras 161
Hughes, Howard 58

India 76
Insight Magazine 147

Internal Revenue Service 91, 93–95, 99–100
Internet 114
Iran 52
Iran Contra 14
Iraq 164
Iraqgate 67
Iron Curtain 133
IRS *see* Internal Revenue Service
Irving, Clifford 58
Israel 35

Jackson, Cliff 69–70
Jackson, Sailor 24–25
Jefferson, Thomas 153
Johnson, Dwayne 23
Johnson, Lyndon Baines 12, 17, 63, 145
Joint Chiefs of Staff 17
Jones, Paula 152

Kansas City Star 37
Kansas City Times 5, 9
Kelley, Kitty 130
Kennedy, Jacqueline 52
Kennedy, John F. 12, 16, 49, 54, 57, 59–60, 127, 152
Kennedy, Robert 117–120, 127, 129
Kent State University 123–124
KGB 55, 59
Kirtland Air Force Base 138
Kissinger, Henry 79
Kurtz, Howard 148, 152
Kutler, Stanley, I. 98

Labor unions 133
Lake Charles, Louisiana 21
Lance, Burt 2–3
Lansky, Myer 22
Lawsuits 118
Lehmann-Haupt, Christopher 120, 149
Levine, Dennis 63–64
Lewis, Jerry Lee 22, 25
Lexus 60
Liberalism 152
Liebling, H.A. 13
Loeb, Bernard 110
London Observer 121
London Times 59
Long, Susan 95

Loomis, Bob 58
Los Alamos National Laboratories 142
Los Angeles Times 47, 50, 68, 72

McGee, Bradley, case 41
McKean, David 63
Mafia 22, 79, 124, 128–129, 160, 169
Manhattan, New York 21
Manhattan Project 138
Marcos, Ferdinand 11
Marshall, Thurgood 145
MCA 118
Meagher, Sylvia 59
Melville, Herman 14
Mencken, H.L. 3
Mengele, Joseph 50–51, 53, 56
Miami Herald 99
Milstein, Gil 168
Milwaukee Journal 122
Money laundering 27–28
Morrison, Allan 94
Moses, Robert 83
Moskin, Robert 53
Mulholland, Bob 165

Nader, Ralph 94
National Association of Manufacturers 97
National Headliner Awards 158
National Journal 5
National Transportation and Safety Board *see* NTSB
Nazis 50, 60
NBC Television 125, 157, 159–161, 164–166, 168, 170
New Republic Books 121
New York City 82–83
New York City Police Department 91, 93–94, 96
New York Press Club 92
New York Times 5–6, 33, 65–66, 72, 75, 79, 81, 91, 96, 99, 117–119, 120–123
New Yorker 149
Newsday 12, 75
Newsweek 33
Nexus 60, 138
NFL 129
Nicaragua 161
Nixon, Richard 3, 12, 76, 78, 124, 127, 145
Nosenko, Yuriy 59

Novak, Robert 147
NRC 92, 95, 99
NTSB 107–110
Nuclear Energy 91
Nuclear Regulatory Commission *see* NRC

Occupational health 91
Oglestreet, Charles 151
O'Leary, Hazel 134
Oswald, Lee Harvey 58–59
Oswald, Marina 59
O'Toole, Patricia 63
Overseas Press Club Award 75, 80

Paddington Press 121
Pakistan 76
Patton, Jim 36, 46
Payne, Ruth 59
Peabody Award 22, 27–28
Penland, Lyndon 162
Pentagon 5, 7–9, 11, 37
People magazine 33
Peretz, Martin 121
Perot, Ross 67
Phelan, Jim 58
Phi Beta Kappa 35
Plagiarism 32
Playboy 122
Plutonium 137–143
Poynter Institute 35–36
Pran, Dith 77, 79–80, 82
President's Commission on Law Enforcement and Administration of Justice *see* Crime Commission
Presser, Jackie 159–160
Privacy 91
Puerto Rico 16
Pulitzer Prize 5–6, 8, 12

Race relations 96
Radio Television News Directors Association 19
Rae, Norma 133
The Raleigh News and Observer 99
Random House 58–60
Reagan, Ronald 118, 145
Red Cross 51
Renaissance 9

Republicans 24, 96, 142, 152
Rimple, Bill 69
Rivera, Geraldo 130
Rockefeller, John D. 2
Romney, George 142
Roosevelt, Theodore 2–3
ROTC 124
Rubin, Frank 166
Rushdie, Salman 60
Russia 55

Sacramento, California 35
Sacramento Bee 35
Safire, William 3, 147
Salinger, Pierre 164
Schwartz, Rhonda 166
Scientology 52
Seale, Barry 29
The Seattle Times 103
Securities and Exchange Commission 70
Serpico, Frank 91
Sexual harassment 145–146
Sharpe, Rochelle 40
Sigma Delta Chi 158
Sihanouk, Norodom 76
Silverman, Ira 157–158, 160, 169
Sinclair, Upton 2
Sirhan, Sirhan 117–119, 127
60 Minutes 88, 98
Sline, Pat 12
Snyder, Dick 121
Snyder, Jimmy "the Greek" 129
Socialism 2
Soviet Union 77
Steffens, Lincoln 2, 4
Stewart, Jim 71
Stone, I.F 130
Stone, Oliver 16
Sudden Infant Death Syndrome 43
Sullivan, Mark 3
Sun Records 25
Super Bowl 35
Swaggart, Donnie 23
Swaggart, Jimmy 19, 22–23, 25–26
Syracuse University 92, 100

Tabloids 31
Tarbell, Ida B. 2, 4
Taylor, Stuart 68

Index

Teamsters Union 1, 121, 124–125, 128, 159–161
Technology 60
Television 16, 87–88
Terrorism 52
Thomas, Clarence 145–146, 149, 153
Time magazine 25, 33
Times-Mirror 39
Three Mile Island 101
Tinning, Mary Beth 43
TRAC 92–93, 95, 99–100
Transactional Records Clearinghouse *see* TRAC
Travelgate 151
Triads 50, 54
Turner, Harry 129
Twain, Mark 14

Union of Concerned Scientists 92
U.S. Attorney General 95
U.S. Constitution 7, 11
U.S. Court of Appeals 122
U.S. Department of Energy 134, 141
U.S. Food and Drug Administration 2
U.S. Justice Department 57, 92–96, 98, 106
U.S. National Security Agency 52
U.S. News and World Report 25, 49, 73
U.S. Nuclear Regulatory Commission 93
U.S. Senate 92
U.S. Supreme Court 123, 146
University of Akron 124
University of Nebraska 35–36
USA Today 33

Vanity Fair 33
Vesco, Robert 157, 162–163
Vietnam War 1, 12, 16, 76–77, 87, 97, 124, 142

W.W. Norton 121
Waas, Murray 67
Waco, Texas 151
Wald, Dick 160
Wall Street 61, 64
Wall Street Journal 31, 40, 106, 125, 148
Wallace, Mike 98
Wal-Mart 166
War on Drugs 160
Ware, John 54
Warren Commission 49, 59–60
Washington, DC 35, 40
Washington Post 33, 59, 100, 148, 165
Washington Times 147
Washingtonian Magazine 129–130
Watergate 1, 3, 13, 57, 97, 99–100
Waterloo, Iowa 157
Weber, Jose 36, 46
Weisberg, Harold 59
Welch, Bob 166
Westinghouse 30
Whitewater Investigation 151
Williams, Pete 164
Woodward, Bob 1, 5, 8, 13, 57, 98–100, 130, 136, 147–148
World War I 97
World War II 60, 97
Wright, Bob 16
Writer's Digest 36

Zacariah, Charles 163

www.ingramcontent.com/pod-product-compliance
Ingram Content Group UK Ltd.
Pitfield, Milton Keynes, MK11 3LW, UK
UKHW042014140426
5217IPUK00015B/1164